Global Trends

The Palgrave Macmillan IESE Business Collection is designed to provide authoritative insights and comprehensive advice on specific management topics. The books are based on rigorous research produced by IESE Business School professors, covering new concepts within traditional management areas (Strategy, Leadership, Managerial Economics) as well as emerging areas of enquiry. The collection seeks to broaden the knowledge of the business field through the ongoing release of titles, with a humanistic focus in mind.

Global Trends

Facing Up to a Changing World

ADRIAN DONE
IESE Business School

First published 2012 by
PALGRAVE MACMILLAN

Palgrave Macmillan in the UK is an imprint of Macmillan Publishers Limited, registered in England, company number 785998, of Houndmills, Basingstoke, Hampshire RG21 6XS.

Palgrave Macmillan in the US is a division of St Martin's Press LLC, 175 Fifth Avenue, New York, NY 10010.

Palgrave Macmillan is the global academic imprint of the above companies and has companies and representatives throughout the world.

Palgrave® and Macmillan® are registered trademarks in the United States, the United Kingdom, Europe and other countries.

ISBN 978–0–230–28486–9

This book is printed on paper suitable for recycling and made from fully managed and sustained forest sources. Logging, pulping and manufacturing processes are expected to conform to the environmental regulations of the country of origin.

A catalogue record for this book is available from the British Library.

A catalog record for this book is available from the Library of Congress.

10 9 8 7 6 5 4 3 2 1

21 20 19 18 17 16 15 14 13 12

Printed and bound in Great Britain by
CPI Antony Rowe, Chippenham and Eastbourne

Contents

Acknowledgements

This book has taken shape over three years and contains a considerable amount of research. The work of searching, collating and organizing facts and figures from the various different original sources has required significant collaboration from a number of people to whom I owe thanks.

Each of my recent research assistants, Gaston Sanchez, Gustavo Rodriguez and Ching T. Liao have worked hard to help me pull all of the disparate elements together. Also, MBA students have taken on the role of developing some of the Global Trend themes. Thanks to Ahmed Akef Mohamed and Ben Wong for their internship project work. Special thanks also to MBAs Pascal Michels and Henley Johnson who went above and beyond the call of duty in their contributions to certain chapters.

In a more general nature, the participants of my courses at IESE Business School have added to this book through their classroom contributions and general enthusiasm for the issues being debated. In particular, my gratitude to those MBA students who signed-up to, and participated so positively in, "The Big Picture" elective during the 2009–10 and 2010–11 academic years. Also to those of the various companies that participated in the "MEGATrend" and "Scenario Planning" sessions and workshops of the many IESE corporate and executive education programs of the last couple of years. More than anything the fun of running these courses has given me the energy to convert all this material into the book you are holding.

Above all I thank my family and friends for the support they have given over the years. Thanks to my Mum and Dad for their efforts to stimulate a young mind, for moving around the world whilst still ensuring a solid education, and encouragement to maintain a healthy degree of awareness of things in general. Thanks to my smart friends who have made me continually look beyond the obvious and to my many work colleagues – past and present – who have shown me the importance of continued learning and seeking new challenges.

This book is dedicated to my ever-supportive, patient and wonderful wife Marta, and my two wonderfully impatient and alive boys – Alex (7) and Max (4).

May we all face-up to the challenges of the 21st century!

Introduction

"This could be our best century ever... or it could be our worst."

Ian Goldin, Ex-Vice President The World Bank, and
Director of the James Martin 21st Century School,
University of Oxford[1]

1876 was not a very good year for the Samurai. After hundreds of years of considerable success in ruling over Japan, several events conspired to bring their powers to an abrupt and unseemly finale. You may well have seen the Hollywood epic drama *The Last Samurai,* starring Tom Cruise, and depicting the westernization of Japanese society towards the end of the 1800s. And, as the title strongly hints the poor old Samurai didn't come off too well in all the confusion. A whole way of life that had emerged during the 7th century AD and been dominant in the region for many centuries came to an end.

As we sit in our 21st-century relative comfort contemplating several worrying clouds on the horizon, the question for us is how on earth did the final curtain come to fall on such an apparently solid political, social, economic and technologically advanced culture? Of course, the Hollywood scriptwriters made much of love, courage, honor and so on, but when I put this same question to my MBA and executive education classes the overwhelming answer from intelligent participants is *"Guns, of course!"* This response corresponds pretty well with the official reasoning given for the decline of the Samurai: the superior firepower of the Western-affiliated Japanese government forces. This is despite the fact that the Samurai had had access to bombs and gunpowder since the first Mongol invasions in the 13th century, and experience in firearms since the Portuguese arrived in 1543. In fact, the story of the Samurai is complex and underlines some important human characteristics when facing changing trends. A combination of turbulent internal and external political changes, mixed with the impact of new, imported technologies and ways of doing things resulted in the last Samurai drawing his last breath. More of this in Global Trend 3: Technological Challenges.

Such historical events should serve as a somber lesson to us now. The Samurai were undoubtedly a tough, well-educated, close-knit social group that had survived many challenges that, frankly, modern societies would struggle to overcome. The same could be said of countless other human civilizations and society structures throughout time. From the Egyptians to the Easter Islanders, the Romans to the Aztecs, the common theme is that they all met their end at some point. And certainly not because they were less intelligent than we are now. Just to be able to make it to the end of the day is proof enough that our ancestors – who managed to colonize the greater part of the globe – were no idiots. Making fire from a couple of stones, or obtaining food (or preventing yourself from becoming food) armed with no more than a sharpened stick is no mean feat.

One of the historical lessons that comes from the many examples of collapsing human civilizations is that, from time to time, humans fail to foresee inescapable trends or to act in a timely and appropriate manner to deal with them. Perhaps we shouldn't feel too bad about this. After all, it isn't just humans that suffer from such an affliction. The same happened to the dinosaurs.

Apparently, every now and then *something* happens to bring an end to an established order. Some refer to such unpredictable and yet highly destructive somethings as "Black Swan" events, and, clearly, history is littered with such catastrophes that demolish the old and open the way for the new… starting with that meteorite (or whatever it was) that ended the reign of *Tyrannosaurus rex* and allowed the mammals to get a look in.

There are two problems for us mammals now that we hold and do not want to relinquish our privileged and comfortable positions: firstly, just how do we spot those black swans? And, second, what should we do when faced with such potential cataclysms? After all, the world always was a pretty complicated place and we have spent centuries making it more complex still. The current subprime-mortgage-induced financial crisis may not rank as ultimately calamitous as that meteorite was for the dinosaurs, but it has been rather devastating in many respects nonetheless. What's more, as we have seen, due to the interconnected nature of the modern globalized world, a ripple in one part of the pond can cause a tidal wave somewhere else.

The first part of the problem is simply a question of *vision*. Most intelligent modern executives, business leaders, politicians (insert any profession you like) share one important attribute with the fern-chewing *Apatosaurus*: they are little inclined to lift their heads from the daily grind to see what's heading in their direction. In both cases, there may well be reasons for not looking-up at the sky or seeing the big picture. After all it takes a lot of effort to move a body weight of over 20,000 kilograms in search of sufficient fibrous food, all the while avoiding predators – just as it does to deal with the complexities of surviving the next press interview, delivering on shareholders' demands or winning an election.

Nevertheless, as we can clearly see from history, and especially in the midst of the current economic crisis, some vision and perspective on important upcoming issues is clearly a virtue. Those species, cultures, companies and individuals that have been able to see what was coming have survived and, often, prospered throughout ancient and modern history. The alternative to having some vision is simply to leave things to those darned black swans that show up at the most unexpected times and places.

Vision is apparently a good thing. Little space needs to be dedicated here to arguing its virtues as it seems to be universally accepted across cultures as a benefit. Vision is synonymous with wisdom. Yet how does one acquire it? Through school, university, work experience? Apparently not. At least not in the manner that qualification-based education is widely executed in today's specialist subject-based "silo" regimes. The modern world is largely set up and run by specialist experts: economists, bankers, engineers, scientists, lawyers, doctors and so on. Even those professionals in positions that, in principle, demand high levels of vision have come through educational and work experiences that severely limit the breadth of their worldview. Perhaps the uncomfortable truth is that the vision of the average mover and shaker or CEO can be restricted and narrowed by the educational route and promotion path necessary to get there – a specialized path rather than one that inculcates a breadth of view and farsightedness that helps one succeed in the long term once in the elevated position. The same is clearly true of local and global politicians and other leaders in whom, as a society, we trust to captain us through turbulent times. It is interesting to note that the ex-Chairman of the US Federal Reserve – Alan Greenspan chose as a title for his memoirs *The Age of Turbulence*, when many now attribute to him and his people the lack of foresight that created the economic conditions underlying the turmoil the new world is currently going through.

With the way that things currently are, acquiring vision, foresight, or perspective on important issues seems to be left to chance. And this is somewhat concerning given the challenges that seem to be facing us as we move into the 21st century. Let's face it, when we consider the reasons behind the fall of the mighty Lehman Brothers' empire in September 2008 and the resulting global financial and economic fallout, it basically comes down to a lack of broader perspective on the part of business executives and political leaders. With just a few moments' thought, anyone suggesting a system based upon lending considerable sums of money to a whole sector of society that was frankly bound to default at some point, and then getting some rocket-scientist bankers to repackage that dodgy debt into fancy-named, complex financial instruments, to be sold on to less sophisticated (and somewhat gullible) institutions and punters looking for easy money should have been told, up-front, by someone serious "*Now hold on a second, that just doesn't make sense!... At least not beyond tomorrow.*"

This was (allowing for a little simplification) the process behind the whole "subprime" debacle and gives some indication as to the lack of general common sense in our "expert"-driven world. In the event, the whole subprime mortgage fiasco was just the spark that ignited an explosion that destroyed other flaky financial set-ups on such a massive scale that, at time of writing, most of the world banking system has been teetering on the edge of the abyss for three years, developed-world governments are at risk of defaulting on their debt, and the future of the world order as we know it has been brought into question. Apparently, no-one who was in any position to inject some common sense into the proceedings had the wisdom to look past the fast buck today, or to see the underlying insanity of the whole set-up. That is what I call a lack of vision.

The second part of the problem, relating to *what to do* about a black swan, in case you actually have managed to see it coming, is equally concerning. It wasn't solely that the Samurai couldn't see what was coming back in the 19th century, or that we didn't realize the economic bubble was inevitably on the verge of bursting back in 2008. It was more that, in both of these very different cases, there was an unhealthy dose of denial – for a whole host of reasons. The status quo is a very absorbing state. As humans we seem to get caught in the hypnotic trance that because things are set up and working in a certain way, they will continue to do so. And so a whole host of factors – inertia, comfort, vested interests, outdated bonus schemes, legacy systems, lack of conviction, etcetera, etcetera – conspire to prevent change. But, as with that bunny in the middle of the road staring blankly into the oncoming headlights, reality often treats such lack of action harshly.

We are now living in a world of uncertain economic outlook, with the prospect of worsening living conditions for millions as a direct result of failure to foresee the foreseeable and act on the actionable. Voices were definitely shouting about the inherently unsustainable nature of things over the last decade (and more). Many of these voices may well have been those of "the end is nigh" doom-mongers, but many more were bearing well-reasoned arguments for moderation and change. The challenge for all of us is to make the distinction, judge what are the serious, well-grounded issues and to act upon them.

The global financial and economic crisis has dropped a heap of uncertainty into our personal and professional lives, and many suddenly look towards the future with increased pessimism. The financial and economic turmoil of the last three years has prized open our sleepy eyes to a view of black clouds on the horizon. To be sure, there are clearly some big, scary and unresolved issues out there, and the apparent inability to really get to grips with them has brought widespread criticism of the way things are done – across political, business and public arenas. Such lack of confidence on important issues clearly impacts our private lives too, resulting in a good deal of confusion as to what is really going on and what the heck we should do about it.

Much of this uncertainty and crisis of confidence is due to a lack of vision – not only on the part of business leaders and political movers and shakers, but also at an individual level. As businesspeople and citizens, we need more tools and skills than we have acquired through our functional, silo-oriented education and experience. In order to make good decisions we also need a dose of general perspective. And to have such perspective requires a firm grasp of the big issues out there in the real world. After all, if, as a species, we were more prone to lift our heads from our daily specialist chores, we might develop that most precious of qualities – common sense. And, if such sense were genuinely more common at all levels of society, it is entirely plausible that we could avoid such setbacks as bursting economic bubbles, and we could face-up to our changing world with greater confidence and sense of purpose.

Therefore, this book argues for a return to a widespread positive valuation by society of *general knowledge*. Not in the form of "How high is the Eiffel Tower?" or "What was Elvis Presley's first hit song?" required by parlor games such as "Trivial Pursuits" or TV game shows, but more the type that is usually attributed to older generations as a result of their broad experiences, often gained through trying times that have required keeping eyes open and brain engaged. Such useful general knowledge and (un)common sense is usually termed "wisdom."

Of course, we need experts: much of human advancement has been due to the specialization of professions. We need specialists in order to keep innovating and improving the way things are done. After all, it takes single-minded dedication to become a successful nuclear physicist, an investment banker, an aeronautical engineer, surgeon... just as is does to break the world record in the 100-meter sprint. Yet, in the athletics world, Daley Thompson, one of my childhood heroes, did not win any medals for being THE best runner, jumper or thrower in the world. He won four world records, two Olympic gold medals, three Commonwealth titles, and the World and European Championships for being an outstanding decathlete... in other words an excellent and dedicated *generalist*.

My question is: Why we do not recognize the merits of such generalists in the political or business arenas, when their sound general knowledge and broad vision could bring real benefits to society? Ultimately, though we need experts with high-quality knowledge of their specialist areas, we also need more generalists in positions of responsibility: people who possess high-quality knowledge across a broad range of important areas. Perhaps by recognizing and promoting such broader vision we could then maintain some high-level common sense.

The way it currently works is that it is hoped that individuals with responsibility will somehow pick up such wisdom by chance as they progress through life. Unfortunately though, from housewives to CEOs, from schoolchildren to presidents, we are all intensely busy in our 21st-century world. Even when we are not busy with our noses to the grindstone, we are surrounded by noise, 24/7. Time-pressed and information-overloaded, people have little time to truly get to grips with general, yet profound, issues. As a result, big mistakes are made: nuclear energy plants are inappropriately sited near to areas of high seismic activity; automobile executives dig themselves into deep holes through misunderstanding fundamental issues governing technological development and changes in societies; hotel chain owners fail to implement adequate scenario planning for pandemic-related health scares; and individuals invest in things they don't understand, can't afford and ultimately regret. The list goes on at societal, business and individual levels.

Otherwise smart, competent human beings fail to take sound decisions or actions due to a lack of any real knowledge of the big picture.

In an attempt to start redressing the balance, I put together a course at the IESE Business School entitled "The Big Picture": in it, my very first question to MBA students and business executives alike is:

> *"How much time do you dedicate to thinking about the big issues that are likely to affect your personal and professional life in the next 20 years?"*

And for all the above reasons, the overwhelming response from the current and future captains of industry is:

"Frankly, not much. Certainly not enough."

What would your answer be?

We treat the past as though it is all obvious, and the future as though it will be an inevitable continuation of what we are currently living. Yet, let's think for a moment about images of the world 20 years ago: George Bush Sr. was in the White House; Lech Walesa was doing amazing things in Poland with his Solidarity movement; the Berlin Wall was still crumbling; the Soviets were leaving Afghanistan; students faced-up to tanks in Beijing's Tiananmen Square; *Raiders of the Lost Ark* was in cinemas; Bryan Adams was top of the Hit Parade; and a Tandy 20 MHz PC with only 2MB of RAM would set you back $8,499!

A lot has happened in the last 20 years, and a lot more will happen in the next 20 years. Yet the majority of people avoid thinking about it.

This book attempts to make a start in filling the hole in generalized lack of forward-looking perspective, through explicitly investigating some global trends that are likely to radically change the world in which we work, rest and play. Trends that will heavily affect the global political and business terrain and that are quite likely to have a real impact within your professional and personal lifetime. The aim is to cut through the media headlines and analyze serious issues in order to help make rational judgments and sound decisions, and, hopefully, to avoid getting into more of the problems currently facing uninformed politicians, time-starved executives and confused world-citizens.

Superficiality is a disease of our times. In the age of sound-bites and ever-decreasing attention spans we are flooded with information of very limited depth. Therefore, this book aims to go beyond the cozy, coffee morning or barroom chat format in which many of the big issues facing humanity seem to be presented to us by the media. To start assessing potential business impacts and possible personal repercussions in the years to come, this book is based-upon the best information I have been able to lay my hands on. It has taken three years of delving through the highest-quality reports I could find, from reputable publicly available sources, to identify the underlying economic, business, historic and scientific facts and drivers behind the main challenges facing us in the 21st century.

From this research, a dozen Global Trends have emerged as being considerable hurdles to be overcome in the continuing survival and progress of humans as a species, along with the world we live in. These twelve global megatrends are in the areas of:

- "The Crisis": What now?

- Geopolitical Power Shifts: China / India versus USA / Europe?

- Technological Challenges: What could possibly trump an iphone?

- Climate Change: What *is* going on?

- Water and Food Supply: Developed versus developing world?*

- Education: Who learns how to read and write?

- Demographic Changes: What is happening to populations?

- War, Terrorism and Social Unrest: Is the world becoming less safe?

- Energy Supply: Fossil fuels versus nuclear and renewables?

- Ecosystems and Biodiversity: Is the human footprint *really* so big?

- Health: What happened to pandemic risks?

- Natural Disasters: Earthquakes, hurricanes, volcanoes, floods...

---

* By the way, my use of the terms 'developed' and 'developing' countries is not meant to be patronising. I use these terms as they are used in the original reports from which data was obtained. Whilst there is no established United Nations convention for designation of these terms, Kofi Annan, former Secretary General of the United Nations, defined a developed country as "one that allows all its citizens to enjoy a free and healthy life in a safe environment." The developing country term on the other hand is generally used to describe a nation with a relatively low level of material well-being: an emerging or developing economy.

You are probably not particularly surprised by this list. In fact, if you could have cited most of it beforehand, congratulations – you are up with the National Intelligence Services of the USA. Many of these issues are, in essence, the core trends identified by the Office of the Director of National Intelligence and the National Intelligence Council – the principal advisors to the President on what to expect in the coming years. As advisors to the President of the USA, they have significant budgets to integrate foreign, military and domestic intelligence, and every five years they assemble hundreds of highly qualified experts to put together an unclassified report on how the world is changing.[2] Also these issues constitute the major big-impact challenges of the "Global Risks Landscape" identified by the global movers and shakers at the 2011 World Economic Forum.[3]

What is surprising – especially since most of us accept that these issues are of grave importance – is just how little we actually know about the underlying facts and what is being done about them. The overwhelming response of most human beings, from the highest politicians and business leaders down, is one of utter incomprehension and/ or denial. A combined burying of heads in the sand: "*As long as it doesn't directly affect us, let's just carry on-regardless*" attitude on a global scale. But hold on: isn't it precisely such attitudes that have got us into the mess that we are now in, with the fallout from the financial and economic crisis?

My contention is that surely, it is better to face-up to inevitable (and evitable) changes in the world and to consider the best courses of action to take based upon sound evaluation of the underlying facts – or as close to "facts" as can be obtained – and consideration of possible outcomes.

While some of them may well be obvious – even to the extent that you may well be bored of hearing about them – make no mistake, these twelve Global Trends are changing our world. They will shape the 21st century: how we live, how societies are shaped and how business is carried-out will be determined by the evolution of these megatrends in the coming years. Have no doubt, each one of these issues has the power to turn your life and/or business upside-down if you are not aware of the underlying forces and fail to take appropriate action.

But don't despair, this book aims to present each of these heavy issues in an accessible and stimulating way to anyone prepared to open their eyes and learn some interesting things that, mistakenly, they assumed they already knew from media headlines or hearsay.

By way of whetting your appetite, consider the following "executive summary" of each Global Trend:

Repercussions of "The Crisis":

OK, it's been tough since Lehman Brothers collapsed and paralyzed the global financial system – but the fallout will make many things tougher. This goes beyond subprime mortgages, collateralized debt obligations (CDO), credit default swaps (CDS) and structured investment vehicles (SIV). As with many historical booms and burst bubbles, a different world will emerge from this, the worst financial crisis since the Great Depression of the 1930s. New economic, financial, political, legal and social structures and regulations will be laid down, and the 21st century will be shaped by how the global economy survives profound uncertainties. After throwing large quantities of public money at underlying problems, excessive debt has moved from the (subprime) family level to the nation level. A central issue now is how to deal with global public debt levels around $39,000,000,000,000,000. Depending on where you live, there are even different ways of saying such an insane number.

Geopolitical power shifts

The BRIC economies are moving fast. China is in the lead, with a GDP having already overtaken western European economies, and predicted to catch the USA by 2035. India next, with a GDP due to overtake most of Europe by 2020 and the USA by 2040. Russia in third place will catch most of western Europe by 2035. Bringing up the rear (but with energy) is Brazil, on track to catch the Europeans by 2040. With such growth rates, the economies of the BRICs en masse could equal those of the G7 by 2032. Other emerging economies are also lining up. With economic success comes political power, and it is inevitable that these countries have a greater say (for good and ill) in the world order. While governance failures are very likely, if you are not involved with these countries, you will find yourself in an ever-shrinking pond.

Technology

Cast your gaze beyond what you think is "high-tech" (extensions to the Internet, electric cars, i-pads and so on). Get ready for some truly disruptive technologies that will profoundly change the way things are done – in the same way the car, air transport and the Internet changed societies in the 20th century. Further incremental changes of existing technologies will continue to impact our modern world – but these will only go so far before improvements diminish. When existing technologies reach maturity, they will be vulnerable to new invasive innovations. Inability to see or adapt to abrupt technological changes, resulted in fewer than 1 in 5 of the top 100 companies of the 1960s surviving the last 40 years unscathed. Be prepared for the "creative destruction" potential of developing technologies that are still off the general awareness radar-screen. How would wireless energy transfer, *Avatar*-style exoskeleton robotics or anti-aging drugs impact your life?

Climate change

It's a fact. Leave the incessant arguments about who or what caused the climate to change and start thinking of ways to live with it. The idea that this goes beyond simple global warming has been hard for many to grasp. This, along with recent media controversies, has derailed many initiatives. Yet the underlying scientific evidence is unequivocal – albeit inconvenient: the warming of the last half century is unusual in at least the previous 1,300 years. This has gone beyond mitigation and will undoubtedly require adaptation as well. Expect some global areas to bake, others to flood, and still others to be blasted by ever-increasing "severe weather events" Seriously look for ways to reduce emission of greenhouse gases for the benefit of future generations, but in the meantime choose where, and how to live and do business with care. The polar bears will have to keep their eyes open and adapt their habits – so will you.

Water and food

Drinkable water is the next oil (gold, diamonds or whatever other precious resource you care for) and without radical changes in its management, it is only going to get scarcer. Only 1 percent of Earth's water is readily available for human consumption. Many economies have become dependent upon finite groundwater supplies that are drying up. About 70 percent of global water-use is in agriculture – so less water, less food. Also, humans are becoming more dependent upon a reducing genetic diversity of crop plants, which adds vulnerability to the human food-chain in the face of many systemic risks. Undernourishment decreased during the last century, but with increasing food prices it has been on the rise again in this. The irony is that while the poor world will continue to starve, the rich world's excessive calorie consumption is leading to obesity, heart failure and diabetes, and food waste is becoming an expensive problem.

Education

By age 15, around 90 percent of OECD kids are studying a variety of fairly complex subjects. Yet at the same age, of the lucky 60 percent to be in school in poorer African nations, over half are still struggling to grasp the basics. Despite overall improvements, Asia, Latin America and Africa remain areas of educational failure. In most countries girls have problems getting into education; boys have problems staying there. Such issues extend into adulthood. Over 775 million adults worldwide – or 16 percent of the world's population – cannot read health advice, manage a bank account, read an advertisement or write a Christmas card. Worse still, they have little or no access to any possibility of learning. Such problems spill-over into the developed world too: 1.5 million adults in the Netherlands are "functionally illiterate" and in France 3 million have literacy problems. If people can't read or write, how can they possibly solve 21st-century problems?

Demographic changes

With increasing life expectancy, lower child mortality and decreasing fertility across both developed and emerging economies come new demographic challenges for the 21st century. By 2050 the world population will rise from the current 6.8 billion people to reach 9.2 billion – with most growth in emerging and developing-economy nations. This may be a lot for the planet to sustain, but this population level is then predicted to level off and stabilize. Within the next few years half of humanity will be having just enough children to replace itself. "Population pyramids" will reshape to "population coffins" as the populations (primarily of developed nations) become older, and thus generate a higher "support ratio" for the working population to sustain. For starters, retiring on full pension at 65 is possibly a thing of the past. Then as populations age worldwide, immigration of younger able bodies to keep things going will be encouraged – or even competed for.

War, terrorism and social unrest

Humans have a history of violence and antisocial behavior. The 20th century was particularly bloody – with anywhere between 69 and 122 million people

killed in major wars – although the Cold War kept much of this violence
at arm's length and out of sight for citizens of many protagonist countries.
The 21st century has started badly, with war, terrorism, social unrest, piracy,
organized crime, illicit trade, corruption, governance failures, fragile states
and proliferation of weapons all high on the global agenda. There is a high
degree of unpredictability with such things, yet high impact geopolitical conflict is perceived to be likely or very likely within the coming decade. Several
very plausible dark scenarios lead to a 21st century that is even more unstable
than the last. If leaders fail to work towards global peace, expect more soldiers,
police and war toys – and less tolerance, compassion and freedom.

Energy

It's what makes our world go round. Each American has the equivalent of 100
servants working for them in the form of powered gadgets. Human demand
for energy is insatiable, and, having grown by 50 percent since 1980, it is likely
to go exponential within the next 30 years – especially with the BRICs so keen
to get up to speed. This will put huge pressure on fossil fuels, which still represent nearly 90 percent of global energy consumption and are found in sensitive
areas like Iraq, Iran, and Libya. Renewables currently represent a small fraction
of power generation and, given the impasses likely with other primary energy
forms, clearly represent a considerable area for further development. Despite
valid concerns relating to nuclear fission energy, keep your eyes open for developments with the potentially safe nuclear fusion option. Also, expect a dammed
valley, wind farm or shiny-topped building near you soon. Otherwise "*Save it!*"

Ecosystems and biodiversity

We currently use resources and dump waste as though we had 1.4 planet
Earths. By 2050, we will be using up the equivalent of two Earths to support
our increasingly unsustainable ways. Many, many creatures have disappeared
from planet Earth as a result of this BIG ecological footprint. Of species we
know about, there is 40 percent less abundance of life now than there was in
1970. With extinction rates predicted to spiral out of control, we are heading towards a "Living Planet Index" of zero by 2050. Yet we are still utterly
dependent upon collapsing bee populations to pollinate about two-thirds
of the world's food intake. And fish will become a rare treat, with as much
as 90 percent of fish stocks already sucked up or poisoned. Ecosystem and

biodiversity concerns will spread beyond the tree-hugging "green" campaigners and have profound "well-being" consequences for us all.

Health

In 1980, the World Health Organization declared the globe free of smallpox, which had killed 500 million in the 20th century alone. But despite such breakthroughs, big barriers still stand in the way of a healthy world: most notably poverty. In poor nations, 34 percent die before 14 years old, and 44 percent between 15 and 69 – many from relatively easy-to-treat conditions such as diarrhea. Without profound change, the UN declaration of health and well-being as a human right is a pipe-dream for over half of the world's population. Yet, while being rich is a help, it is no guarantee of health. A Tajikistani can expect equal health and longevity as an American – while paying 25 times less on healthcare. Spiraling costs, pandemics, drug resistant superbugs, new child illnesses, more old-age, sedentary and urban chronic illnesses: burdens are increasing upon public and private health systems already showing stretch-marks. Will they reach breaking point? Take care.

Natural disasters

Over 200 million people are now affected by disasters each year. In the 1970s it was *only* 50 million per year. Earthquakes and droughts remain the main killers, but floods and storms are the hazards that affect most people. Crowded cities, unsafe constructions, lack of urban planning, destruction of natural buffers, and climate change have all combined to expose over 3 percent of the world's population to natural disaster per year. In Haiti around 40 percent were affected when 70 percent of buildings collapsed, causing an economic impact of 123.5 percent of GDP. Wealthy countries are also at risk: the Japan earthquake of 2011 is the most costly disaster in history. The probability of a major earthquake occurring within 30 years in San Francisco is 67 percent. Those that can, implement immense projects to protect themselves, while the UN classifies poor, populous cities such as Dhaka in Bangladesh as "disasters waiting to happen."

And yet, in the face of all these 21st century challenges, the World Economic Forum report *Global Risks 2011* states:

> The world is in no position to face major, new shocks. The financial crisis has reduced global economic resilience, while increasing geopolitical tension

and heightened social concerns suggest that both governments and societies are less able than ever to cope with global challenges. Yet… we face ever-greater concerns regarding global risks, the prospect of rapid contagion through increasingly connected systems and the threat of disastrous impacts.

With all of these issues, it would be easy to take a negative outlook, yet this book is not about pessimism. Nor is it about optimism. It is about realism. It is about facing up to a changing world just as human beings have always done. It is about recognizing that the human trajectory has never been an easy ride and that those that prosper have always been the ones with their eyes open and most flexible to change.

In comfortable Western cultures this is a challenge. After all, simply mention the word "crisis" to a passer-by on any street in Europe or North America and you will get a negative response. The very concept of crisis is a threatening one with sinister connotations. Yet, interestingly, those clever Chinese (about whom we will be hearing more in Global Trend 2) have two characters representing the notion of "crisis":

The first character denotes what we in the West would expect: *threat/ danger*. However, the second character is perhaps surprising. It stands for *opportunity/ chance*. So if you were to stop a passer-by on the streets of Shanghai with the word "*weiji*" maybe the response would be a more considered balancing of positives and negatives. Perhaps this is wishful thinking. But certainly any crisis or challenge, if properly managed, doesn't have to be all negative.

Clear threats emerge from each of the above megatrends, but so, too, do new possibilities. This book aims to serve as guide to charting the turbulent waters of the years to come: mitigating the risks whilst maximizing opportunities. Whether you are a political leader, a business high-flyer or merely a concerned human being, my belief is that you should know more about these things. In fact this project started out a few years ago with a mission to inform myself across these interlinked Global Trends.

In some ways, this book attempts the impossible: to collate the main issues around such a diverse array of subjects that nobody can possibly call themselves an expert in them all – certainly not me. Furthermore, there is a high chance that you are more of an expert in some of the topics than me. As such, I have no intention of "teaching Grandmother to suck eggs" – you have my full blessing to skim over or omit altogether certain chapters that are within your realm of knowledge. There is no way a single publication can achieve a complete analysis of all these 21st century Global Trends. Nor, probably, could any single publication achieve such a thing, even for any individual Global Trend. What this book does do is distil a huge amount of expert economic, historical and scientific information that is already out in the public domain into a coherent presentation of the important aspects of each of the twelve Global Trends. The treatment of the topics is necessarily somewhat varied due to their different underlying dimensions. However, the overall thrust of providing an overview of the main issues and related key facts, and some perspective on potential upcoming threats and opportunities, remains constant throughout the following chapters. My hope is that any expert skimming through the chapter relating to their specialist knowledge would conclude with a: "*Hhhmmm. Not a bad summary of the main issues.*"

Of course, issues relating to these Global Trends are continually debated at institutional, regional, national and international levels and, as such, at least some of the details are likely to be out of date by the time you read this. However, since the focus is upon the underlying trends, the overall messages that this book conveys should remain largely on course and more-or-less palatable for years to come. Perhaps consider the insights contained in this book as a "canned condensed milk" version of what is happening out there – without all the media "froth" of the fresh daily news.

My goal is that by reading this book you will not only be improving your general knowledge on these specific issues, but obtaining a broader perspective, and developing a greater vision with which to take sound personal, professional and leadership decisions. And, perhaps more importantly, ownership of where you, your family, your organization and your society are heading in the coming years. Wisdom is not something I promise as a result of reading this book. Nevertheless, I would like to think that this book might help you avoid kicking yourself in 10 to 20 years' time for being ill-informed about upcoming life-changing events, and for failing to act on mitigating the risks or – most importantly – maximizing the opportunities that are heading your way!

Repercussions of "The Crisis"

"The crisis… has brought some transformation, much acceleration of previous trends and, above all, great uncertainty. That uncertainty was present all along. But now we know."

Martin Wolf, Chief Economist, *Financial Times*[1]

On 15 September 2008, Lehman Brothers, the 158-year old investment bank, became the largest bankruptcy in US history, an event that subsequently paralyzed the global financial system. Governments pumped in cash, but the crisis deepened and broadened, crippling industries and crushing hopes with a force not seen since the Great Depression hit in 1929. Over the last couple of years, as commentators and participants have attempted to explain what happened, we have all been exposed to a dazzling range of new financial terms including such gems as: subprime mortgages, collateralized debt obligations (CDO), credit default swaps (CDS) and structured investment vehicles (SIV).

Just as physicists continue to debate what happened in the first few seconds after the Big Bang that formed our universe, there is still tremendous discussion by economists as to the underlying causes and initial dynamics behind the credit crisis. In a nutshell (and much simplified), however, the underlying issue was the bringing together of both homeowners – represented by their mortgages on houses – and investors – represented by money from large institutions such as pension funds, insurance companies, sovereign funds, mutual funds etcetera. This was done by the banks and brokers commonly known as "Wall Street."

In the wake of the "dot.com" bust in 2000, and the terrorist attacks of September 11 2001, the Federal Reserve Chairman Alan Greenspan lowered the interest rate to a low 1 percent to keep the US economy growing. Thus, those investors that had traditionally invested in very secure treasury bills started to look elsewhere for better returns. Meanwhile, Wall Street could now borrow from the Federal Reserve at an abnormally low interest rate. Add to that general surpluses from the likes of China, Japan and the Middle East and there was an abundance of cheap credit. Banks could now borrow money and go crazy with "leverage" – borrowing money to amplify the overall profits from a deal.* So, highly leveraged Wall Street institutions (such as Bear Stearns, JPMorgan Chase, Citigroup Incorporated, Goldman Sachs, Morgan Stanley, Merrill Lynch and Lehman Brothers) borrowed lots of money, made good deals, got very rich and then paid the borrowed money back. Traditional treasury-bill investors saw this and wanted some of the stellar returns. Wall Street obliged by connecting these investors to homeowners through mortgages.

With ever-higher house prices, increasing numbers of families wanted to get onto the housing ladder and contacted a mortgage broker – who connected them to a lender eager to put his (borrowed) money to work. The family bought their dream house, the broker made a good commission, and the lender obtained a revenue stream from the monthly mortgage payments of the family.

Everyone was happy.

The next step was for investment banks to borrow millions of dollars to buy up thousands of similar home mortgages (paying a nice fee to the original lenders), and start collecting all the monthly payments from the homeowners. This in itself was a good business, but then with true Wall Street wizardry, these mortgage revenue streams were repackaged into further structured investment vehicles in the form of cascading safe (Triple A), okay (triple B) and frankly dodgy (unrated) mortgage debts – or *collateralized debt obligations* (CDOs). Each of these tiered products could then be sold on to investors looking for specific types of investment with associated returns on investment: from safe products (with lower return-on-investment e.g. 4 percent) to the less safe (with higher-return-on-investments e.g. 10 percent). While the banks

---

* Businessmen A and B have $10,000 each. A buys a box for $10,000 and sells it for $11,000 making a $1,000 profit. Not bad. But, Businessman B goes and gets a bank loan for a further $990,000 and buys 100 boxes. He then resells these 100 boxes for $1,100,000. Then he pays back the $990,000 bank loan plus $10,000 in interest- leaving him with a profit of $90,000.

bought the safer CDOs, and insured themselves with a credit default swap, the flaky mortgage-loan CDOs, which received a higher rate of return to compensate for the higher risk of default, were bought by non-risk-averse investors such as hedge funds. The investment banks made millions from selling these CDOs and repaid any outstanding loans they had.

By now, traditional investors saw this as a great investment (certainly much better than the 1 percent being offered by the Federal Reserve), and wanted more CDOs. The investment banker went back to the lender to buy more home mortgages, and the lender went to the mortgage broker to drum up more mortgage business to sell. But everyone qualifying for a standard mortgage already had one – so, in combination, the lender and broker came up with an idea to squeeze things a bit further. As Dr. Seuss's Grinch would say: "*A wonderful, awful idea.*" Add further risk to new mortgages. After all, if homeowners defaulted the lender would get to keep the house in any case, and in a world of perpetually increasing house prices the lender could still sell the house for profit. Brilliant! Instead of lending to responsible homeowners (prime mortgages), brokers and lenders started providing mortgages to the somewhat less responsible. And so the infamous subprime mortgage was born, with no down-payment or proof of income necessary.

As before, the mortgage broker got his commission for pushing another mortgage, and families of limited and unstable income bought big houses. The subprime mortgages were sold to investment banks in their thousands and were then converted into CDOs and sold on to investors (… still represented by large institutions such as pension funds.) Again, the least risk-averse investors got the highest returns from the repackaged flaky-debt CDOs. No-one was unduly worried since in this game of pass the parcel, as soon as the bundle was sold to the next person it was not their problem.

Not surprisingly, less-stable home-owners started to default on their mortgages, and banks started to foreclose.

This meant that what had been a stream of monthly payments became a house. No problem – the house was put up for sale. But as more of the sub-prime homeowners began to default, and banks put more houses on to the market, supply exceeded demand and the unthinkable happened: house prices started to fall. In an area of dropping house prices, anyone still paying their mortgage of $250,000 dollars was strongly incentivized to default too when all their neighbors' houses were now valued below $100,000. Default rates swept through the USA and house prices plummeted.

Now there was a big problem.

With revenue streams from these investments drying up, and the assets supporting them now close to worthless, balance sheets throughout the global financial chain had truly enormous holes in them. What was worse, institutions throughout the world had borrowed many millions to buy into this until-recently highly profitable game and now had no way of paying back their loans. What started with subprime individuals unable to pay-back their mortgages worked its way up the chain to highly leveraged institutions across the board unable to pay their mountainous debts of millions of dollars. At this point the whole financial system simply froze. No-one would buy any of the previously highly desirable CDOs and institutions across the board started to go bankrupt.

For the months following the collapse of Lehman Brothers, the whole global financial system was apparently teetering on the edge of oblivion. Fear was palpable across the political, financial and business communities as total meltdown, and all its fearsome implications, became a significant possibility. The sting in the tail after all this, though, is that the investor and the homeowner were still linked. The homeowner's previously high-performing savings and pension plans were, after all, very possibly invested in those riskier CDOs.

Incredible. Yet such events are far from rare in human history.

As such, one of the better commentators during the unraveling of the crisis has not been an economist, a banker or a businessman, but a historian – Niall Ferguson of Harvard and Oxford Universities. In his book *The Ascent of Money*,[2] he makes the point that ever since the second millennium BC, when Mesopotamians were inscribing "IOUs" on clay tablets, there have been repeated booms and burst bubbles. Charles Kindleberger and Robert Aliber make similar revelations in their book *Manias, Panics and Crashes: A History of Financial Crises*[3] and define the term "financial crisis" as applying broadly to a "variety of situations in which some financial institutions or assets suddenly lose a large part of their value."

In the 19th and early 20th centuries, many financial crises were associated with banking panics, and many recessions coincided with these panics. Other situations that are often called financial crises include stock market crashes and the bursting of other financial bubbles, currency crises, and sovereign defaults.[4] Financial crises directly result in a loss of paper wealth; they do not directly result in changes in the real economy unless a recession or depression follows. Many economists have offered theories about how financial crises develop and how they could be prevented. There is little consensus, however, and financial crises have remained a regular occurrence around the world.

According to George Soros, financier and philanthropist, the financial crisis of 2007 to 2010 has been somewhat different from other crises which have erupted at intervals since the end of World War II in that "[It] marks the end of an era of credit expansion based on the dollar as the international reserve currency."[5] As such, this global financial crisis has been seen to be triggered by a liquidity shortfall in the United States banking system. It has resulted in the collapse of large financial institutions, the bailout of banks by national governments and downturns in stock markets around the world. In many areas, the housing market has also suffered, resulting in numerous evictions, foreclosures and prolonged vacancies.

> **It is considered by many economists to be the worst financial crisis since the Great Depression of the 1930s.**

Even those disagreeing with it being compared to the severity of the 1930s, have agreed that it has been the worst recession since World War II – eclipsing in global terms the 1980s Latin American debt crisis and the Japanese financial crisis of the 1990s. The current crisis has contributed to the failure of key businesses, declines in consumer wealth estimated in the hundreds of billions of US dollars, substantial financial commitments incurred by governments, and a significant decline in global economic activity. Many causes have been suggested, with varying weight assigned by experts. Both market-based and regulatory solutions have been implemented or are under consideration, while significant risks remain for the world economy beyond the current periods.[6,7,8]

The collapse of the housing bubble, which had peaked in the USA in 2006, caused the values of securities tied to real estate pricing to plummet thereafter, damaging financial institutions globally. Questions regarding bank solvency, declines in credit availability, and damaged investor confidence had an impact on global stock markets, where securities suffered large losses during late 2008 and early 2009. Economies worldwide slowed during this period as credit tightened and international trade declined. Critics argued that credit rating agencies and investors failed to accurately price the risk involved with mortgage-related financial products, and that governments did not adjust their regulatory practices to address 21st-century financial markets.[9,10]

The underlying causes and potential repercussions of this financial and economic crisis are varied and complex and are topics of continuing debate. In a G20 workshop held in May 2009, the members agreed that the following had contributed to the crisis:[11]

- Regulatory inefficiencies and mistakes, and arbitrage between regulations.

- Failure in the operation of the International Monetary System (IMS) and the resulting constellation of economic policies.

Yet the G20 workshop concluded that the most likely primary cause of the crisis was that:

"Credit was expanded too rapidly and to increasingly risky borrowers through instruments which dispersed exposure in such a way that end investors did not realize the extent or correlation of risks they had taken on."

This last point refers to the previously mentioned subprime mortgage debacle in the USA, and the associated dressing up of this unsafe debt into complex financial products (or financial "weapons of mass destruction") that were of unfathomable risk level to end-purchasers of this debt. As outlined earlier, apparently all-too-often these hoodwinked end-investors were large institutions such as pension funds. In addition, quite apart from the amplitude of Lehman Brothers bankruptcy, the G20 workshop identified several other features of the financial and economic cycles that were unusual and may have exacerbated the effects of crisis:

- Bank credit was growing in excess of Gross Domestic Product (GDP): Low interest rates across the yield curve together with rapid development in financial innovation led to bank credit growing at rates more than that of GDP. For example, in both the USA and Euro areas "excess credit level"* rose by about 40 percent between 2000 and 2008. By comparison, in Japan over the same period it had dropped by approximately 20 percent.

• A background of rising house prices: Housing construction expanded rapidly to reach historical highs in terms of GDP in many countries.

• The economic downturn has been global: the economic crisis has affected developed and emerging economies alike. Indeed, the slowdown in growth between the second half of 2007 and end-2008 seems to have been of broadly similar magnitude in the two regions. While the pre-Lehman prediction for growth in OECD† countries was to maintain the previous trend of 2 percent growth, their economies actually shrank by 7 percent during 2008: a 9 percent reduction of growth compared to predictions. Similarly, in non-OECD countries the previous predictions were expecting continued growth rates of around 8 percent, whilst actual growth fell to nearly 1 percent during 2008: a 9 percent reduction of growth compared to predictions. So, both OECD and non-OECD worldwide economies took a nearly 10 percent hit to their growth as a direct result of the financial crisis going global.

• Capital outflows and inflows in the main advanced economies: There was a major retrenchment in cross-border banking flows in the 2nd quarter of 2008, which was particularly dramatic in banking centers such as the United Kingdom and Switzerland, but also significant for the United States and other advanced economies. From a consistently positive trend over several years, total capital outflows‡ in the first quarter of 2008 were nearly 2 trillion US dollars. However by the second quarter of 2008 total capital outflows had dropped to MINUS 1 trillion US dollars across main advanced economies. Total capital inflows also dropped off the cliff at the same time. In other words, no money was moving to or from these

---

* The deviation of domestic bank lending to the private non-financial sector as a share of GDP from the long-term trend. 3-month moving average.

† Organization for Economic Co-operation and Development (OECD) is an international economic organisation of 34 countries founded in 1961 to stimulate economic progress and world trade. It defines itself as a forum of countries committed to democracy and the market economy, providing a platform to compare policy experiences, seeking answers to common problems, identifying good practices, and co-ordinating domestic and international policies of its members.

‡ Including FDI, Portfolio, Banks and other capital flows.

economies. No-one wanted to move, and capital flows remained low throughout 2008 and 2009.

- Globalization and the propagation of the crisis: The rapid process of globalization over the past two decades played a major role in both the run-up and the propagation of the crisis. Over the past decades sectors such as manufacturing have become increasingly dependent on imported materials, with production supply chains having clearly become more international. In 1970 the share of imported goods in manufacturing production was a meager 8 percent, but by 2000 this had grown to nearly 30 percent. Yet, whilst quarterly world trade growth rates had been ticking along rather nicely, by the end of 2008 world trade had contracted for the first time in nearly two decades (apart from a minor hiccup in 2001).

- Was the US Federal Reserve policy of maintaining low interest rates sustainable?: In a devastating commentary in September 2009, David Blake, an asset manager and former Goldman Sachs analyst, pointed a finger at Alan Greenspan, long feted as the doyen of central bankers and architect of global prosperity during his 18 years at the Federal Reserve. The Financial Times article "How gamblers broke the banks" quoted Blake as saying:

Where Mr. Greenspan bears responsibility is his role in ensuring that the era of cheap interest rates created a speculative bubble... To create one bubble may be seen as a misfortune; to create two looks like carelessness. Yet that is exactly what the Fed under the leadership of Greenspan did.

So, after the causes and effects of the crisis, what of the solutions?

Well, governments and central banks responded with unprecedented actions in three areas: fiscal stimulus,* monetary policy expansion,† and institutional bailouts by government to prevent further bankruptcies of key institutions. In other words, developed-country governmental institutions felt obliged to throw money at the problem: public money, both in order to

---

* The use of government expenditure and revenue collection (taxation) to encourage economic growth
† Monetary policy that seeks to increase the size of the money supply.

fill the very many holes that had appeared in the balance sheets of organizations that were "too big to fail," and to keep their national economies from imploding.

Considering each of these three solutions in turn:

Most citizens of developed-world economies would have noticed the huge fiscal stimulus efforts, throughout 2008, 2009 and 2010, in the form of impressive and immediately apparent building of new schools, roads, bridges, airports and whatever other forms of public spending in order to pump cash liquidity into the economy. In many countries this has been quite amazing to behold. Where has this money come from? Firstly, from increased taxes and secondly from increased government borrowing (or selling of government bonds to investors.)

Then came monetary policy expansion – which traditionally has meant turning the presses on to print more money. The problem for modern governments, though, is that such antics are usually confined to the toolbox of incompetent military junta banana republics. Furthermore, when base interest rates are either at, or close to, zero, normal expansionary monetary policy of lowering interest rates by the central banks can no longer function. Hence the emergence of the rather unconventional monetary policy tactic of "quantitative easing" (or QE, and subsequent QE2) – whereby the central bank creates money which it then uses to buy back government bonds and other financial assets from investors (such as other banking institutions) in order to increase money supply in the economy. Of course, such actions raise the prices of the financial assets being bought. In addition, the effectiveness of such measures is potentially limited if banks opt to keep the cash earned (in order, for example, to increase their capital reserves in a climate of increasing loan defaults) instead of pumping that credit into the broader economy.

And last, but by no means least, came the institutional bailouts by government to shore-up those banks and other at-risk institutions considered too big to fail – deemed necessary to prevent the entire global financial and economic system from going down the drain. One such example was the famous (or infamous) TARP: The Troubled Assets Relief Program. On October 3 2008 the United States created TARP as part of the Emergency Economic Stabilization Act of 2008. The program originally allowed for $700 billion in spending, including three tranches of $250 billion, $100 billion, and a final $350 billion available upon request from the President and approval from

Congress. These funds were taken-up by such diverse beneficiaries as financial firms such as Citigroup ($50 billion), Bank of America ($45 billion) and AIG ($69.8 billion). But also funds were provided for automakers such as GM ($85.3 billion), homeowners ($50 billion) and small businesses ($15 billion).[12] In addition to national governments initiating such similar troubled assets protection schemes, the World Bank Group committed $58.8 billion in fiscal year 2009 to help countries struggling amid the global economic crisis, a 54 percent increase over the previous fiscal year and a record high for the global development institution.[13]

Of course, the upshot of these solutions has been a growing amount of public debt.

Some world economies which had billions in public debt, now had trillions. According to *The Economist's* Global Public Debt Clock,[14] as of 6.19 p.m on 14 February 2011 (St. Valentine's Day!), the global public debt is $38,885,000,641,143... no wait $38,885,003,333,298... no sorry, $38,886,106,931,836... now $38,886,209,629,658... you get the gist.

In 2011, the global public debt is $38,886,213,522,479 (... and growing.)

Do you even know how to say such a large number?

If fact, depending on where you live there are different ways of saying it. In other words, this number is so big that there is no single internationally recognised way of saying it. Most English-speaking countries, as well as Brazil, Russia, Indonesia and Turkey use a "short-scale" whereby this number would be nearly $39 TRILLION. In French, German, Spanish, and Scandinavian-speaking "long-scale" countries this would *only* be $39 BILLION.*

The big question is:

Are such levels of public debt sustainable?

At time of writing, the United Kingdom has a public debt of $1,554,843,835,616 or 69.3 percent of GDP. Or to make it more personal, with a population of 61,849,315, that works out at $25,139.23 cents per per

---

* In the original English version, the rest of this book uses the short-scale convention.

man, woman and child. Given an average 2009 annual income of $42,320,*
and 18,844,000 available jobs in the UK,[15] and an average income tax level
of 20 percent... that yields $8,464 tax revenue per working person per year...
or $159,495,616,000 total tax revenue per year... and hence 9 years and
9 months to repay the current national debt. (Assuming of course that the
debt burden doesn't grow, salaries stay high and employment and tax levels
stay stable during this time.)

The United States has a public debt of $8,004,352,054,795 – 55.0 percent
of GDP. Or, with a population of 307,145,205 that is $26,056.71 per man,
woman and child.

How is it that governments can borrow so much? Well, given that they
have the power to tax their citizens into the future, investors are prepared to
buy those government bonds (or elaborate IOUs) with the relative certainty
that the government will pay them back at some point.

A problem comes when the debt gets so large that investors start to baulk
at the proposition that citizens will be unable to shoulder such a tax burden.
Let's take a look at how some of the economies that have recently been in
the news stack-up – including some of the "wobblier" economies at time of
writing (see Table 1.1).

Not surprisingly, investors have taken a look at these numbers, done a
few calculations and decided that there is a significant possibility of certain countries defaulting on their loans. Now you have a sovereign debt
crisis. At time of writing, Iceland, Greece and Ireland have been deemed
bankrupt, with the European Central Bank and International Monetary
Fund (IMF) stepping-in to impose harsh conditions upon their governments to protect the rest of the system from "contagion." To give some idea
of just how likely investors felt that certain countries might default, the
ten-year government bond yields of Germany, Spain, Portugal, Ireland and
Greece were approximately 3 percent, 6 percent, 7 percent, 8 percent and
12 percent respectively in January 2011.[16] Back in 2009 all of these Euro
area nations had been able to borrow money in the markets paying an
interest level of around only 4 percent. Such increases in interest payments
on national debt puts the sustainability of modern growth-dependent
economies further into question, and thus investor confidence goes into a
vicious-circle tailspin.

---

* Exchange rate: GBP 1 = USD 1.6.

Table 1.1: Public debt, some examples

Country	Public debt	Population	Public debt as percent GDP	Public debt per capita
Belgium	$461,615,068,493	10,600,000	97.4 %	$43,460.29
France	$2,101,847,945,205	62,636,986	78.3 %	$33,560.77
Germany	$2,493,428,767,123	82,824,657	73.6 %	$30,107.77
Greece	$400,145,205,479	11,000,000	120.5 %	$36,411.38
Iceland	$13,736,986,301	300,000	115.8 %	$42,959.52
Ireland	$148,115,068,493	4,287,671	66.5 %	$34,931.10
Italy	$2,483,542,465,753	59,924,657	116.2 %	$41,465.14
Japan	$10,043,172,602,740	127,063,013	193.4 %	$79,053.36
Portugal	$182,923,287,671	10,600,000	77.7 %	$17,205.22
Spain	$802,531,506,849	45,812,328	28.3 %	$17,529.85

Source: *The Economist*, Global Debt Clock, 2011.

The Economist article "Time for Plan B," summed up this situation with a downbeat conclusion: that the current European bail-out strategy is failing in its intended purpose of calming investors and protecting the Euro area's central countries from the goings-on in peripheral nations. Fundamental contradictions in the "Plan A" response implemented in the rescue of Greece and Ireland, along with uncertainty regarding which nations may be deemed insolvent in the medium term, has led to investors becoming more nervous. Borrowing costs have thus risen for several nations, and the Euro crisis is deemed likely to continue spreading. Thus, as a "least bad" solution, *The Economist* proposes the restructuring of debt of the struggling "plainly insolvent" countries – starting with Greece, and probably including Portugal and Ireland.[17]

So – previously stable European countries are at risk of defaulting on their loans (just like those subprime mortgage holders) and the crisis of confidence that had started with individual borrowers has moved to the level of insecure nation borrowers, with risk of contagion to not-so-insecure nation borrowers.

As a result, confidence levels in the whole European project and the Euro currency have plunged in the markets. Furthermore, because of all the austerity measures imposed, the economies of the European periphery have plunged further into recession and their outlook looks bleak. Not surprisingly, many European citizens (a lot of them unemployed) have taken to the streets, both in peaceful and very nonpeaceful demonstrations, against all sorts of things, from the level of bankers' bonuses to the severity of austerity measures.

Apparently, the road to recovery in the coming decade is not going to be short and dull, but rather long, complicated and – for certain countries at least – somewhat painful. According to the Organization for Economic Co-operation and Development (OECD), up to 25.5 million people will have lost their jobs by the end of 2010, and this will, in all likelihood, keep rising. At the time of writing, the damage has been the greatest in America, Britain, Ireland and Spain, where the collapse in house-building has cost many construction workers their jobs. However, many believe that in other advanced economies, the worst is yet to come. The unemployment rate in the United States surpassed 10 percent, the highest level in 26 years, and is expected to stay at an elevated level well into 2011. According to the OECD, "the economic recovery now spreading across OECD countries is still too timid to halt the continuing rise in unemployment."[18]

Emerging economies have not escaped the turmoil and have also demonstrated clear vulnerabilities. According to the IMF, "corporate defaults are rising in all regions, with loan losses thus putting pressure on banking systems. Refinancing needs of emerging market businesses and banks are large, revealing substantial rollover risks. For instance, debt service of bonds and syndicated loans denominated in foreign currencies is estimated at $400 billion over the next two years."

As a result of increasing defaults across the board, banks have needed more capital and are less prone to providing the much needed credit to stimulate economies in recession. The IMF projects that the lending capacity of banks will continue to remain in the doldrums since:

Even though bank earnings are recovering, they are not expected to be able to offset fully the anticipated write-downs over the next 18 months. Insufficient earnings, combined with continuing deleveraging pressure, means banks will have to raise more capital. Additionally, banks must refinance a massive amount of maturing debt over the next two to three years.

An unprecedented $1.5 trillion in bank borrowing is due to mature in the euro area, the United Kingdom, and the United States by 2012.[19]

As to future trends, *The Economist* article "The long climb" sets out three possible scenarios for postcrisis economic development in the coming years: 1. a full recovery; 2. a permanent loss; and 3. a scenario of widening loss. Thus in the fallout from the crisis, these distinctly plausible scenarios indicate possible opportunities for return to precrisis conditions as well as very real potential threats of lasting damage to rates of economic growth, and failure to recoup losses.[20]

Threats and opportunities

At the time of writing, the World Economic Forum (WEF) 2011 has just finished. This is where all the worlds' leaders and thinkers get together in the lovely Swiss ski resort of Davos-Klosters. One of the many outputs from the forum is the report *Global Risks 2011*, outlining a landscape of threats that the world is likely to confront in the next ten years. At the top of the list of 38 global risks in terms of impact is the continuing threat of fiscal crises (plural), with a perceived economic impact around the trillion-dollar level and "very likely" to occur within the coming decade. Several other economic-crisis-related threats are also identified as being either likely or very likely within the next ten years: "liquidity/ credit crunch," "asset price collapse," "global imbalances and currency volatility," "regulatory failures," "slowing Chinese economy," "retrenchment from globalization," "extreme commodity price volatility," "infrastructure fragility" and "extreme consumer price volatility"; all with economic impacts in the hundreds of billions of dollars.[21]

The OECD's 2010 Economic Outlook points to slowly improving financial conditions supporting economic growth but "weaker than in previous recoveries." Furthermore, Pier Carlo Padoan, OECD Deputy Secretary-General and Chief Economist, indicated that unemployment remains persistently high and there is the risk it will prove long-lasting in many countries. Also, while postcrisis growth has been stronger in emerging market economies, it remains weak, uneven and faltering across OECD nations. As he states:

> Against such background, the challenge will be to guide the transition from a policy-driven recovery to self-sustained growth. As stimulus is

withdrawn, policy will have to provide a credible medium-term framework, including for the financial sector, to stabilize expectations and strengthen confidence. To this effect, international collaboration, notably within the G20 process, will be essential... There are significant risks on the downside, notably those stemming from renewed declines in house prices in the United States and the United Kingdom, high sovereign debt in some countries, and possible abrupt reversals in government bond yields. Were some of them to materialize and threaten to derail the recovery, additional policy responses would be warranted in countries that still have room for maneuver. Global imbalances remain wide, and in some cases have started widening again, and there are rising concerns that they may threaten the recovery ... Some countries have been reacting to capital inflows through unilateral measures to stem the consequences on their domestic economies. Protracted unilateral action of this sort is likely to have little – or even counterproductive – effects and risks triggering protectionist moves. However, such unilateral actions also signal dissatisfaction with the progress that has been achieved because of the lack of a cooperative response...

A continuing paranoia that any upturn in economic activity is yet another "dead cat bounce" is also weighing heavily on market sentiment and general confidence levels. The apparent inability of governments to provide quick solutions has led to political and social unrest across many countries and the risk is that this instability will continue for years to come. To mitigate such risks, governments will need to be careful not to cut, and even to increase, core security spending – despite austerity measure cuts in other areas. If policing is not up to scratch, widespread dissatisfaction with politicians could easily lead to further social unrest and increases in crime.

It goes without saying that such instability would lead to challenging business operating conditions and decreased foreign direct investment – making matters worse. Clearly therefore, any austerity programs aimed at regulating government spending and public debt will need to be carefully moderated to keep key sectors intact, and with adequate stimulation programs to keep the economy afloat and to maintain competitiveness into the future. Corporate and personal tax revenues will most likely need to be increased to combat the high sovereign debt levels, but this will need to be tempered with the need to continue encouraging business growth and skilled people to stay put.

A further exacerbation of the social unrest trend comes with prolonged high unemployment levels leading to deterioration of skills – and businesses finding it hard to find the talent required. Without appropriate policy and business measures, unemployment could foreseeably continue growing in certain countries – with yet more social unrest and increased crime. Also, with increased job uncertainty comes decreased consumer purchasing and businesses in affected sectors going bust – thus driving-up unemployment more. A very vicious circle.

With reduced opportunities for work in certain regions comes a "brain drain," as capable people move to find work and better career options elsewhere. If governments and business leaders fail to stimulate investment, especially in R&D, this could lead to loss of national and regional innovation and competitiveness in the longer term. Of course, a quick and populist fix is that of trade tariffs, subsidies and general protection of local industries. The problem with this is that global trade diminishes. Deeper and longer-term negative consequences become likely as importing businesses suffer decreased range and quality of imported goods and exporting businesses suffer from reciprocal trade barriers at the other end.

Despite the grim tones of much of the previous text in this chapter, outlining the very real threats, the continuation of the OECD's Pier Carlo Padoan's economic outlook gives some definite cause for optimism:

> A rebalanced policy regime must provide substance to the notion of 'growth-friendly' fiscal consolidation, by looking more closely at the composition of public finance both on the spending and the revenue sides, and facilitating new sources of growth. Measures should include improving public sector efficiency, while preserving outputs, in growth-enhancing areas, such as education and innovation. The tax structure should move away from corporate and labor income taxes towards higher taxes on consumption, property and externalities such as greenhouse gases.
>
> Robust growth will also require a decisive acceleration of structural reform, which has slowed during the global recession… Structural reforms are urgent in labor markets to increase employment, facilitate reallocation of jobs and workers and help ensure that the unemployed and vulnerable groups remain attached to the labor market. Implementing this labor-market agenda is urgent, since otherwise the large and growing number of long-term unemployed may become permanently and structurally

unemployed. Product market reform is also needed. Reduction of barriers to competition, especially in service sectors, and of restrictive housing policies would increase flexibility and set the stage for renewed sustainable growth...

Rebalancing needs to be implemented gradually but decisively, leaving no doubt as to the direction the global economy is taking. Resolute and collaborative policy action to restore macroeconomic balance and a renewed commitment to structural reforms will boost confidence, hasten the exit from the recession and revitalize sustained growth in living standards worldwide.

Hence there is the distinct chance of improving upon ways of doing things – but any optimism relies upon a big IF... if appropriate and decisive actions are taken by the world's movers and shakers. This represents a tremendous opportunity for political, institutional and business leaders to act in the interests of the broader global society, but will require new economic, financial, political, legal and social structures and regulations being laid down – both at local and global levels.

At a business level, every cloud has a silver lining. Many new business opportunities will be spawned from the mayhem. Even during the worst depths of the Great Depression in the 1930s, Hollywood boomed, with 60 to 80 million Americans going to the movies each week. Beyond media and entertainment that provided escapism for the masses, other winners of the Great Depression were advertising, travel (especially by air) and any low-cost-oriented business model. Similarly in the wake of the current crisis, many asset prices have decreased – for example the value of equity markets in 2008 dropped by up to 70 percent. But many of these will have had a strong rebound and represent opportunities for business investors willing to take the risk and "ride the wave." Also, with increased competition for decreasing demand in certain sectors come opportunities for buyers to negotiate better prices and payment terms. A whole new emphasis will be placed on low-cost businesses – both in Business to Consumer (B2C) and Business to Business (B2B) arenas. With many businesses fighting to survive there have been new opportunities for consulting services in organizational restructuring and "lean" operations. Overall, the crisis has been seen by many organizations as a chance to implement new, better ways of "doing more with less." After the turmoil, many organizations will emerge stronger, fitter and healthier. As the adage goes – "what doesn't kill you, makes you stronger." And this is probably true, as long as you rise to the challenge and make any necessary changes to stay alive.

The same goes at a personal level. With a tough job market, those that keep their eyes open, remain flexible and take the initiative to gain more relevant knowledge and skills will thrive. This in turn will create a need for education and training services. Above all, there is likely to be a change in career opportunities in the public sector. With the large governmental economic stimulation packages implanted over the course of the last couple of years, career opportunities in certain sectors of government have blossomed. Nevertheless, as worldwide governments now strive to implement austerity programs to reverse public deficit and pay back sovereign debt, several public sectors will be cut back or outsourced to privatized lower cost providers. While the total number of public sector employees is likely to decrease as a result of austerity measures, appropriately qualified managers will be highly sought after to manage the processes of change – both in public and private sectors.

As the 20th century was molded by the end of two world wars, the 21st century will be shaped at its outset by how the global economy survives the current profound global economic uncertainties and how the sky-high public debt levels of developed economies are brought under control. Of course, a new role will be forged for emerging countries in driving the global economy. As developed nations grapple with their sovereign debt issues and developed nation consumers cut-back on their consumption, populations in emerging economies (starting with Brazil, Russia, India and China) may just start to pick up some of the slack. If they do, these nations will take on a greater importance, not only in their historical role as low cost production countries, but as important markets in their own right. As a result, emerging countries, trading on both the production and consumption sides, are likely to claim more significant roles at the international negotiating tables – leading to rapid and profound shifts in global geopolitical power; the topic of the next Global Trend.

Global Trend 2

Geopolitical Power Shifts

"Our future history will be more determined by our position on the Pacific facing China than by our position on the Atlantic facing Europe."

Barack Obama, President, United States of America.[1]

In 1905, Britain was the ruler of the waves and watched with concern as the United States of America rose to become a potential challenger. While a shared heritage between the two nations helped avoid military conflict as the USA inevitably overtook British international power, the rise of Germany and Japan in the 20th-century global power struggle did precipitate war. Now, in the 21st century, *The Economist* special report on China and the America explains that, with the rise of a richer and defiantly authoritarian China, President Barack Obama is likely to face a far more "nettlesome" challenger to the world order than his own country had been a century ago. Since the USA is still struggling to emerge from the crisis, and China's economy is still growing at pace (albeit somewhat slower than before the crisis), many experts see the balance of power shifting rapidly in favor of China. Recent references to a USA–China "G2" indicate a shift in relative nation-strengths and that these two countries are now seen as "near-equals, whose co-operation is vital to solving the world's problems."

Apparently world geopolitics* is on the move again. Actually, it never stopped – it just felt like it with over fifty years of post-World War II deadlocks and, from the end of the 20th century, a world policed by the only superpower left standing: the USA. Yet, under the surface there have always been undercurrents of change operating out of sight within global governance systems.

---

* Geopolitics is the study of geographic distributions of power among states. Multidisciplinary in its scope, geopolitics includes the study of reciprocal relations between geography, politics and power.

In addition to China, world political and business leaders have also been watching the other rapidly developing economies of Brazil, Russia and India, which, with China, form the often-seen acronym of the BRIC countries. In addition, some commentators include South Korea within these emerging powers – conveniently turning BRIC into BRICK.* Indeed, Bloomberg argues that South Korea is in fact "another 'BRIC' in the Global Wall."[2] Whether Korea is included in the party or not, few would argue that between them these countries are likely to be pivotal in directing the course of future politics, business and contributing to the success or failure of institutions such as the World Trade Organization (WTO).

The 2011 World Economic Forum (WEF) had a catchy theme: "Committed to improving the state of the world." And, by the forum's own accounts in its report, *Global Risks 2011*, the state of the world does indeed need some improving, given that:

Within the next ten years global governance failures is perceived to be "very likely" – with an estimated potential economic impact of over $500 billion.[3]

Such potential global governance failure is seen to be a direct consequence of the inevitable geopolitical power shifts with the (re)emergence of the BRICKs et al. So, what is fuelling the meteoric rise of these new world upstarts? In two words: *economic growth*. And this economic growth is expected to continue. The United States and the European Union are still the world's largest economic entities by far and, to all intents and purposes, currently remain the leaders of the world trading system. Yet change is in the air, since in terms of size, speed and directional flow, the transfer of global wealth and economic power now under way – roughly from West to East – is without precedent in modern history. As Martin Wolf, chief economics commentator at the *Financial Times*, put it: the West is looking at the "youthful vigour of emerging economies with admiration, envy and even fear."[4]

These shifts in economic power are derived from two principal sources: firstly, increases in oil and commodity prices have generated windfall profits for the likes of the middle east states, Brazil and Russia; and secondly, lower costs combined with government policies have shifted the locus of

---

* North Korea can largely be ignored in an economic sense.

manufacturing and some service industries to Asia – the lion's share of which has gone to China and India.

As a result, the contribution of the BRICKs to global exports has been continually increasing. In 1993, Brazil, Russia, India, China and Korea originated 10 percent of world exports. By 2007 this had more than doubled: 22 percent of world exports emanated from these five countries. China alone contributed an incredible 57 percent of that export growth in that time period.

By 2007, Brazil, Russia, India, China and Korea were a major focus of EU and US trade policy, accounting for 26.2 percent and 19.2 percent of total EU and US merchandise, respectively. Between 2000 and 2007, EU trade with the BRICKs more than tripled to almost $970 billion (of which 42 percent was with China). US trade with BRICKs increased two and a half times over this period and totaled about $612 billion in 2007 (of which 66 percent was with China).

Of course all this growth in trade has resulted in economic growth for these countries. The combined 2008 GDP of the BRICKs was almost $10 trillion or almost 70 percent of the United States and almost twice as large as the Japanese economy. According to the International Monetary Fund (IMF), the GDP of the BRICKs has been growing at a much faster rate than the USA, Japan and the EU. While the USA, Japanese and European economies dawdled along at approximately 2 to 3 percent between 2004 and 2008, the corresponding approximate figures in the BRICKs were: Brazil 3 to 6 percent; Korea 4 to 5 percent; Russia 6 to 8 percent; India 8 to 10 percent; and China at a breathtaking 10 to 13 percent.[5]

With the 2009 recession following the 2008 global financial crisis, the IMF calculated that many of the world economies shrank: the USA to about minus 3 percent; Japan to an estimated minus 6 percent; and Europe to approximately minus 4 percent. All in all, the crisis knocked about 6 to 8 percent off GDP growth year on year. The BRICKs did not escape unscathed: most of them experienced similar 5 to 8 percent dents in growth rates.

However, the economies in India and China continued to grow at a fairly healthy (by Western standards) estimated rate of 4.5 percent and 6.5 percent respectively. Nonetheless, while most of the Western world would love to achieve such real GDP growth rates even in normal times, by their own standards such growth was rather lackadaisical. With the crisis, both countries GDP growth slowed by about 5 to 6 percent – but at least they have kept growing. Each of the other BRICK economies shrank in 2009, affected by the repercussions of the global economic crisis: Brazil dropped to about minus 1 percent; Korea to an estimated minus 4 percent; and Russia dropped to an estimated minus 6 percent – about 13 percent below previous growth levels. Ouch.

Despite the recent economic turmoil, most indicators are that China, India, Russia, and Brazil will continue to be a huge potential powerhouse for driving the world economy.

A not-so-positive indicator of this, perhaps, is just how far they have still to go to catch-up in certain aspects. For example, while their GDP growth figures would indicate a rise to stardom, the average population of the BRICs is relatively poorer compared to that of the G7.* In 2000, the GDP per capita in BRICs was $2,618 compared with $29,651 in the G7. By 2014 these figures are predicted to rise to $8,654 in BRICs and $45,780 in the G7.[6] The gap remains big but in percentage terms is closing, and pretty fast by historical standards. Such statistics point to the enormous drive and motivation that well-positioned, but poor, populations experience to continue working hard to attain a better standard of living. Now they have seen and tasted some of the trappings of the rich world they are unlikely to slow down of their own accord.

GDP growth in BRIC countries has been and is expected to continue to be higher than G7 countries in the years to come.

The following table highlights the predicted continuing meteoric evolution of the share of world GDP for the BRIC countries compared to other major economies. It is clearly evident that as the economies of USA, Japan, Germany, UK and France (and all the other usual suspects) suffer a decrease in their global clout, the BRICs are on the up. There is simply a transfer of GDP growth from the mature to the new economies. For every apparently unstoppable percentage point increase in world share of GDP within the BRIC economies, there is a corresponding drop in share in the developed economies. And nowhere is this clearer than in a direct comparison of the statistics for

---

* G7 is a group of seven industrialized nations that include Canada, France, Germany, Italy, Japan, the United Kingdom and the United States.

the USA and China. Also, such figures would indicate that a touch of humility is required of individual countries within Europe when it comes to economic importance in the global arena (see Table 2.1).[7]

With such growth rates, the economies of the BRICs en masse could equal those of the G7 by 2032.

The interesting question is: *when will these upstart countries' GDPs overtake those of the individual G7 nations?*

Of course, we already know that China has overtaken France, UK, Germany and Japan within the last few years. But, according to the investment bank Goldman Sachs, China's economy is likely to surpass that of the USA by as soon as 2027. But beyond the China story, their predictions put India catching up with Canada in 2011, with Italy by 2020, followed by France, UK, Germany and Japan by around 2030. Russia next, has already overtaken Canada, and is set to overtake the Europeans by 2030, and her old rival Japan by 2038. Nor should we forget the feisty Brazilians, who are moving up fast on Russia's tail

Table 2.1: Share of world GDP for major global economies and BRICs

		2009 (%)	2010 (%)	2011 (%)	2012 (%)	2013 (%)	2014 (%)
Major global economies	USA	20.02	19.60	19.33	19.02	18.64	18.26
	Japan	6.20	6.04	5.92	5.79	5.62	5.46
	Germany	4.09	3.96	3.82	3.70	3.59	3.48
	UK	3.11	3.03	2.98	2.94	2.91	2.87
	France	2.99	2.92	2.87	2.82	2.77	2.72
BRICs	China	12.05	12.73	13.37	14.02	14.72	15.45
	India	4.95	5.09	5.23	5.38	5.55	5.71
	Russia	3.28	3.33	3.35	3.36	3.38	3.41
	Brazil	2.87	2.89	2.88	2.86	2.84	2.81

Note: Each group is ordered in descending order of size.

Source: *The Financial Times*, 2010.

and predicted to have overtaken Canada in 2011, the major European nations by 2032, and Japan also by 2038.[8]

Yet what of other non-BRIC emerging markets? Goldman Sachs identifies, in addition to the BRICs, the "Next-11" countries:

Bangladesh, Egypt, Indonesia, Iran, Mexico, Nigeria, Pakistan, Philippines, South Korea, Turkey and Vietnam also have a high potential of becoming the world's largest economies in the 21st century.

Of this other cohort of economies, apparently Mexico is currently in the lead and projected to overtake Canada by 2020, the Europeans by the late 2030s, and Japan by the 2040s. Next up, South Korea is expected to catch Canada by 2026 and Italy by 2035, and Indonesia, which will have overtaken Canada, the European nations and Japan between 2030 and 2050. Nigeria is on course for catching Canada, Italy and France in the 2040s; and Turkey, Vietnam and the Philippines will each overtake Canada and Italy also in the 2040s.

Can you imagine such a new world order in which the likes of humble Brazil will be bigger than even the biggest of European heavyweights, or that traditional underdogs such as Indonesia and Nigeria will be successfully taking economic power from the waning Europeans? And all this based on current growth rates (which also have the potential to accelerate) and predicted within ten, twenty, or thirty years. Certainly, if such predictions do come to pass, they will take major readjustment of attitudes across the globe.

Now that I have your attention with the impact of the rising economies, let's return to consider some salient aspects of each of the BRIC economies, starting with China…

As is patently obvious to any Wal-Mart shopper, the economies of the USA and China have become interlocked over the past decade.

America is the world's biggest debtor and China its biggest creditor. By September 2008 China had surpassed Japan as the largest holder of US Treasuries. According to *The Economist* magazine, China owns $800 billion of American government debt, enough to give it power of life and death over the American economy.[9] By comparison, the $200 billion of US Treasury securities held in Britain seems rather paltry, although Britain and China had started at similar levels back in 2000.

As a driver of national economic growth, China is following the tried and tested path of establishing an automotive sector. This is what many developed economies did throughout the 20th century to propel growth and modernization of society. In 2004, the *21st Century Business Herald* – one of China's leading newspapers – concluded an article on the rival centers of China's fast-growing car industry with:

Shanghai, Guangzhou, Changchun, Beijing, Wuhan, Chongqing: six cities with six dreams. But what they really all dream of is the same—Detroit.

Yet, with the Chinese government wanting to emulate America's use of the automotive industry as a driver of economic growth, *The Economist* article "Tug-of-car" states that:

Now Detroit dreams of China.[10]

In 2001, approximately 2 million light vehicles (cars, vans etc.) were sold in China compared to about 19 million in the USA. By 2009, both countries had sales levels of around 12 million. For the next decade this trend in car manufacturing is only likely to continue: USA less, China more.

But the story is not only about outsourcing low-cost manufacturing.

China has experienced the strongest growth in scientific research over the past three decades of any country.

Thomson Reuters, which indexes scientific papers from 10,500 journals worldwide, analyzed the performance of the four emerging-markets countries – Brazil, Russia, India and China – over the past 20 years. While in 2008, Brazil, India and Russia each published around 30 to 40,000 peer-reviewed scientific journal articles, China produced 112,318. This is still lower than innovative countries such as the USA, which published 332,916 articles in 2008. However, bear in mind that China was not really in the research game back in 1990 – but subsequent growth rate has been astounding and indicates a desire to take ownership higher-up the value chain than simply working on production lines.[11]

Throughout history, economic and technological development has led to increased military muscle. China is no different and has engaged in a rapid military build-up that could challenge America as the defender of Asian peace. Unannounced, China is building its first aircraft-carrier. Hence there are growing worries in Washington that China's military power could challenge America's wider military dominance in the region. Yet the Chinese government insists there is nothing to worry about and that it has no plans to displace American power in Asia. In fact, in 2009 the defense budget of China was a meager $80 billion. This compared to a US defense budget that has ramped-up considerably this decade to over $600 billion (and with additional funding likely to be approved).

According to the US National Intelligence Council (NIC), few countries are poised to have more impact on the world over the next 15–20 years than China. If current trends persist, by 2025 China will be the world's second-largest economy, a leading military power, the largest importer of natural resources and an even greater polluter than it is now. However, the biggest risk for China is that the government will find it difficult to maintain the high levels of autocratic control over the population's lives that they do today. As the country becomes wealthier and is exposed to alternative political and social systems, there is a significant chance that the Chinese people will reject their current subjugated lifestyle. Political turmoil could slow, or even derail, recent economic successes.[12,13]

India is the world's second-fastest-growing big economy after China. Since 1980, India's GDP growth has rarely dropped below 4 percent, and between 2003 and 2008 it has hovered somewhere between 8 and 10 percent.

> **Over the last few years, India's economy has grown
> at an average annual rate of 8.8 percent.**

Services, which contribute more than half of the GDP, have grown fastest; above all, India's computer-services companies.[14] Over the last five years the level of outsourcing call-centers to the Indian subcontinent has been astounding. Most English-speaking consumers are likely to have heard at some point the gentle, usually very polite, Indian accent of a Mumbai, Delhi or Bangalore call-center operator.

In certain aspects, confidence in India's growth exceeds that of China – in spite of the apparent Indian chaos compared to the Chinese efficiency. There are a couple of reasons for this: the first is that India is blessed with a young and growing workforce – a "demographic dividend." India has one of the world's lowest dependency ratios (of children and old people being supported by working-age adults) and this will remain so for a generation. By 2020, the working population in India is predicted to increase by close to 150 percent. The second reason for optimism is also one of the causes of so much chaos in the first place: democracy. While the democratic state may appear an inefficient mess, in the long run it is liable to be more robust. In addition, millions of innovative Indian entrepreneurs are permitted freedoms to develop businesses at home and across the globe. This has given the Indian private sector firm foundations in innovation and a competitive resilience. Thus, India probably will continue to enjoy relatively rapid economic growth and will strive for a multipolar world in which New Delhi is one of the poles. Although India faces lingering deficiencies in its domestic infrastructure, skilled labor, and energy production, the nation's rapidly expanding middle class, youthful population, reduced reliance on agriculture, and high domestic savings and investment rates will propel continued economic growth.[15]

Now let's consider the B, R and K of the BRICKs.

Brazil has established a solid economic foundation for steady growth based on political stability and an incremental reform process. Brazil is hosting the FIFA World Cup in 2014 and the summer Olympics in 2016, and as such will be in the spotlight over the coming few years. A recent study by the government said Brazil will invest $18 billion in infrastructure, and more than 700,000 permanent and temporary jobs will be created. On a more general level, Brazil has vast potential for sustained growth. Foreigners are pouring money into Brazil on a massive scale as the country is enjoying a new wave of trust and optimism – and foreign direct investment:

Brazil has become the 2nd largest destination for flows of foreign direct investment (FDI) into developing countries after China.

FDI in Brazil has risen from next to nothing as recently as 1995 to close to $50 billion of investment inflow by 2008. Furthermore, it appears that Brazilian society is stabilizing – with a score on the GINI coefficient, a measure of social inequality, falling and nearing comparable equality levels with the United States.[16]

Also we should not forget Brazil's natural resources: it has the world's largest freshwater supplies and history indicates a strong link between economic development and water resources (see Global Trend 5: Water and Food); it has the largest chunks of tropical forests – which may become important if carbon-trading ever truly takes off (see Global Trend 4: Climate Change); and Brazil is self-sufficient in oil and, with large new offshore discoveries in 2007, is likely to become a big oil exporter (see Global Trend 9: Energy). Brazil has actively been pursuing regional trade deals. It has sought to broaden its Mercosur* partnership with its other South American neighbors, and opened new talks with South Africa and India. It's noteworthy that Brazil's number-one trade priority is to have a comprehensive World Trade Organization (WTO) deal that would open US and European markets to Brazilian agricultural exports.

In the coming decades, therefore, in all likelihood Brazil will be exercising greater regional leadership, as a first among equals in South America. Nevertheless, aside from its growing role as an energy producer and its role in trade talks, it may demonstrate limited ability to project beyond the continent as a major player in world affairs. Nevertheless, its progress in consolidating democracy and diversifying its economy will serve as a positive regional model.

Russia will play a potential role in key areas like energy, climate change and investment and upon its accession to the WTO, in tandem with the new Asian trading powers. In 2008, it is estimated that Russia had 1,245,000 active military personnel and 2,400,000 active military reserves.

Significant numbers of military personnel, in addition to nuclear capabilities, make Russia still one of the strongest military powers on earth.

Cooperation between the USA and Russia has been crucial to world stability in the past decades. On the June 24 2010, Russia and the USA agreed to renew military cooperation and to work on nonproliferation.[17] Russia has the potential to be richer, more powerful, and more self-assured if it invests in human capital, expands and diversifies its economy, and integrates with global markets. On the other hand, the NIC's report *Global Trends: 2025* indicates that Russia could experience a significant decline if it fails to take these steps and oil and gas prices remain low or volatile.

South Korea has a significantly higher Growth Environment Score[†] than any of the other BRICKs.

---

* Mercosur is a Regional Trade Agreement (RTA) between Argentina, Brazil, Paraguay and Uruguay whose purpose is to promote free trade and the fluid movement of goods, people, and currency.
† Goldman Sachs' measure of the long-term sustainability of growth.

Of all the BRICKs, South Korea has followed the most aggressive strategy in terms of pacts with trading partners: forming the South Korea–ASEAN* pact; signing a Free Trade Agreement (FTA) with the USA in June 2007; launching negotiations on a similar deal with the EU, and establishing an economic partnership agreement with India in 2009; reviving FTA talks with Japan that had been stalled; and advancing consultations with China with the aim to open negotiations on a bilateral trade pact. The South Koreans have been busy.[18]

Having considered the various conditions in and around these countries, it is now time to consider another question:

Will economic clout translate into political muscle and a shift in power?

The US NIC reckons the answer is "Yes," based upon an international futures model measuring defense spending, population and technology for individual states. There will be a shift in the center of gravity of political weight by 2025. The two main losers will be the USA and Europe, with state power as a percentage of global power dropping from about 23 percent to 21 percent, and from approximately 18 percent to 13 percent, respectively between 2005 and 2025. The obvious winners will be China (with state power rising from about 11 percent to 15 percent of global power between 2005 and 2025) and India (7 percent to 9 percent of global political power 2005–2025). Japan also loses power, while Russia and Brazil marginally gain: all three standing at a similar level of about 4 percent of global political power by 2025.

So, China is set to overtake the European Union as a political power by 2025.

Furthermore, Europe will remain heavily dependent on Russia for energy for years to come, despite efforts to promote energy efficiency, renewable energy and lower greenhouse gas emissions. Another immense challenge facing Europe is its shrinking and aging population. Nor are there any easy fixes for Europe's economic deficits except likely cutbacks in health and retirement benefits, which most states are only just beginning to contemplate. A further sign of Europe's declining geopolitical weight may come in the form

---

* Association of South East Asian Nations.

of reduced defense expenditure to stave off the need for serious restructuring of social benefits programs.

But will the USA maintain its position of power? Apparently so. Despite losing a few percentage points of global power, the USA is predicted to remain the strongest player in 2025. But there is a twist. As per their 2008 report on global trends, the Director of National Intelligence and the NIC will be advising the President and policy-makers of the USA that by 2025, the United States will find itself in the position of being one of a number of important actors on the world stage, albeit still probably the most powerful one. The USA probably will continue to be seen as a much-needed regional balancer in the Middle East and Asia. Developments in the rest of the world, including internal developments in a number of key states – particularly China and Russia – are also likely to be crucial determinants of US policy.

None of the above analysis really considers changing patterns in the Muslim world. Clearly countries such as Iran, Indonesia, and Turkey could play increasingly important roles on the world stage and especially for establishing potential new directions for Muslim countries. Iran has the second-largest reserves of natural gas in the world (See Global Trend 9: Energy). Additionally it is strong in human capital. If there is political and economic reform in Iran in addition to a stable investment climate, economic resurgence could take place quickly. However Iran's determination to follow a nuclear program has increased its isolation from the world – as demonstrated when the UN Security Council passed resolution 1929 on June 9 2010 imposing sanctions.[19]

According to the IMF, Indonesia is currently the 18th-largest economy in the world. It also has the fourth-largest population in the world and has abundant natural resources, giving Indonesia huge potential for growth. Apparently, Indonesia could rise economically if its elected leaders take steps to improve the investment climate, including strengthening the legal system, improving the regulatory framework, reforming the financial sector, reducing fuel and food subsidies, and generally lowering the cost of doing business.[20]

By the same IMF estimates, Turkey is currently the 17th-largest economy in the world. It has also been playing a very active role as a mediator within the Middle East. Turkey is actively trying to find a negotiated solution to the Iranian nuclear crisis, is working with the Iraqis and the Kurds to manage conflict in Iraq, and recently played a leadership and mediation role between Israel and Syria. Turkey was also previously pushing for progress on the peace process between Arabs and Israelis. Clearly this is a country with increasing self-confidence in playing at a global level.

Threats and opportunities

At a society and business level, there are continuing threats on the radar screen for those based in slow-moving mature nations that have benefitted from the 20th-century status quo. With the foreseeable continuing rise of BRICs and many others, it is likely that certain functional business areas will keep moving to these lower-cost countries, with corresponding continued loss of employment in developed countries. As the emerging markets climb the social scale, they are likely to go beyond poaching low-paid manufacturing jobs and move towards the higher-end research and development roles that most developed nations have considered their exclusive domain. Exacerbated by the fallout from the economic crisis (Global Trend 1) this could lead to continuing social problems.

All of the above changes in geopolitical dynamics will lead to shifts of power, pressure on resources and increased potential for conflict. Apparently, the world is shifting towards a multipolar system, with a less dominant USA and Europe and a more powerful China and India, and a historic transfer of wealth generally from west to east. While the USA will probably remain the most powerful country in 2025, the rise of emerging powers and regional blocs will constrain its ability to "call the shots" across the world. According to the Director of National Intelligence and the National Intelligence Council of the USA, the whole international system – as constructed following World War II – is likely to prove inadequate in dealing with the new geopolitical challenges. Not only will the new players, starting with Brazil, Russia, India, China, but also including several other potential rising challengers, have a seat at the international high table, they will bring new stakes and rules of the game.

Of course, one threat for societies and businesses of the increased global influence of the likes of China and Russia would be a potential corresponding decrease in democratic processes in an international context. Neither of these countries has an exemplary record in open, transparent ways of doing things, clear legal systems or a solid stance on human rights. Rather there is a risk that the corruption, bribery and coercion that appear to be normal practices in some aspects of BRIC life could potentially spill over onto the wider geopolitical stage. On a business level, such issues could lead to conflicts of interest.

As companies expand their global network and try to benefit from the advantages of moving their operations to other, less democratic countries, they may face some ethical dilemmas. For example: a major German car manufacturer was recently accused of paying bribes in China and Nigeria to win business deals,[21] and in order to renew its Internet Content Provider license in China, Google had a long series of run-ins with the Chinese authorities and compromised certain principle of freedom of access to information.[22]

Similarly, there are potential environmental threats as geopolitical power shifts to countries that have demonstrated less concern regarding actions such as reducing pollution. When the goal is economic growth above all else for new world players, it will be harder to enforce regulations to reduce environmental damage (see Global Trends 4 and 10).

A particular geopolitical sticking point is likely to be the pressure upon resources. Unprecedented economic growth of the emerging nations, coupled with 1.2 billion more people (see Global Trend 7), will put pressure on resources – particularly energy, food, and water – raising the probability of demand outstripping supply and severe shortages. The pace of technological innovation will be key to outcomes during this period. At present though, it would seem that all current technologies are inadequate for replacing traditional energy architecture on the scale needed. It should be no surprise, therefore, that China is currently busying itself with buying up oil, minerals, metals and all manner of other natural resources across Asia, Africa and Latin America in order to fuel its growth.

The smoothness in transition of power from old to new will depend in large part on how well-disposed the incumbent nations are to relinquishing their power and how open the upstarts are to accept alternative ways of doing things. Hence the concern of the world's movers and shakers at the 2011 World Economic Forum over the likelihood of global governance failure and geopolitical conflict within the next ten years. At time of writing, the oil-rich and unstable countries of North Africa and the Middle East are proving, yet again, to be potential catalysts of wider geopolitical turmoil and global change. The ousting of President Hosni Mubarak from the presidency of strategically important Egypt has startled the global community – not least because he was one of the very few Muslim leaders not to be an intransigent enemy of Israel. Also, the world's eyes will always be trained on political events in Egypt given that two-thirds of European oil and nearly 8 percent of global shipping traffic passes through the Suez Canal.

The same is true of Libya – also undergoing, at time of writing, turmoil, with its eccentric leader Muammar Gaddafi fighting for his political life against rebel forces, and UN intervention looking increasingly likely to persist and play a key role in the country's political development.[23] Given that the oil reserves in Libya are the largest in Africa and the ninth-largest in the world – and that these reserves are particularly attractive due to low costs of production and close proximity to European markets – recent events are causing concern across the global geopolitical arena.

The wider threat to stability is that other political regimes in the Middle East oil-producing nations will become infected by the pro-democracy "Jasmine Revolution" that started in Tunisia and spread to Egypt and Libya. While the West has turned a blind eye towards the political and social faults of these regimes in the past, in the interests of keeping the oil flowing, the status quo has now been brought into question. Now there is the very real possibility of oil supplies being disrupted because of political turmoil in countries like Bahrain and even the world's largest oil producer, Saudi Arabia.[24] Given the ongoing trials of a world attempting to emerge from the economic crisis, disruption to oil supply, resulting in increasing energy prices and slower economic recovery would be the worst-case scenario, one that many countries – including the USA, China and most of Europe, might be unwilling to accept. The geopolitical stakes are high, with several contenders jostling to act as regional balancer in Africa and the Middle East.

Assuming the almost inevitable geopolitical friction doesn't translate into all-out Armageddon (which is not really in anybody's interests) but rather can be resolved through good old-fashioned diplomatic dialogue, then there are tremendous areas of opportunity within the changing geopolitical landscape. Facing up to the challenges presented by the new geopolitical realities, the World Economic Forum's Geopolitical Global Agenda Council[25] summarized several opportunities, stating that at the national level governments of medium-sized rising powers like Brazil, Indonesia and Turkey will have the opportunity to redefine their roles on the regional and international stages. As a result, new international forums will emerge to include the upcoming nations and to resolve geopolitical issues. In order to avoid conflict, nations will need to adopt the alternative of greater levels of collaboration over global issues, and in the medium- to long-term that has to be a good thing. This should make many of the emerging governments of the world more responsible. Most world leaders are aware that belligerence only gets you so far in the modern world. With the fallout from the crisis there have already been unprecedented levels of global cooperation between the most unlikely of political partners. While it would be naïve to think this will magically resolve all of the big global sticking points tomorrow, the major nations of the world are so interconnected that it is in everyone's interests to keep talking and bringing solutions to the table. The financial crisis has been a big wake-up call for the world's politicians, and the shifting geopolitical sands presents a huge opportunity for them to resolve some underlying weaknesses in the outdated world governance structures.

Certainly, at the economic level David Ricardo argued, in 1817, that there was a positive impact when two countries trade: each country gaining by specializing in the good where it has comparative advantage, and trading that good for another. As power shifts and more regional markets with distinct competitive advantages emerge, the world's GDP will increase along with per-capita economic standards. In theory at least, everyone wins – society, business and individuals – as long as (often tempting) local protectionist measures can be avoided. From increased geopolitical collaboration will emerge the opportunity to improve global financial stability. This will take considerable work, but again it is in the interests of all. Just look at how hard European politicians are working together to keep Europe on track despite their national differences. Faced with a stark alternative, human beings seem to fight extra-hard to do the right thing.

In this process of geopolitical evolution, nations, businesses and individuals will have the chance to decouple from the constraints of previously flawed ways of doing things. For example, despite the colonial hyperbole, Africa has to all intents and purposes been a forgotten continent for many decades. Now, particularly with an upcoming geopolitical struggle for resources, it is squarely on the agenda for development. China, in particular, is investing huge sums in infrastructure development in Africa. Notwithstanding corruption and other ills, at least some of this investment will filter down to improve living standards, education and health in certain African nations.

For international companies and investors the Geopolitical Global Agenda Council forecasts that CEOs who understand the increased role of governments in market activity in many countries, particularly in state-capitalist emerging markets, will be best positioned to benefit from first-mover advantage. Also, companies with diversified risk exposure will be better placed to survive an inevitable period of volatility in global markets. Thus, those players who understand the dynamics behind emerging markets will be best placed to profit. Of course, at the business level, strong emerging markets are synonymous with new growth opportunities. Those firms who best adapt their strategies to fit the realities of these new markets will be the winners. In addition, local firms from the BRICs and other emerging nations will enjoy greater success at home and greater learning opportunities through partnerships with foreign firms. This may enable them to gain the financial strength and skills necessary to become multinational players competing with existing large companies in Western markets. The medium – to long-term continued expansion of these emerging economies is almost inevitable – albeit with occasional hiccups or even gastroenteritis. The road will not be easy for businesses in these countries, but as the BRICKs and other rapidly developing nations provide new sources of growth, and as investment grows, better infrastructure will be built, new local companies will appear and the countries' local markets will become even more attractive for foreign investment.

On a personal level, those individuals who are well informed, prepared to be flexible in the face of geopolitical change, and prepared to adapt will have the chance to prosper. Such profound worldwide change will open up new spaces for entrepreneurs to address new market needs across the globe. In developed nations such entrepreneurial activities could maintain current standards of living. In emerging nations such activities offer the potential of lifting millions of people out of poverty and providing them with access to basic services to ensure adequate provision of food, health and education to help create the next productive generation. Beyond this, however, perhaps individuals should be aware of the need to demonstrate the upcoming nations the benefits of mature-country principles – starting with fundamental human rights.

Of course, geopolitical power has historically come from a nation's ability to provide the conditions for innovation and technological development in order to lift standards of living, to drive productivity growth and to exert some power at the global level – on an economic and/or military level. This brings us to the matter of technological challenges… the topic of the next Global Trend.

Global Trend 3

Technological Challenges

"Any sufficiently advanced technology is indistinguishable from magic."

Sir Arthur C. Clarke, Author, Inventor and Futurist[1]

What is your favorite technology? An iPhone? Laptop with wireless Internet connection? Cellphone with built in digital camera? Facebook? Or something more traditional, like home cinema projectors?

If you're interested, my favorite technology is a hammer. You may be surprised, but frankly it is somewhat better at hitting nails into things than any of the above modern gizmos. Judged on dimensions of cost, durability, reliability, and a simple-to-understand instruction leaflet it clearly stands out from other technologies. It doesn't need batteries or recharging, is fairly environmentally inert and user-friendly (apart from the odd black fingernail from time to time.) What is more, this technological device has been in existence in different forms since pretty much the first human being who lifted a rock, tied it to a stick and used the resulting contraption to crack a nut about 2.5 million years ago.[2]

In other words, "technology" does not just apply to new stuff. Technology is a broad concept that deals with human (as well as other animal species'*) usage and knowledge of tools and crafts, and an ability to control and adapt the environment. While technology does keep advancing, it has been with us since the very first human beings. In fact, managing technological development is pretty much what we as a species are about. From the first control of fire, ceramic cookware, through the invention of the wheel, wind and water mills, bronze, iron, steel, the printing press, steam power, the car, the mobile

---

* Until recently it was believed that the development of technology was restricted to human beings, but recent scientific studies indicate that other primates and certain dolphin communities have developed simple tools and learned to pass their knowledge to other generations.

phone the Internet and the Space Shuttle, technological development has followed step-by-step the trajectory of human development. Or vice versa.

Human history has always been about keeping up with technological advances in order to make life more comfortable (fire), easier (the wheel), more productive (the printing press, steam power), more mobile (the car) etcetera etcetera.

As we sit at the beginning of the 21st century with Internet and a whole plethora of fancy gadgets at our disposal it is worth remembering that the world we live in is not only the result of recent – often fantastic – breakthroughs in science and technology. It is also the result of legacy technological breakthroughs made throughout history.

The importance of legacy technologies is quite nicely demonstrated by a favorite anecdote of mine about the Space Shuttle. Apparently, it was neither designed in metric (meters and centimeters) or imperial (feet and inches) measures – but rather in widths of the average Roman horse's bum.

Let me explain. It goes without saying that the clever Romans designed their wheeled chariots to fit the width of the said equine *derriere*, and so ended up with a fairly standard axle width across the various chariot models. Any nonstandard chariot would be constantly bobbing in-and-out of the ruts made by countless previous (standard) chariots, thus resulting in a very uncomfortable ride for passengers and the high likelihood of broken wheels, axles and chassis.

With the Roman exploits across Europe all those roads were rutted pretty much to the same width. Even after the Romans had long since departed, the rutted roads remained, and any carriage maker worth his salt would make wagons and carriages offering comfort and durability to the end user – with a workshop and tooling based on that Roman horse's backside measure. Not much changed for centuries in the roads of Europe until steam power arrived, with subsequent roll-out of train transport. And who made the first trains? The existing carriage makers did, with their existing workshop and tool facilities. Thus the British and European railway width gauges were also derived from the same horsey anatomy measure (apart from cases such as Spain, where rail gauges were set deliberately differently to stop invading forces just hopping on the 10.38 from Calais). Again, this gauge became more or less standard, and when trains and railways were exported to the new lands across the Atlantic the machinery and bits and pieces that were installed there were based on the same dimensions as Europe. The "standard gauge" (also named the Stephenson gauge, after George Stephenson, or Normal gauge) is a widely used rail gauge. Approximately 60 percent of the world's existing railway lines are built to this measure. The distance between the inside edges of the rails of standard gauge track is a somewhat improbable 1,435 millimeters or 4 ft 8½ inches (… or could this be exactly twice the width of an average Roman horse's backside?).

Now, fast-forward to the 21st century. The Space Shuttle's solid rocket boosters need to be transported into the NASA Kennedy Space Station along a railway connecting to the Florida East Coast Railroad – constructed in the 19th Century on these same Roman horse dimensions. The route from the supplier of solid rocket boosters goes along this railway line and through some tunnels also based upon the same measure. As a result, one of the main criteria for the rocket boosters' design was that they had to be able to pass through these tunnels. So there you have it, the Space Shuttle (or at least the boosters) are measured in widths of the average Roman horse's bum.

While the accuracy of this anecdote is probably open to considerable debate, it is a nice story which illustrates the concept of legacy technologies.

Emerging technologies are often *incremental* developments upon previous generations of technologies.

Even Wall-E (the futuristic robotic star of the film of the same name) has a start-up tune of existing models of Apple computers. Wherever we go with technological development we will always be constrained somewhat by key past and present legacy technologies.

Having said that, though, technology WILL continue to develop and find new, surprising ways of making our lives more enriching, enjoyable, confusing, and frustrating, and generally cause our societies to change irreversibly. The inevitable march of technological development will open our businesses to new markets and make them more productive – or conversely make them outdated and nonviable.

Apparently, some sectors of Victorian society assumed that with steam power they had reached the summit of human technological advancement, with no further innovative breakthroughs left to be found. Of course they were wrong, just as anyone today is wrong to believe that we are at the peak of technological genius with the Internet, mobile phones and genetically

Figure 3.1: The S-curve

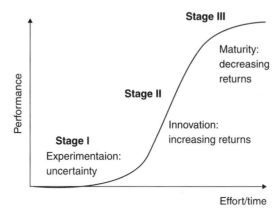

modified breakfast cereal. There will be further technological developments that will have profound impact on the way we work, rest and play.

While most technological development is through *incremental* changes to past inventions, occasionally a *disruptive* technological advancement comes along that can radically change the way things are done. Such disruptive technologies can come in the form of either a new breakthrough (such as fire, controlled flight, the Internet) or a clever combination of previously unlinked inventions (such as the car, heart surgery, the iPad).

It was just such a disruptive technological advancement that flummoxed the last Samurai and resulted in their downfall (as presented in the Introduction). Let's explain with Figure 3.1.

What in business circles is called the technology "S-curve.*"**

From the 7th century AD to the 1100s the Samurai culture emerged and went through a great deal of experimentation and uncertainty as they developed stage I of their technological base and society structure. Amongst other things they experimented with early forms of warfare, bows and arrows, armor, swords and so on. Yet as they entered the 13th century, the rate of innovation and technological advancement increased, for good reason: they had to use all their

---

* Since its form is of a flat S.

ingenuity to repel the Mongol invaders. This was stage II of their technological trajectory, as they developed steel that was (and still is) really very impressive, along with a whole battlefield strategy that led to them wipe the floor with any enemy they encountered. They incorporated cannons and some firearms into their arsenal upon meeting the Portuguese and Dutch visitors in the 1500s, but preferred to base their warfare upon their far more reliable *katana* swords and *yumi* longbows with a range of 100 meters. They were, at this point, the masters of the universe, and for very practical reasons probably viewed the fire-sticks with some disdain. So a mix of practicality, arrogance and cultural inertia prevented them from taking things further with the new "pop-gun" technology, which they probably considered dirty, awkward, noisy, unpredictable, often dangerous for the user, and frankly dishonorable (possibly rather similar characteristics to those Europeans that brought them.) After several centuries of successfully waging war, the Samurai leaders knew best. Or at least they thought so.

But they didn't account for stage 3 of the S-curve. After all, you won't squeeze many more meters out of a bow and arrow, and there is a limit as to how many heads one person can chop off with a sword, however good he may be at writing poetry about cherry blossom. So moving into the 1700s and 1800s the Samurai entered maturity and a phase of diminishing rates of improvement.

Very unfortunately for them, another technology S-curve was busy entering the high-innovation stage II during the 1800s (ironically, across the Pacific Ocean). During the American Civil War, those early European fire-sticks were being developed into pretty lethal pieces of kit. A decisive moment occurred in 1861 when a certain Dr. Richard J. Gatling decided to attach several barrels together with crank handle and gravity-fed reloading mechanism. The Gatling gun was born: a disruptive technology if ever there was one. Now three uneducated farm hands from Kentucky could shoot down a whole army of highly educated, experienced and motivated warriors.

The Samurai had glued themselves to a set of technologies that was always going to run out of gas.

Ultimately they paid for it, not because they weren't aware of firearms, but because they chose largely to ignore their potential for further development. Even when the writing was on the wall, their response was to try harder using the techniques they were familiar with. It may seem blatantly obvious now that a Gatling gun will always beat a *katana,* but the Samurais' initial response is actually typical throughout the history of technological development – not just for societies but also on the business level.

Take the Tudor Ice Company for example. A fantastic, well financed company, recruiting the smartest managers and engineers; sales figures increasing year-on-year for the last 50 years; and the most global company in the sector – producing and exporting throughout the Americas, Europe and Asia via highly efficient operations and logistics networks. At the Boston Trade Association, the founder Mr. Frederick Tudor stated: "This industry has been growing and extending itself with no successful competitor for more than half a century, and there is reason to think it is yet in its infancy."

So, would you like a job there?

Oh, I forgot to mention, the Tudor Ice Company produces ice... cutting it from the frozen lakes around Boston. And we are in the 1860s.

Perhaps you are suddenly not so tempted by the job offer, but actually the Tudor Ice Company was an incredible organization that made millions for the Tudor family. Imagine shipping approximately 160,000 tons of spring-water ice annually from Boston to the gin & tonic drinking elite of the Caribbean, Bombay and Hong Kong in the 1800s. The only blot on the landscape was that ice was clearly more expensive in hot areas, thus prompting meat distributors to look for alternatives to natural ice. They became aware of the first practical refrigeration demonstrations in England in 1834, and by 1868 the first commercial man-made ice plant was opened in (hot) New Orleans.

As with the Samurai, Tudor came up against a rival technology S-curve entering high rate of improvement (stage II), just as its own technologies were apparently reaching maturity (stage III).

Yet, the Tudor Ice reaction was to renew efforts to boost natural ice production with new innovations such as steam-powered circular saws, mechanical conveyors from ponds to warehouses and better distribution systems. All these innovations helped the Tudor Ice Company to reduce prices and continue to compete. In fact, 1886 was the record year for natural ice production in the USA at 25 million tons.

But there is only so long a company cutting ice from lakes in Boston can compete against a refrigeration plant that is already located in a hot destination. And with the advent of electrical household refrigerators the game was up and lugging big blocks of pond-ice around the globe was no more.[3]

Again, it was not that Mr. Tudor et al. were not aware of the new technologies, but rather that they ignored them and thought their traditional way of doing things was best. If the Samurai, or Tudor Ice, had kept an eye on emerging technologies and absorbed them into their own ways of doing things, perhaps they would have survived longer. But they didn't – so they didn't.

What makes the job of keeping abreast of new technologies harder is that they usually come from somewhere else. As a result of vested interests, corporate and social inertia, herd instinct, myopic or tunnel-vision executive decisions and so on, disruptive technologies rarely come from within the sector. An expert in swordsmanship may come up with some incremental innovations in hand-to-hand combat weapons, but is highly unlikely to come up with a disruptive firearm innovation. An expert in cutting ice from ponds may develop faster, more efficient ways of extracting the natural ice, but is unlikely to push any new-fangled refrigeration technologies.

Steamships did not emerge from the sailing fraternity. Digital cameras did not originate from the conventional photography sector. Word-processing software was not innovated by typewriter manufacturers.

> **Disruptive technologies are invariably developed somewhere else and, all too often, take the incumbents by surprise when they "invade" the established market by offering improved performance.**

What is sobering is that many of the incumbent cultures and companies associated with the previous technologies simply do not survive. Newcomers

Figure 3.2: Disruptive technology invades an established market

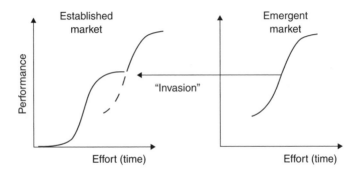

bring a different perspective and set of skills, with limited legacy investments and so less to lose. As Clayton Christensen points out in his book *The
Innovator's Dilemma*, such disruptive technologies can result in the death of
"well managed companies that have their competitive antennae up, listen to
their customers, invest aggressively in new technologies, and yet still lose market dominance."[4] Christensen argues that business practices such as focusing
efforts on the most profitable current products and customers can ultimately
weaken a company in any sector. Mainstream customers often reject innovations, which can lead firms with strong customer-focus to allow strategically
important innovations to languish – unwittingly bypassing opportunities and
creating space for more nimble, entrepreneurial companies to "catch the next
great wave of industry growth."

Let's think mechanical typewriters for a moment. Would you prefer to be a
typewriter manufacturer in the late 1960s before word-processing PCs came
along, or at the beginning of the 21st century? Let's face it life was good for
them in the 1960s, and now there are no mass-markets for them anymore.
Right? Well, it could just be the other way round. From the 1970s things got
pretty treacherous for the average typewriter supplier and most simply did
not survive the competition from the disruptive word processor technologies. On the other hand, those few that did manage to survive, would have
incorporated some of the new technology and perhaps have a relatively
comfortable niche market right now.

Consider this for a moment:

> **How many of the top 100 companies of the 1960s have
> survived unscathed the last 40 years?**
> **Answer: less than 1 in 5.**

Only 19 percent of the top 100 companies in 1966 were still top 100 companies in 2006. Another 15 percent still existed, but had shrunk (often considerably). A full 66 percent of the top companies had died within 40 years.[5]

Much of this change in top companies is driven by disruptive new technologies that can rapidly change ways of doing things, kill incumbent companies'
competitive advantage or simply sweep aside whole industry sectors within
the blink of an eye. Of course this can have a profound impact at a society
and national level, and thus political and business leaders need to be very
conscious of the threats that invading technologies pose to the status quo. As

such, the World Economic Forum's report *Global Risks 2011* identifies "threats from new technologies" as being likely to occur within the next decade, and attach a perceived negative economic impact of around $200 billion to such a threat. One technological issue that concerns leaders is around the still-developing technology area of the Internet, and particularly the thorny topic of online data and information security: perceived as likely to pose a threat within the next ten years and also to the tune of around $200 billion.[6]

While the WEF Global Risks report understandably focuses upon the risks, there are considerable opportunities presented by new technologies. The flip side of the coin is that, while many companies die as a result of not being able to adapt to new ways of doing things, even more new companies are created as a result of innovations.

In fact, on the upside, 81 percent of the top 100 companies in 2006 were new to the list since 1966, and many did not even exist in 1966.

This is what is called the "creative destruction" power of technological innovation. If you play your cards right, technology can open up considerable new opportunities to new players. Not much explanation needs to be given here of the benefits of technology in creating new sectors, new markets, new products, new methods of production, new ways of transporting products from different areas of the world, and so on. Just look at the meteoric rise of Apple and the plethora of products emerging each year from similarly technologically gifted companies.

On the other hand though, just as getting involved with a new technology too late can be disastrous, it can also be counterproductive to get involved with technologies too early in their S-curve evolution. As most early users of technologies find out, it can be pretty uncomfortable, frustrating, time-consuming, or downright dangerous to get involved with crude new innovations before they have fully emerged from the development phases. After all, the S-curves of different technologies can take different forms – with some technologies spending a long, long time in stage I before finding a widespread use. Many, or possibly most, innovations simply die at this early stage and never see the light of day.

Just consider the early mobile phones that first emerged on the market in the 1973. They were about the size of a briefcase and weighed in at 2 kilos. "Lead users" of such devices would have had to deal with comparatively astronomic prices, with relatively abysmal battery life and erratic coverage. Even with modern mobile phones, while there is apparently no firm evidence to link mobile phone use to health issues, scientists still caution that further surveillance is needed before conclusions can be drawn – and there is still some concern, particularly for children. A major research study running from 2000 to 2010 across Australia, Canada, Denmark, Finland, France, Germany, Israel, Italy, Japan, New Zealand, Norway, Sweden and the UK to see whether mobile phone use is associated with an increased risk of head and neck tumors concluded:

> *"The possible effects of long-term heavy use of mobile phones require further investigation."*[7]

So even now, the jury is apparently still out, and it would seem that perhaps with mobile telephones we may still be relatively low down in the S-curve in the experimentation and uncertainty of Stage I. Quite apart from the risk of physical harm caused by getting involved with still unproven technologies, there are the potential psychological and emotional impacts of overuse of such relatively new technologies. This is rather concerning given the huge take-up rates of mobile phones – particularly amongst youngsters. According to the *Emerging Health Threats Journal*,[8] levels of ownership (and possible excessive use) of mobile phones amongst the young are: 90 percent of 11–16-year-olds in the UK; 95 percent of 14-year-olds in Sweden; 76 percent of 10–11-year-olds in Hungary; and over 95 percent of 14–19-year-olds in Germany. These ownership and usage rates are still increasing and moving to ever-younger age-groups.

A quick glance over the early history of X-rays after Röntgen's discovery in 1895 reveals a rather gory story of misunderstanding the potential health threats behind new technologies. Early users of X-ray equipment commented on deep sunburn, dermatitis, hair loss, painful sores and swollen fingers with prolonged exposure – but often seemed to dismiss such things somewhat jovially as minor ailments hardly worth bothering with. Yet a few years later these ailments had developed into severe cancerous tumors, amputations, and radiation-induced cancer deaths. As Geoff Meggitt explains in *Taming the Rays*:[9]

> The explosion of interest in the rays meant that exploitation far outstripped understanding and when potential hazards were seen they were

widely ignored. So, the absence of shielding around the early X-ray tubes resulted in considerable injury to the operators, and the problem was compounded by the common practice of operators looking at their own hand with a fluorescent screen to test the apparatus.

Many X-ray lead user operators suffered delayed but appalling injuries. By 1936 there was a memorial erected in Hamburg to commemorate the deaths of these "heroic pioneers for a safe and successful application of X-rays to medicine." Marie Curie died in 1934 of leukemia caused by exposure to high-energy radiation from her research. It took several years for the lethal effect of X-rays on unborn fetuses to be understood, while physicians continued to examine pregnant women with X-rays. And it took yet more years to pin down widespread safety measures and protocols for the safe use of X-rays.

> **Many of the early X-ray users died from their injuries and even more were to die from unsuspected long-term effects that were a long-way from being fully understood.**

Perhaps there is a message here: as an individual avoid being a lead user with any untested or unproven new technology that could affect your health. And societies should beware of widespread roll-out of such technologies without understanding the longer-term consequences. With companies too, timing is everything. Become attached to a new technology during the experimentation phase and you risk wasting money, time and effort in the short-term and potential collapsing market and law suits in the medium and long term. On the other hand, waiting too late could mean that you could miss the boat, losing out on some important beneficial breakthroughs and new strategic opportunities for growth.

The way we live as people and as families, the way we do business, and the way societies are structured have changed hugely as a result of technological development through the ages. Yet, while technology in all forms has been advancing throughout human history, it would appear that as a result of the sheer number of people and efforts being devoted to innovation, the rate of technological progress is increasing. Of course there have been huge positives emerging from all this innovation: running water and sewage control; medicine and healthcare; improved housing; better mobility and communications.

In fact, a lot of the improvements in quality of life are due to technological advances.

However, there are also clear negatives. If you are on the wrong side of technological advances, or of technologies that go awry, it won't only fail to improve your quality of life – it may significantly reduce the length of it. Just consider the horrors of weapons of war and the health impacts of increased pollution, contamination and increasing amounts of rubbish. Even new, sexy, and "always-on" technologies such as Internet-enabled mobile phones have their downsides and have been blamed for excesses – in the form of increased stress and information overload, reduced social skills amongst incessantly "texting" youth and the Facebook generation. Of tremendous concern to any parent is that developments such as the Internet also permit increases in traditionally unacceptable behaviors, such as child pornography.

There are winners and losers. As an individual you want to be on the right side, and the same applies to societies and businesses. Drawing lessons from both the costly BP Deepwater Horizon oil spill in 2010 and the potentially catastrophic Fukushima Dai-ichi nuclear plant failure in 2011, *The Economist* article "In place of safety nets" recommends:

> *"Don't assume disasters won't happen at the frontiers of technology – presume they will."*[10]

The article goes on to recommend that three rules are applied to implementation of new "brittle" technologies:

- *Rule 1*

  Even if day-to-day operations seem to be safe and secure, disasters still happen. For years the oil industry planned on the fail-safe functioning of "blowout preventers," yet the Deepwater Horizon disaster indicated that such devices do not always live up to their name. Similarly, records indicate that partial meltdowns such as that at the Fukushima nuclear power plant are more likely than the nuclear industry routinely tells itself.

- *Rule 2*

  Develop technologies for repair and remediation before they are needed. Oil companies operating in the Gulf of Mexico are now developing a system to cap leaking wells. But such efforts could have been implemented before the Deepwater Horizon incident. *The Economist* also remarks that "Fukushima and other nuclear plants seem oddly lacking in robotic access to places where workers cannot or should not go."

- *Rule 3*

  When the safety nets of rules 1 and 2 fail for some reason, improvisation is needed and "situational awareness is invaluable." In effect this means that information-gathering sensor systems should be deployed routinely, widely and even in seemingly redundant ways. Apparently, the US Energy Secretary, Steven Chu, was shocked that the only source of information from the Deepwater Horizon's blowout preventer was a single gauge. Furthermore, *The Economist* considers that appropriate sensor systems "should also be kept independent of the related systems used for control; you want them to work even if – especially if – the control system does not."

So, both history and recent bitter experience have shown that new technologies should be treated with care. Furthermore, when so much can be at stake, wide-scale implementation of recent innovations should be undertaken on the assumption that things can go wrong, rather than naïvely relying upon keeping fingers crossed.

Threats and opportunities

Clearly, all of the above represent considerable threats and opportunities at society, corporate and individual levels. The key question is: what are the threats and opportunities? And for whom? Perhaps a good starting-point is to consider the technologies that surround us today (which, by the way, are very different to those surrounding our parents, grandparents, great grandparents…).

A typical family in a standard house in any average socioeconomic level part of the Western world will most probably have a couple of modern petrol or diesel powered cars, several hands-free telephones, plus mobile phones (with digital camera), a computer or two with broadband Internet connection, satellite TV, video-DVD home cinema set-up, and microwave oven. There will even be robots in the form of washing machines, dishwashers, and dryers. And this is not even a particularly avant-garde household in technological terms. Higher-tech households may have even fancier robots in the form of self-guiding automatic vacuum cleaners and lawnmowers. But this is all the normal stuff we think comes under the "technology" umbrella. Yet there is more: the boxed breakfast cereals and fresh strawberries we eat 365 days per year represent huge technological leaps in agriculture and distribution. Gas central heating has changed living habits over the last few decades. Cheap artificial-fiber clothing means that Granny has put down her knitting needles. The list goes on and on.

The beginning of the 21st century has already seen an incredible pace of change. In the area of computing and Internet technology, there has been a huge jump in broadband internet usage globally: for example in the US from 6 percent of internet users in 2000 to over 80 percent of users by 2007.[11] There were 77.4 million broadband subscribers in the USA in 2008, and 264 million broadband subscribers in the top 30 countries.[12] By the time you read this book, there will almost certainly be tens of millions more. With the use of data compression to transfer music over the Internet came the boom in music downloading, with a corresponding rise of portable digital audio players such as the Apple iPod and Microsoft's Zune. By 2005, online digital music sales were already 6 percent of all music sales.[13] The word "google" has become a verb. Flash technology reached the point of being able to make video players, and YouTube emerged as the default website for uploading and viewing videos. USB flash drives rapidly replaced zip disks and 3.5-inch diskettes. Blogs, portals, and wikis have become essential communication methods for amateurs, professionals and businesses. Wireless networks are becoming ever more commonplace. Internet usage surpassed TV viewing in the same year that videogame industry's profits surpassed the entire movie industry's: 2004. Social networking websites like Myspace and Facebook, and microblogging platforms like Twitter, have gained so much in popularity that they are being credited with significantly contributing to the downfall of Hosni Mubarak's regime in Egypt.[14]

In the area of communications technology, small, powerful, accessibly priced mobile phones became highly common, and expanded quickly in third-world countries. Traditional telephone lines were rapidly replaced, with major telecommunications carriers converting their networks, and offering new services. This has led to near-saturation of cell phone ownership, and corresponding decline in the use and availability of public payphones. Similarly, with audio visual technology, digital cameras have become immensely popular due to rapid decreases in size and cost while photo resolution steadily increases. Sales of film-reel cameras have almost died. Flat-panel displays are displacing cathode ray tubes. Television has gone through the big "digital switchover." Digital video recorders (DVRs) allow consumers to modify content they watch on TV, and to record TV programs and watch them later. DVDs, and subsequently Blu-ray discs, have replaced VCR technology as the common standard in homes.

As for transport technology, there have been advances in "hybrid" petrol-electric vehicles such as the Toyota Prius, Ford Escape, and the Honda Insight. "Biodiesel" has also emerged as a fuel alternative. Photovoltaic energy generation has increased in popularity. Under the bonnet and console, several other technologies have been incorporated into vehicles such as self-diagnosing systems, advanced precollision safety systems, memory systems for car settings, back-up sensors and infra-red cameras, keyless start and entry, satellite radio, and voice-activation. Robotics has continued to develop, with applications in medicine and surgery. By 2006, domestic robotics had found their place, with 1.5 million units of iRobot's "Roomba" in homes. Humanoid robots have improved considerably, to the point of retailing as (still expensive) toys such as the "RoboSapien."

Other technological developments that have likely changed your personal and professional life already this century (even if you didn't notice) include: corrective eye surgery; GPS (Global Positioning System); and RFID (Radio Frequency ID), to name but a few.

The key, though, is where all of these technologies are on the S-curve. Probably, most are in stage II with further improvements possible. Yet several existing technologies are likely to be entering the mature stage III of slowing performance returns, which makes them susceptible to being superseded by new disruptive technologies.

Are there any technologies out there that could represent new disruptive technologies?

Of course there are. As you are reading this, there are more people than you would possibly care to imagine working away in their white coats in laboratories around the globe searching for further breakthroughs to keep advancing all of the above, as well as a whole load of totally new things. Weird and wonderful things such as: artificial intelligence, 3D displays, genetic engineering, anti-aging drugs, powered exoskeleton robots (have you seen the film *Avatar*?), quantum computing (which would permit *much* faster computing than we currently have), superconductivity, wireless energy transfer, "clean" nuclear fusion (as opposed to the currently available and controversial nuclear fission*). Just imagine a world with any of these potential technologies being unleashed.[15]

Any of these may, or may not, prove to be a disruptive technology, displace existing ways of doing things and change the way we live, work and play. On their own they have the potential of being important, but in combination their power could be enormous. Add the *Avatar*-style exoskeleton robots, for example, to wireless energy transfer and you have a changed world. No more petrol stations, no more cars – after all you could run to work in a self-charging 200 mile-per-hour suit. This is still in the realms of science fiction, but remember, the way we live now would be pure science fiction to our great grandparents. With the current trajectory of developments in anti-aging drugs, it is entirely conceivable that in 20 years' time those who can afford the treatment will stop aging.

Another example of an emerging technology that could prove to be hugely creatively disruptive is 3D printing. The idea behind this quirky technology is essentially the same as normal two-dimensional printers: a design is sent from a computer to a nearby printer. But instead of printing a single layer of ink, a 3-D printer continues superimposing a multitude of thin layers of material on top of each other until a three-dimensional object is built-up directly from the original computer generated blueprint. In fact 3-D printing has been around for many years in stage I of the S-curve. It has been applied in niche applications such as "rapid prototyping" to create conceptual design models directly from computer-aided design (CAD) systems – eliminating the need for laboriously handcrafted prototypes. But many now believe the technology has reached a point in development that it could find wider, more mainstream uses. Thus the technology is entering stage II, whereby rapid improvement could potentially open up new applications that displace established ways of doing things.

Mass production changed economies and societies in ways that would have been difficult to imagine before the industrial revolution of the late 18th century. Now, could 3D printing reverse the trend of economies of scale? Certainly, 3D printing is capable of creating a single item as cheaply as through mass-producing thousands of them. If the technology continues on its current developmental trajectory, it is conceivable that in the not-too-distant future

---

* Fission is the main process behind nuclear weapons as well as nuclear power stations – such as Chernobyl (Ukraine), Three Mile Island (USA) and the Fukushima plant (Japan), recently damaged by earthquake and tsunami. See Global Trend 9.

it might make business sense to download from the Internet a generic design of, say, a replacement car part and print-off a single piece at a local 3D printer. Such an efficient process would severely jeopardize current systems involving complex supply chains and mass-production factories in far-off lands. Similarly, complex crafted items – such as violins – might be created more economically by 3D printers that do not need highly skilled artisans or expensive equipment installations. Already, 3D printers, capable of creating a diverse array of fairly complex articles, are not much larger than early 2D desktop printers and are retailing at affordable prices for home users.

In the article "Print me a Stradivarius: How a new manufacturing technology will change the world," *The Economist* magazine proposes that 3D printing may have as profound an impact on the world as the coming of the factory did. Yet, just as the full impact of technologies such as the car, the airplane or the Internet were unclear at their outset, it is difficult to predict the long-term impact of 3D printing. Nevertheless, it is likely to create winners and losers and disrupt many ways that things are currently done. As a result, *The Economist* recommends that "companies, regulators and entrepreneurs should start thinking about it now."[16]

The emergence of such innovations should not come as any great surprise. Throughout human development there have been many key breakthroughs. Each of these has radically changed the way we live. The subsequent innumerable incremental innovations have simply enhanced these radical innovations, but without the same sudden and dramatic impact, changing things forever.

Within the coming decades we are likely to witness more disruptive technology breakthroughs that will change the way we live at society and individual levels, and how business is done. Where will such disruptions come from no-one knows for sure. But history has shown that one thing is fairly certain – that there is a disruptive technology out there that is likely to change life as we know it. Those societies, businesses and individuals that are open-minded enough to jump S-curves at the opportune moment and embrace such a technology will flourish. Those laggards that do not are likely to have problems.

However, timing is crucial as widespread adoption of unproven technology too soon can also prove a waste of effort – or worse may result in later environmental, social or individual harm. This is a particular concern, in a highly interconnected world with opportunists pushing to rapidly roll out new technologies before they are fully proven. Historical events and recent disasters, such as the Deepwater Horizon oil spill and the Fukushima nuclear plant failure, have shown that it is possible to push certain technological envelopes too far, too fast. As described earlier, *The Economist* article "In place of safety nets" lays out some commonsense rules for managing such challenges, pointing out that regulators and companies will need to work together to prevent harmful incidents, while still obtaining maximum social and business benefits from continued technological advancement.

In this respect, one potential solution that could be applied in certain areas of new technology application is that of "safety case" regulation. Rather than the requirement for companies to meet predefined, often outdated or simply arbitrary safety standards, it might make more sense for companies to make a reasoned case that their technology-related actions are safe under all plausible scenarios – and for this safety case to be comprehensively put to the test by themselves and skilled regulators. Such an approach has been widely seen as having helped the oil industry in the UK's North Sea avoid more accidents like Piper Alpha, a rig explosion in 1988 that claimed 167 lives. Beyond making a case for safety, it would also make sense for companies to demonstrate their ability to react when things do go wrong in the "uncharted space" of new technology implementation. As *The Economist* states:

"It really does help to think the unthinkable."

That said, if a serious technology does emerge, and it stands up to rigorous safety-case-type testing in the field, it's probably best not to wait too long before making that jump. After all, while being careful to avoid the very real potential pitfalls of rashly adopting unproven technologies that we still don't fully understand, none of us want to be another last Samurai.

Undoubtedly, technological development since the industrial revolution has caused pollution and the contamination of our atmosphere, for example, through the burning of fossil fuels to power everything from our cars to our iPads. This has had clear negative impact in a reduced quality of life for millions, and a continued negative impact at an environmental level. Yet, the other side of the coin is that technological development and roll-out of innovative and potentially disruptive new energy technologies is likely to represent part of the human response to climate change... the next Global Trend.

Global Trend 4

Climate Change

"I've been trying to tell this story for a long time and I feel as though I've failed to get the message across... There are good people in politics... who hold this at arms-length because if they acknowledge [climate change] and recognize it, then the moral imperative to make big changes is inescapable."[1]

Al Gore, 45th Vice President of the United States,
Nobel Peace Prize Winner*

This is a chapter that many will probably choose to skip, believing that they have heard it all before and with a firm opinion on the matter. Two apparently irreconcilable camps seemed to have formed: the "let's get on with living" pragmatists versus the "if only it were different" idealists. Many supposedly well-informed people are fed up of the whole issue given that no intelligible conclusions seem to have emerged. The media has largely squeezed all the juice they can out of the polar-bear-stranded-on-melting-icebergs story and moved on from the warming issue to other "hotter" topics. To put it bluntly the world is fed-up with the whole climate-change issue.

While Al Gore's 2006 book and film *An Inconvenient Truth* successfully raised public awareness about the whole issue it also provoked considerable negative reaction. While almost everyone agreed with the "inconvenient" bit, many were – and still are – somewhat less disposed to believe the bit about "truth." After all, here was an ex-politician trying to persuade us all to give up many hard-earned 21st-century comforts on the basis of some apparently inconclusive evidence from a bunch of eccentric scientists. In retort to the idea that the world may be warming up a few degrees a common response has been "So what?" or "Well, life would be quite nice if the world were a bit warmer."

---

* With the International Panel on Climate Change.

Even now, simply mentioning the name Al Gore to any group of business-people and world citizens will invoke a strong reaction that either puts the man into "hero" or "villain" status, with not many opinions falling in between. After Al Gore failed to win the contentious 2000 US presidential election against his Republican rival George Bush Jr., many people would rather have seen him simply retire from the public scene.* If he had won that election the world might well be in a different state, but his very image makes a lot of people uncomfortable. Furthermore, the 2007 Nobel Peace prize awarded jointly to Gore and the Intergovernmental Panel on Climate Change (IPCC) only seemed to ramp up much of the controversy surrounding the whole climate change issue.

Such diametrically opposed and emotional opinions do not make for rational debate or unbiased media coverage on the issue of climate change. There are the believers and the nonbelievers and that seems to be that.

Recent variable weather patterns have not helped to shed any light on a clear answer. The winter of 2009–2010 in Europe was unusually cold. There were atypical snowfalls in several parts of the Northern Hemisphere: on March 8 the Mediterranean city of Barcelona was paralyzed by the heaviest snowfalls since 1962; in April the city of Kyoto, Japan, experienced simultaneous snowfall and cherry blossom blooming, which had not happened in decades. Such events made the general public ask themselves what had happened to Al Gore's "global warming," and further doubted his "truth" in the light of their daily experiences.

Yet a few months later Europe was indeed wilting in a heatwave. Reports of heat-related deaths in Russia, of passengers being evacuated from German trains with faulty air-conditioning, and losses in harvests around Europe, were backed up by statistics: 2010 had the warmest average temperature for the January–June period on record according to the National Oceanic and Atmospheric Administration in Washington.[2]

The concept that climate change goes beyond simple global warming, and that extreme weather events are indeed a sign of how long-standing patterns are being disrupted, has been hard for the broader public to grasp.[3]

---

* The Florida election recount of 2000 will possibly go down as one of the strangest episodes in democratic history in which 'hanging chad' (or an incomplete hole punched in voting cards) votes were not registered by the counting machines. Gore ultimately lost the presidential election to George W. Bush when the US Supreme Court settled the legal controversy by ruling 5–4 in favor of Bush.

With a confusing climate message, public opinion polls have been confirm-ing *decreasing* public concern with the whole issue. In a 2009 poll among US residents, only 1 percent cited the Environment as America's most important problem, compared to 26 percent for health care and 29 percent the economy. A poll published by the European Commission showed a fall in the number of EU citizens who saw climate change as the world gravest problem – from 62 percent in 2008 to 50 percent by 2009.[4]

Added to this "is it or isn't it getting warmer?" confusion was the contro-versy in November 2009 surrounding "Climategate" – in which some personal emails of climate scientists (at the University of East Anglia's Climate Research Unit in the UK) were hacked and released into the public domain. Despite the fact that the hacking and releasing of email content was an illegal act, allega-tions of misconduct were pointed at certain scientists and a trial by public opinion ensued. Yet more controversy was heaped upon the whole question of "truth" behind the climate change issue.

However, several official inquiries and reports into the allegations of scientific malpractice have turned up little that undermines the conclusions of the largely rigorous climate science community. Thus despite "a noxious campaign against the credibility of environmental science in general, and climate science in par-ticular" the case for acting to limit carbon emissions remains largely intact. *The Economist* explained that "the science of climate change has seemed to be derailed by Climategate and the discovery of some errors in IPCC reports, even the gravest of which come far short of undermining its conclusions."[5]

The Internet allowed the doubt in climate science to "go viral." Interestingly, though, one example of these anti-climate-science blogging websites "Climategate: Anthropogenic Global Warming, History's Biggest Scam" stopped blogging operations in March 2010 and, as at time of writing, was posting the following message: "This site/domain name will entertain offers for sale in the low to mid $xx,xxx range."[6]

And while anti-climate-science bloggers have been cashing in on their websites, diligent climate scientists have worked on. With all the confusion and passage of time the underlying scientific evidence for climate change has gone largely uncontested and the climate change process itself has continued unabated.

So what is behind all this? Let's put opinions, prejudices and emotions to one side and take a look at the science underlying the climate change argument. What are the findings of the climate science community?

To make some sense out of all the nonsense, we have to ask three basic questions:

1. Is the world heating up: yes or no?

2. If yes, what is the most likely underlying cause?

3. If a cause can be identified, what can be done about it?

So, firstly, is the world heating up? According to the majority of serious scientists the answer is a definitive "Yes!"

Most of the scientific basis for climate change comes down to work collated, assessed, and endorsed by the scientific body called the Intergovernmental Panel on Climate Change. The IPCC was created in 1988 by the World Meteorological Organization (WMO) and the United Nations Environment Program (UNEP) as an effort to provide the governments of the world with a clear scientific view of what is happening to the world's climate.[7] In 2007, the IPCC released its Fourth Assessment Report on Climate Change, which summarized current understanding of climate change.* The report took 6 years to produce, involved over 2,500 scientific expert reviewers and more than 800 authors from over 130 countries. Interestingly, in this report the IPCC modified their definition of climate change from previous ones that focused upon an *a priori* assumption that humans are to blame:[†]

Climate change in IPCC usage refers to… any change in climate over time, whether due to natural variability or as a result of human activity.[8]

Thus the IPCC neatly sidestepped the need for attributing climate change – directly or indirectly – to human activity and could focus first on identifying

---

* The next IPCC Assessment Report (5th) is currently in progress and is not due for release until 2014- so the 2007 report represents the most up-to-date collation of data available.
† For example, the United Nations Framework Convention on Climate Change (UNFCCC) definition for climate change refers to a change of climate that is attributed directly or indirectly to human activity that alters the composition of the global atmosphere and that is in addition to natural climate variability observed over comparable time periods.

whether climate warming was happening or not – and *then* look for possible causes. In this respect their conclusion was:

"Warming of the climate system is unequivocal, as is now evident from observations of increases in global average air and ocean temperatures, widespread melting of snow and ice and rising global average sea level."[9]

This has to be one of the most definitive scientific statements I have ever read. While scientists usually speak in terms of likelihoods and confidence intervals to express levels of certainty, here the IPCC leaves no room for doubt.* The following is a synopsis of the evidence supporting such a strong statement.

There have been significant changes in the Earth's surface temperature, average sea level and snow cover over extended periods of recording. While there is clear short-term "noise" variation in each of the graphs for temperatures, sea levels and snow and ice cover, the trends over longer periods of time are unmistakable. From 1850, average surface temperatures have been going up, and the trend over the last 50 years is of warming that is nearly twice as fast as the previous 50 years. Eleven of the twelve years from 1995 to 2006 rank among the twelve warmest years in the instrumental record of global surface temperature (since 1850). The temperature increase is widespread over the globe and is greater at higher northern latitudes. Average Arctic temperatures have increased at almost twice the global average rate in the past 100 years. Land regions have warmed faster than the oceans. Observations since 1961 show that the average temperature of the global ocean has increased to depths of at least 3000m. New analyses of balloon-borne and satellite temperature measurements of the atmosphere at different levels (lower and mid troposphere) show warming rates similar to those observed in surface temperature.

An increase of around 1°C in average global land temperature, from around 13.5°C to about 14.5°C, over the past century and a half may not seem a lot, but it is enough to have a significant impact upon sea levels,

---

* The IPCC defines a framework for treatment of uncertainty: virtually certain >99%; extremely likely >95%; very likely >90%; likely >66%; more likely than not > 50%; about as likely as not 33% to 66%; unlikely <33%; very unlikely <10%; extremely unlikely <5%; exceptionally unlikely <1%.

which since 1870 have shown a clear upward trend – rising over 200 mm. Global average sea level rose at an average rate of 1.8 mm per year from 1961 to 2003 and at a faster average rate of about 3.1mm per year from 1993 to 2003. Since 1993 thermal expansion of the oceans has contributed about 57 percent of the sea level rise, with decreases in glaciers and ice caps contributing about 28 percent and losses from the polar ice sheets contributing the remainder.

Another indication of increasing global temperature is that snow and ice extent has decreased. Satellite data since 1978 show that annual average Arctic sea ice extent has shrunk by 2.7 percent per decade, with larger decreases in summer of 7.4 percent per decade. Mountain glaciers and snow cover on average have declined in both hemispheres. The maximum areal extent of seasonally frozen ground has decreased by about 7 percent, from around 38 million km^2 to approximately 35 million km^2, in the Northern Hemisphere since 1900 – with decreases in spring of up to 15 percent.

Temperatures at the top of the permafrost layer have generally increased since the 1980s in the Arctic by up to 3°C. It is important to remember that such a modest – even apparently "nice" – increase in temperature is capable of turning a *lot* of solid ice into liquid water, and this can have profound impacts.

Furthermore, at continental, regional and ocean basin scales, numerous long-term changes in other aspects of climate have also been observed. Trends from 1900 to 2005 have been observed in precipitation amount in many large regions. Over this period, precipitation increased significantly in eastern parts of North and South America, northern Europe and northern and central Asia – whereas precipitation declined in the Sahel, the Mediterranean, southern Africa and parts of southern Asia. Globally, the area affected by drought has likely (i.e. >66 percent probability) increased since the 1970s. Some extreme weather events have changed in frequency and/or intensity over the last 50 years:

- It is *very* likely (i.e. >90 percent probability) that cold days, cold nights and frosts have become less frequent over most land areas, while hot days and hot nights have become more frequent.

- It is likely (i.e. >66 percent probability) that heatwaves have become more frequent over most land areas.

- It is likely (i.e. >66 percent probability) that the frequency of heavy precipitation events (or proportion of total rainfall from heavy falls) has increased over most areas.

- It is likely (i.e. >66 percent probability) that the incidence of extreme high sea levels has increased at a broad range of sites worldwide since 1975.

There is also observational evidence of an increase in intense tropical cyclone activity in the North Atlantic since about 1970, and suggestions of increased intense tropical cyclone activity in some other regions where concerns over data quality are greater. Multi-decadal variability and the quality of the tropical cyclone records prior to routine satellite observations in about 1970 complicate the detection of long-term trends in tropical cyclone activity.

Average Northern Hemisphere temperatures during the second half of the 20th century were very likely (i.e. >90 percent probability) higher than during any other 50-year period in the last 500 years and likely (i.e. >66 percent probability) the highest in at least the past 1,300 years.

Again, this is pretty categorical for a scientific study – indicating that the majority of the evidence collected is showing trends in similar directions.

It is not just the IPCC that is identifying such evidence. The National Aeronautical and Space Administration (NASA, no less!) has also been monitoring trends from the sky and collating research that largely corroborates the findings published by the IPCC. For example, according to NASA the extent of arctic sea ice is shrinking yearly, with the last measured (2009) summer ice coverage being the third-smallest recorded since satellites began measuring sea ice extent in 1979.[10]

However, not everybody shares the view that the earth is warming. This is a complex issue, after all, and there may quite possibly be contradictory empirical data. For example, some information sources such as blogs, websites, media articles and other voices have highlighted that the planet has been cooling since a peak in global temperature in 1998. According to NASA though this cooling is only part of the picture – and they indicate that it is easy to "cherry-pick" a period to reinforce any particular point of view. NASA quotes from another report stating:

> It is possible, and indeed likely, to have a period as long as a decade or two of 'cooling' or no warming superimposed on a longer-term warming trend... [Yet] claims that global warming is not occurring that are derived from a cooling observed over short time periods ignore natural variability and are misleading.[11]

So, it would seem that our best current estimate – and certainly the *official* view – is that the world is, indeed, warming up and that there are knock-on climate impacts. The evidence presented is certainly compelling.

The next question is: if there is warming what is the most likely cause?

Now, it has to be said that this is a *very* difficult question to answer given the complex nature of planet Earth. While there is apparently little controversy regarding the climate changing, there is more when it comes to identifying the cause of this warming – and especially when it comes to whether the drivers of this climate change are "anthropogenic" (or human induced).

Changes in the state of Earth's climate system can occur due to alterations in "external" extraterrestrial factors – such as solar output, Earth-Sun geometry etc., upon which humans can have little or no influence. Also, climate change can occur as a result of changes in terrestrial factors related to the oceans, atmosphere and land.[12] Such "internal" factors include geological changes like volcanic emissions, mountain development, continental drift and so on. Again, such factors are largely beyond the influence of human beings. If any of these factors were driving climate change it would be a natural phenomenon.

Yet certain potential terrestrial climate driving factors can be, and almost inevitably are, affected by the activities of *Homo sapiens*: atmospheric chemistry and reflectivity, surface reflectivity and the heat exchange between atmosphere and oceans. Here is where the famous "greenhouse" effect comes in. The theory is that when sunlight passes through the atmosphere and warms the Earth's surface, some heat is radiated back towards space. If there are not enough "greenhouse gas" molecules in the atmosphere to trap it, too much of this radiated heat escapes and the planet cools down. Conversely, if there are too many greenhouse gas molecules too much of the radiated heat gets trapped and the planet heats up.[13]

In fact, without the greenhouse effect life on Earth as we know could not exist, given that it regulates temperatures within certain livable bounds. In effect, life on Earth has evolved in sync with the levels of greenhouse gases naturally present in the atmosphere. The greenhouse effect is a natural process that has been in operation for millions of years that has ensured an adequately cozy blanket over the Earth to ensure we don't freeze or boil. The debate surrounding anthropogenic climate change focuses upon whether human activities are responsible for making this blanket too thick and trapping too much heat in. As Al Gore said in *An Uncomfortable Truth:*

> The most vulnerable part of the Earth's ecological system is the atmosphere. Vulnerable because it is so thin. If you had a big globe with a coat of varnish on it, the thickness of that varnish relative to the globe would be pretty much the same at the thickness of the Earth's atmosphere compared to the Earth itself. And it is thin enough that we are capable of changing its composition.

It has to be said the theory of us changing the delicate regulatory balance of the greenhouse effect is plausible given that mankind has indeed been contributing heavily to the amount of greenhouse gases in the atmosphere for some time now. The gases that contribute to the greenhouse effect are water vapor, carbon dioxide (CO_2), methane (CH_4), nitrous oxide (N_2O) and chlorofluorocarbons (CFCs) – all of which humans have become pretty good at belching out as byproducts of the way we live. Of particular concern have been CO_2 emissions, which have increased drastically since the industrial revolution as a result of burning fossil fuels (see Global Trend 9: Energy.)

A comparison of atmospheric samples contained in ice cores and more recent direct measurements, provides evidence that atmospheric CO_2 has increased sharply since the Industrial Revolution. For 650,000 years atmospheric CO_2 has risen and dipped in cycles, but rarely exceeding 280 parts per million. Since the industrial revolution, though, atmospheric concentrations of CO_2 have continued rising, and in 2005 were at 379 parts per million (see Figure 4.1).[14]

Thus, according to NASA and the IPCC, the view of most scientists is that human activities are changing the natural greenhouse gas composition and hence driving climate change – mainly through these unprecedented

Figure 4.1: Atmospheric CO$_2$ concentration over time

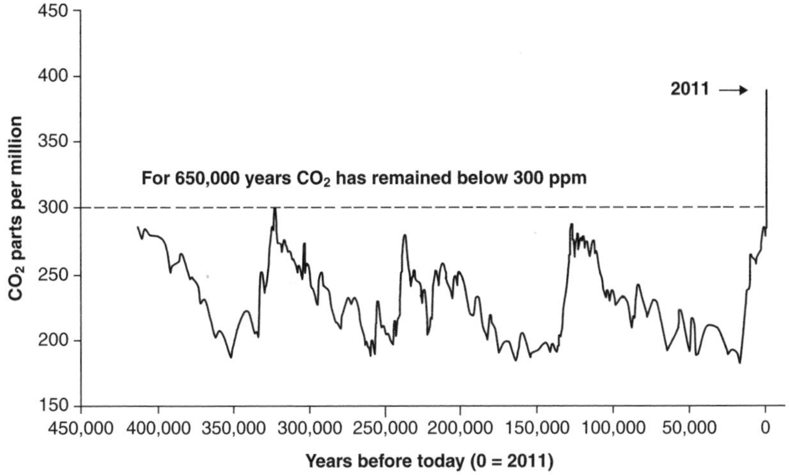

Source: NASA/National Oceanic Atmospheric Administration (NOAA) Paleoclimatology

emissions of greenhouse gases, and particularly CO$_2$. The IPCC Fourth
Assessment Report on Climate Change states:

> Global atmospheric concentrations of CO$_2$, CH$_4$ and N$_2$O have increased
> markedly as a result of human activities since 1750 and now far exceed
> pre-industrial values determined from ice cores spanning many thousands
> of years. The atmospheric concentrations of CO$_2$ and CH$_4$ in 2005 exceed
> by far the natural range over the last 650,000 years. Global increases in CO$_2$
> concentrations are due primarily to fossil fuel use, with land-use change
> providing another significant but smaller contribution. It is very likely that
> the observed increase in CH$_4$ concentration is predominantly due to agri-
> culture and fossil fuel use. The increase in N$_2$O concentration is primarily
> due to agriculture

And hence:

> *"There is very high confidence that the global average net effect of*
> *human activities since 1750 has been one of warming...Most of the*

observed increase in global average temperatures since the mid-20th century is very likely [i.e. >90 percent probability] *due to the observed increase in anthropogenic greenhouse gas concentrations."*

Therefore, the IPCC models using both natural and anthropogenic "forcings" indicate that the man-made impact is by far the more significant of the two. And, given such a high-certainty link between man-made greenhouse gases and increased warming, most worrying perhaps is that:

Global greenhouse gas emissions due to human activities have grown since pre-industrial times, with an increase of 70 percent between 1970 and 2004.[15]

According to *The Economist* article "Getting warmer," CO_2 emissions are now 30 percent higher than they were when the UN Framework Convention on Climate Change was adopted 17 years ago. Atmospheric levels of CO_2 and other greenhouse gases reached 430 parts per million (ppm) in 2008, compared with 280 ppm before the industrial revolution. At current rates of emission, these levels could treble by the end of the century – equating to a 50 percent risk of global temperatures rising by 5°C. By comparison, the world is only 5°C warmer now than it was during the last ice age. The impact of such an increase in temperature would include "fast-melting ice sheets, rising sea levels, drought, disease and collapsing agriculture in poor countries, and mass migration." As *The Economist* concludes: "But nobody really knows, and nobody wants to know."[16]

So, "*Inconvenient*"? Definitely.
The "*Truth*"? Maybe not an utterly conclusive absolute truth, but certainly our best current approximation to one for the time being.
So, to the third question: if a cause can be identified,
what can be done about it?

The biggest single possible action would be to reduce the emissions of greenhouse gases by burning less fossil fuel. While there may be other complicating mechanisms in the climate change process, none of them offer "a remotely satisfactory alternative explanation" for the global rises in temperature. The underlying and uncontested facts are that carbon dioxide and other greenhouse gases act to warm planets and their levels on Earth continue to increase significantly. *The Economist* article "Flawed scientists: The Intergovernmental Panel on Climate Change needs reform. The case for climate action does not" concludes that: "The temperature rose over the 20th century in a way that follows from these basic truths."

Clearly it is impossible to predict with certainty just how much harm global warming will do in the 21st century. However, *The Economist* states that moving away from fossil fuels should be a global priority, given there is "a far from trivial chance of things turning catastrophic."

It was with this potential catastrophe in mind that the UN Kyoto protocol was adopted in 1997 to try to get governments to accept binding targets with the goal of achieving "stabilization of greenhouse gas concentrations in the atmosphere at a level that would prevent dangerous anthropogenic interference with the climate system."[17] As of July 2010, 191 nations have signed and ratified the protocol (with the significant exception of the USA – the major CO_2 emitter when Kyoto was formulated).[18] Yet, even since the protocol was adopted, CO_2 emissions have risen by 20 percent. As the Kyoto protocol deadline approaches in 2012, it seems that the countries that did sign will be unable to meet their promised target reductions.

Given the failure to live up to the Kyoto protocol's objectives, the international community sought to reach a new global agreement at the UN Climate Change Conference in Copenhagen, Denmark in December 2009.[19] Yet again, there was a failure to reach a global agreement despite a group of nations recognizing the scientific view that the increase in global temperature should be below 2°C to combat climate change. For rich countries that would mean an 80 percent cut in their emissions or a reduction to 2 tonnes of CO_2 equivalent per head per year. At present, emissions are around 24 tonnes per head in the United States and around 10 tonnes in Europe. The IPCC suggests the developed world should aim to cut by 25–40 percent below 1990 levels by 2020.

Throughout this, it has been interesting how the tone has changed in *The Economist*'s reporting of climate change. Back in December 2009, before the United Nations Climate Change Conference in Copenhagen, Denmark, the onus was upon obtaining an international consensus to halt climate change in its tracks. Arguing for more leadership from politicians and support from voters in order to drive more national policies towards cutting CO_2 emissions, *The Economist* article "Stop climate change – Rich and poor countries have to give ground to get a deal in Copenhagen" stated: "The leaders gathering in Copenhagen need to come to an agreement, even if it isn't a very good one."[20]

Yet no such consensus was reached in Copenhagen. Following the Climategate email scandal, another call to arms was launched by *The Economist* in March 2010, under the title "Spin, science and climate change: Action on climate is justified, not because the science is certain, but precisely because it is not." Given the uncertainty regarding the range of climate possibilities – with catastrophe being a distinctly possible "scary" outcome – the argument behind this article was that "the costs of averting climate change are comparatively small. Just as a householder pays a small premium to protect himself or herself against disaster, the world should do the same."[21]

Another UN Climate Change Conference was scheduled in December 2010 in Cancún, Mexico, as a last-ditch effort to push through some global political consensus. In the end, those with low expectations of the Cancún summit were proved right. Some consensus was achieved – but for much-reduced emissions targets with little climate change improvement. *The Economist* report on the conference concluded that, while the UN climate process may have done well from the summit "the climate, [did] not [do] so well."[22]

Resignation appears to have set in. While the global politicians squabble, it is accepted that climate change is moving ahead and it looks like humans – and the rest of life on Earth – will just have to find ways of dealing with it. *The Economist* article "How to live with climate change: It won't be stopped but its effects can be made less bad" recognized that "since the beginning of time, creatures have adapted to changes in their environment" and that such adaptation has involved many deaths in past evolution. Nevertheless, unlike other species, humans are somewhat gifted in their ability to plan ahead and prepare for inevitable changes. With climate change being quite possibly the "craziest experiment mankind has ever conducted," there is a chance that it is brought under control sometime in the future. But in the meantime temperatures are likely to continue rising and "the human race must live with the problem as best it can."[23]

This change in focus taken by *The Economist* in the year between December 2009 and December 2010 is significant. The move has gone from mitigation of climate change to one of accepting that change is inevitable and that mankind must adapt to the consequences of climate change as best we can.

So, let's recap.

The world is warming-up. Our best explanation for this is that man-made greenhouse gas levels – especially the drastic increases in CO_2 levels in recent history – are the main cause. Thus, acting to reduce CO_2 emissions is the prime identified action to mitigate climate change – but nothing credible is being done due to lack of global political consensus

Oh dear. This realization that the only course of action left is to adapt to potentially catastrophic changes served to put climate change even higher on the agenda at the meeting of the world's political and business leaders at the World Economic Forum meeting in Davos in January 2011. Despite all the media confusion and negative publicity towards climate science in the previous year, in terms of combined risk-impact, climate change was perceived as *the* Global Trend that most concerned panel members of the WEF's Global Risks survey.[24]

Threats and opportunities

The underlying threat of this Global Trend comes from the (thus far) slow and gradual nature of climate change. *En masse*, human beings find it hard to get excited about an increase in temperature of a degree or so over several decades. Yet such a passive response is dangerous and reminds of the metaphor of the frog and the pot of water. If thrown into a pot of hot water the frog, it is said, will instinctively jump out to save itself. However, if the frog is placed into cooler water which is then gradually heated up, the frog does not realize what is happening and boils to death. I must point out that I have never tried this experiment, so cannot vouch for its accuracy. Nevertheless, the metaphor does seem to make some sense in the context of humans' response to such a slowly unfolding threat. This is exacerbated further by the emotional inclinations of many to entrench themselves into an immovable opinion despite an overwhelming body of good-quality scientific evidence to the contrary. Many seem inclined to ignore "global warming" on the basis that it may be inconvenient for others but frankly quite nice for those in northern latitudes – rather than attempting to grasp the underlying issues at hand.

There are clear threats to individuals, businesses, societies and to life on Earth as we know it. The IPCC Synthesis Report highlights that many social systems and business sectors will bear the brunt of the negative impacts of unequivocal warming upon ecosystems, water, food, coastlines, settlements, health, and industry of all forms. And the report clearly indicates that this is not purely a clear and present danger, but rather one whose repercussions will become clearer and even harsher as time goes by:

> Anthropogenic warming over the last three decades has likely had a discernible influence at the global scale on observed changes in many physical and biological systems... With current climate change mitigation policies and related [economic] development practices, global greenhouse gas emissions will continue to grow over the next few decades.

The understanding is that temperatures follow CO_2 (and other greenhouse gas) levels. Thus there is a time-lag between pumping out the emissions and feeling the resulting increased heat trapped in the atmosphere. While we continue to belch out fossil fuel fumes at an increasing rate, there is simply no knowing what temperatures will rise to in the coming 10, 20, 30, 40, 50... years. The global temperature difference between now and the last ice age is only 5°C. Knowing that in the last ice age there were ice sheets over two miles thick that extended as far south as New York, we can only postulate what another 5°C could do to the planet.

Climate change is as close to a "fact" as humans are capable of identifying: no-one appears to disagree with the IPCC claim that "the warmth of the last half century is unusual in at least the previous 1,300 years."[25]

Yet, let's for a moment consider the scientists' very strong claims that this warming is linked to evidence that "global atmospheric concentrations of carbon dioxide, methane and nitrous oxide have increased markedly as a result of human activities since 1750 and now far exceed pre-industrial values determined from ice cores spanning many thousands of years."

Only very few question this statistically supported link. And, again, no-one contests that greenhouse gases overall – whether man-made or natural – contribute to the heating of the planet. Thus if there is any way for humans to control the *total* greenhouse gas levels this would represent an important lever for humankind to maintain the essential atmospheric balance with which we have evolved. And clearly the most realistic way for us to do this would be to control our own greenhouse gas emissions. It makes no sense to blame the only other potential suspect (in this case Mother Nature) for global warming, when we are busying ourselves with producing the very gases – and in quite literally industrial volumes – that directly contribute to the effect. While the scientists' arguments and evidence for man-made climate change are very plausible, even if they turn out to be wrong (which is very unlikely) our actions should come down to the same thing: self-restraint and not messing on our own doorstep – especially when we are the first in line to lose out to the projected "warming of about 0.2°C per decade... for a range of emission scenarios."

Thus, any way you look at it, working towards international agreements on reducing CO_2 and other greenhouse gas emissions appears to be the main opportunity for mitigating climate change. Of course, political and business leaders, and the citizens and consumers to whom they are answerable, will have a role to play in obtaining such agreements. To date, one of the main sticking points in international climate negotiations has been that we are largely dependent upon the burning of fossil fuels to power economic growth. Thus there has been an eternal blame game: developed countries refusing to adopt restricted emissions on the premise that emerging nations are still polluting; and emerging nations have been reticent to restrict their emissions because they are embarking along the exact same polluting path to wealth that others have been on for over a century. "It's not fair to stop us doing what you've been doing for years to get rich" seems to be a common emerging nation retort to the richer nations' demands.

To get past this childish schoolyard impasse at a global level requires someone to make a concessionary or innovative move – and perhaps the moral imperative does fall on the political and business communities of richer, more developed countries. After all, it is the richer countries that must own up to the lion's share of historic atmospheric pollution that has resulted in current global warming levels. And the richer countries have more means at their disposal to lead by example and find alternative economic development models or invent technologies offering cleaner energy alternatives (see Global Trend 9: Energy). This may be seen as a moral issue but there are also likely to be benefits in being amongst the first cohort to adopt such new sustainable ways of working.

Beyond mitigation of future climate change impacts, humans are going to have to adapt to inevitable changes. Rather disconcertingly the IPCC states that: "anthropogenic warming and sea level rise would continue for centuries due to the time scales associated with climate processes and feedbacks, even if greenhouse gas concentrations were to be stabilized."

The IPCC's report, *Climate Change 2007: Impacts, Adaptation and Vulnerability* concludes that "evidence from all continents and most oceans shows that many natural systems are being affected by regional climate changes, particularly temperature increases. Impacts due to altered frequencies and intensities of extreme weather, climate and sea-level events are very likely to change. Adaptation will be necessary to address impacts resulting from the warming which is already unavoidable due to past emissions."[26]

In order to combat the risk of climate change becoming a self-reinforcing phenomenon, a portfolio of adaptation and mitigation measures will need to be considered by policy-makers, business leaders and individuals. Then action will be required in order to diminish the risks associated with climate change; to avoid, reduce or delay negative impacts. Policy-makers need to ensure the right mechanisms are in place to incentivize appropriate adaptation and mitigation actions. Business leaders need to work with government to ensure economically viable and workable solutions are created in the short and long term. Everyone will have to remain flexible as new knowledge emerges relating to this dynamic and shifting problem. Above all, it would appear sensible to address the combined issues of economic growth, demand for increased GDP and insatiable appetite for more fossil fuels in parallel with climate change. What appears to be happening at present is the subjugation of the potentially catastrophic climate to a lower priority position in the global "to do" list. In the face of overwhelming – and frankly sometimes scary – evidence, relegating actions on preparing for and limiting future climate change is unlikely to be a good move.

A good deal rests on the shoulders of global politicians and business leaders to find solutions – and fast. Yet in this respect there is some cause for optimism. The "ozone hole" is perhaps the best example of an undisputedly anthropogenic atmospheric change that met with a rapid international agreement. After the discovery of a severe depletion of the ozone layer above Antarctica, in 1985 it was established that chlorofluorocarbons (CFCs) were causing this depletion. It was also established that such a depletion in the ozone layer resulted in increased exposure to UV-B radiation from the Sun and increased levels of skin cancer, cataracts, and suppressed immune systems in humans and animals, and also damage to terrestrial plant life, single-cell organisms, and aquatic ecosystems.[27] In September 1987 the "Montreal Protocol on Substances that Deplete the Ozone Layer" was agreed upon, requiring the international phasing-out of production and consumption of these substances. This ban on CFCs effectively led to a reduction in size of the ozone hole and demonstrates that the international community is indeed capable of addressing such problems in a timely fashion when it is in the common interest.

However climate change is likely to be more complex to overcome. The forecasts are that many in the world will be suffering with extreme temperature highs and lows, increased storms and flooding, severe droughts, diminishing ice extent and general increasing sea levels. We should expect to see an increase in public health issues, water shortages, agricultural problems, business expense increases, food shortages, disruptions in global travel, and potential waves of climate change refugees: the first of whom moved away from the low-lying, previously idyllic Cateret Islands in the South Pacific in 2008.

The Cateret Islands however are in stark contrast to another low lying area: the Netherlands, where, historically, there have been the human and financial resources to implement measures to protect against rising sea levels. The difference between these two places indicates that the changes induced by climate change will probably generate losers and winners (at least in the medium term). In addition to threats, many of the major anticipated impacts imply certain opportunities for some. Those fortunate to be in certain geographical locations, or those wealthy enough or able to position themselves relatively favorably, may be in a position to benefit from some of the climate changes. Increasing temperature will make growing seasons longer in certain geographic regions, as well as opening up new arctic shipping routes for international trade and resource exploration. More rainfall could make previously arid areas viable for agriculture.

Furthermore, as more evidence is likely to emerge supporting the existence of the climate change phenomenon more governments, businesses and consumers will be increasingly prone to increase spending in adaptation and mitigation measures. Governments, businesses and individuals are likely to look towards better building infrastructure and improved technologies to allow sustainable and comfortable living at increased temperatures and in the face of unpredictable climate patterns. Similarly, managing food and water supplies may reduce the tendency towards migrations from stricken areas.

Yet, given the great deal of uncertainty surrounding the whole climate-change process, there is likely to be a great deal of luck involved as to whether you are one of the winners or one of the losers. At the very least, just as the polar bears are having to adapt and find new ways of making a living, we human beings are going to have to keep our eyes open and be prepared for change.

In the first line of battle against the climate lies the very sustenance upon which we depend: water and food supply. This is the topic of the next Global Trend.

Global Trend 5

Water and Food

"The water crisis that seems possible within the next 10 to 20 years will quite probably trigger significant shortfalls in cereal production and, as a result, a massive global food crisis."

Peter Brabeck-Letmathe, Chairman of Nestlé[1]

That the Chairman of the board of directors of a company that produces numerous different brands of bottled water is concerned about water supply is probably not particularly surprising. On the other hand, given that he is likely to know better than most of us the challenges of getting sufficient volumes of quality drinking water into bottles around the world, he is perhaps worth listening to when he says that water is "by far the most valuable resource on this planet."

Furthermore, given that Nestlé is one of the world's largest food and nutrition companies, its supply chain brings together a multitude of agricultural producers – large and small – across the globe. Therefore Mr. Brabeck-Letmathe is in a good position to draw a link between a possible water crisis and any resulting food crisis. He has repeatedly warned that water is becoming a scarce resource, and that this is likely to become a particular problem in areas, such as India, where water tables are falling particularly fast while agricultural output is increasing. Clearly there is something unsustainable about such goings-on.

After all it is "Water and Food" – in that order. Not "Food and Water" as may sound more natural in everyday speech. Nor does this book treat these topics separately in distinct chapters. Why? Well, it is simple: 70 percent of global freshwater withdrawals are used in agriculture. That means that if there is no water there is no agriculture and no food. When water becomes scarce so does food. Water scarcity imposes limits on food production and supply, putting pressure on food prices and increasing countries' dependence on food imports. Furthermore, while we need both to sustain life, a lack of clean, safe and reliable water is usually the first to bring problems.

Of the two issues, water security is ranked by the World Economic Forum's report *Global Risks 2011* as a "very likely" risk within the next ten years, with a perceived economic impact of around $500 billion. Food security follows closely behind with a slightly lower perceived risk of occurrence in the coming decade and economic impact of about $300 billion.[2] The US Office of the Director of National Intelligence underlines the importance of the twin water–food issue:

> Experts currently consider 21 countries with a combined population of about 600 million to be either cropland or freshwater scarce… 36 countries, home to 1.4 billion people, are projected to fall into this category by 2025. Lack of access to stable supplies of water is reaching unprecedented proportions in many areas of the world and is likely to grow worse owing to rapid urbanization and population growth.[3]

Yet, while there is an inherent link with water, the issue of food does bring several additional challenges and further concerns to the 21st century dining table. According to the Food and Agriculture Organization (FAO) of the United Nations, food security exists when all people, at all times, have physical, social and economic access to sufficient, safe and nutritious food that meets their dietary needs and food preferences for an active and healthy life. Clearly, we do not live in a world in which such food security exists for the majority. For a whole host of reasons, the number of undernourished people in the world has been increasing for the last decade, mostly in poorer nations.[4] Yet, somewhat perversely, at the same time richer nations have been experiencing increasing levels of health problems related to *overconsumption* of food. In addition, the environmental impact and sustainability of modern intensive agriculture has been brought into question, along with ethical considerations related to issues such as genetically modified crops. We will take a look at such issues later in the chapter, but first let's get to grips with the underlying issues of water supply.

Water

Clearly, water scarcity is a key global issue at both political level and business levels. In an interview with the management consulting firm McKinsey & Company, Peter Brabeck-Lethathe stated:

> Water is, for us, a strategic issue. The main challenge is no doubt water security for the farmers who supply our factories all over the world. Farmers worldwide are the main users of water – 70 percent of withdrawals, more than 90 percent of actual consumption – and they will be the most affected parties in case of a massive water shortage. In 2003, Frank Rijsberman, then the head of the International Water Management Institute, had expressed his concern: "If present trends continue, the livelihoods of one-third of the world's population will be affected by water scarcity by 2025. We could be facing annual losses equivalent to the entire grain crops of India and the US combined." This is a frightening scenario. Needless to say, such a global crisis would affect all companies, not only those from the food industry.

Nor, it has to be said, is McKinsey a slouch when it comes to identifying future consulting opportunities; so it is worth taking notice when they dedicate an entire issue of their flagship quarterly business journal to "The water imperative" of the 21st century. Clearly the problems associated with water go beyond the nutrition and beverage business arenas. Given increasing pressure upon fresh water supplies, the challenges surrounding this issue have been receiving increasing attention from a broad range of scientists, politicians, media, business professionals and the general public over the last decade. For example, Tom Albanese, CEO of Rio Tinto, one of the world's largest mining groups, explains that water management has become a strategic issue given that the company's water-intensive operations tend to be located in areas that are either arid or plagued by torrential rains.[5]

In *The Economist* article "Running dry," Andrew Liveris, the chief executive of Dow Chemical refers to water as "the oil of the 21st century." As with oil, water is critical to the global economy. Yet, unlike oil, water has no substitute and supplies of clean, easy-to-access water are coming under pressure as the result of growing populations and emerging middle-classes that desire a water-intensive Western lifestyle. The investment bank Goldman Sachs, estimates that worldwide water consumption is following an unsustainable growth rate – doubling every 20 years. Furthermore, climate change is having profound and complex impact upon the availability of freshwater, through more frequent and severe droughts.[6]

In 2010, *The Economist* also ran a special report "For want of a drink," remarking that the words "water" and "crisis" often appear together in print nowadays. With clear evidence of decreasing aquifer levels, disappearing glaciers, reservoirs drying-up, rivers no longer reaching the sea, as well as possible wars between nations currently at odds over water rights, apparently "everyone must use less water if famine, pestilence and mass migration are not to sweep the globe."[7]

But how is it that our "Blue Planet" is so beset with water problems?

Although 70 percent of earth is covered with water, only 1 percent of that water is readily available for human consumption: 97 percent of the water on our planet is salt water and the remaining 2 percent is in the form of ice.[8]

The 2009 United Nations *World Water Development Report* outlines the importance of water to both the human and natural world in which we live:

The amount of freshwater on Earth is finite, but its distribution has varied considerably, driven mainly by natural cycles of freezing and thawing and fluctuations in precipitation, water runoff patterns and evapotranspiration levels. That situation has changed however. Alongside natural causes are new and continuing human activities that have become primary "drivers" of the pressures affecting our planet's water systems. These pressures are most often related to human development and economic growth.

History shows a strong link between economic development and water resources development. There are abundant examples of how water has contributed to economic development and how development has demanded increased harnessing of water. Such benefits came at a cost and in some places led to increasing pressure on the environment and increasing competition among users. Our requirements for water to meet our fundamental needs are our collective pursuit of higher living standards, coupled with the need for water to sustain our planet's fragile ecosystems, make water unique among our planet's natural resources.[9]

The UN water development report goes on to link crises across the various domains of climate change, energy and food supplies, and troubled financial markets to water resources management. As competition between demands on water increases, society will need to respond with improved water management – ensuring the provision of water of a given quality, quantity and reliability at a specified place.

In 2002, the United Nations Committee on Economic, Cultural and Social Rights took the unprecedented step of declaring water as a fundamental human right which "entitles everyone to sufficient, affordable, physically accessible, safe and acceptable water for personal and domestic uses."[10] However, to live up to such an ideal is going to be a challenge given that:

Freshwater consumption worldwide has more than doubled since World War II and is expected to rise another 25 percent by 2030.[11]

The UN FAO outlines that our renewable freshwater supplies come from the 110,000 cubic kilometers of precipitation that fall on land every year. Almost two-thirds of this amount evaporates from the ground or transpires from forest, rangeland or cropland vegetation. The remaining 40,000 cubic kilometers per year becomes surface runoff that feeds rivers and lakes, and groundwater that feeds aquifers. Part of this water is removed from these rivers or underground aquifers for human consumption by installing infrastructure. This removal of water is called "water withdrawal." Most of the withdrawn water is returned to the environment some time later, after it has been used – though the quality of the returned water may be poorer than the quality when it was originally removed.[12]

So where does this freshwater go to and how is it used? Water usage is very uneven across countries. The big three water users are: India which gulps a colossal 646 cubic kilometers of water per year; China 630 cubic kilometers per year; and the United States 479 cubic kilometers per year. Following these big consumers, in order of consumption are Pakistan, Japan, Thailand, Indonesia, Bangladesh, Mexico and the Russian Federation. Unsurprisingly, these top-ten consumers roughly follow the top-ten most populous countries: 1. China, 2. India, 3. USA, 4. Indonesia, 5. Brazil, 6. Pakistan, 7. Bangladesh, 8. Nigeria, 9. Russia and 10. Japan (For more population details see Global Trend 7: Demographics).

However, the different order of water consumption compared to population size as well as the unlikely appearance of Thailand and Mexico in the top consumers list would indicate that there are different drivers of water consumption at a per capita level. There is no apparent simple relationship between water availability and consumption levels. It would appear to be more a question of lifestyles. While some arid areas have extremely low levels of consumption, others have extremely high levels – depending upon the activities in which the local human populations are engaged.

A better indicator of water consumption activities is given by the amount of water withdrawal (in cubic meters per year) per inhabitant for agricultural, domestic and industrial purposes. In this respect:

Several countries consume more than 1,000 cubic meters (or 1,000,000 liters) per person per year – about half an Olympic-sized swimming pool per man, woman and child on a national level.

Such countries include those with somewhat limited rainfall in certain areas but which support an intensive agriculture sector, such as Canada, USA, Australia and Portugal. Also in this group of high per-capita water consumption is a group of rather arid countries including Iran, Iraq, Pakistan and Sudan. Then come a bunch of ex-Soviet Union states: Turkmenistan, Uzbekistan, Kazakhstan, Bulgaria and Romania. And finally some "odd" ones with no immediately apparent reason for such high water withdrawals: Thailand, Ecuador, Guyana and Suriname. As a general trend though, it would seem high water consumption comes down to a combination of lifestyles in arid countries with high levels of agriculture and/or poor water management.

At the other end of the scale of water withdrawals per capita lie broad swathes of sub-Saharan Africa (including Angola, Congo, Chad, Nigeria, Ethiopia, Kenya, Uganda, Cameroon, Gabon and others) where inhabitants withdraw less than 100 cubic meters of water per year as a result of traditionally leading water conserving lifestyles and having little water infrastructure to speak of.

The UN FAO goes on to indicate the specific uses of withdrawn water:

Three types of water withdrawal are distinguished: agricultural, municipal (including domestic), and self-abstracted industrial water withdrawal.

A fourth type of anthropogenic water use is the water that evaporates from artificial lakes or reservoirs associated with dams.

Excluding evaporation, the UN *World Water Development Report*[13] indicates the specific regional variations for water withdrawals across agriculture, industry and domestic uses as shown in Table 5.1.

So, in most world regions the lion's share of water goes to agriculture, and this usage has been increasing for several decades – as the UN *World Water Development Report* explains:

The last 50 years have seen rapid acceleration in water resources development for agriculture. Development in hydraulic infrastructure (dams and large-scale public surface irrigation), as well as private and community schemes (particularly groundwater pumping), have put water at the service of populations as part of the global effort to rapidly increase staple food production, ensure food self-sufficiency and avoid famines. As the global population grew from 2.5 billion in 1950 to 6.5 billion at the beginning of the 21st century, food production growth outstripped population growth,

Table 5.1: Regional variations in water withdrawals

Region	Water Withdrawals		
	Agriculture (%)	Industry (%)	Domestic (Urban) (%)
Africa	86	4	10
Asia	81	11	7
Latin America	71	10	19
Caribbean	69	8	23
North America	39	48	13
Oceania	73	12	19
Europe	32	53	15
World	**70**	**20**	**10**

Source: UN *World Water Development Report 3: Water in a Changing World,* 2009.

irrigated area doubled (particularly in Asia), and water withdrawals tripled...

This success in agricultural production led to a 30-year decline in food prices in most countries, a trend that lasted until very recently. In real terms, food prices declined, until recently, to their lowest levels in history, so that consumers in many countries could eat better while spending less of their budget on food. Today, food supply accounts for a very small part of household income in rich countries, but it can constitute as much as 80 percent of income of poor people in developing countries.

Declining food prices... also led to reduced investment in agriculture, particularly in irrigation, resulting in neglect of maintenance of public irrigation schemes and a sharp slowdown in the growth of irrigated agriculture. [See Figure 5.1.]

Therefore, improvements in water management – such as irrigation – have led to improved agricultural production and a 30-year decline in food prices.

Figure 5.1: World food prices (line) vs global irrigation activity (bars)

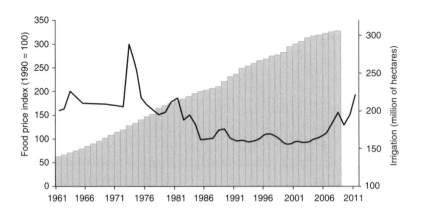

Source: UN *World Water Development Report 3*: Water in a Changing World

Yet, since 2000, food prices have started to rise again, with all manner of global implications, such as the wave of unrest across the Middle East. More of such food issues later.

After agriculture, the next biggest user of water worldwide is industry – especially in industrialized North America and Europe. Of course, water has many uses in industry, including cleaning, heating and cooling, steam generation and as a solvent and an ingredient of a plethora of industrial products. Different industries demand different water quantities and qualities – for example the high-technology industry can require water of a higher quality than drinking water, and in large volumes.

Next time you throw away a newspaper, consider this:

> **The volume of water used to produce a tonne of paper**
> **can be up to 2,000 cubic meters – or 2 million liters.**

That is a lot of water. Yet others manage to produce a tonne of paper with "only" 80 cubic meters. Similarly, to produce a tonne of sugar requires anywhere between 3 and 400 cubic meters of water. Steel needs between 2 and 350 cubic meters per tonne; petrol between 0.1 and 40 cubic meters per tonne; soap between 1 and 35 cubic meters per tonne; and between 8 and 25 cubic meters of water are required to produce one tonne of beer!

With industrial growth comes the demand for energy to provide heat, light, power and transportation. This also has potentially important impacts upon water availability since water cooling is needed for all thermal sources of power (See Global Trend 9: Energy). In industrialized countries a significant proportion of water withdrawals go towards power generation: for example, in the USA total water withdrawn for cooling in power generation is equal to the entire share of the nation's water use in agriculture – 39 percent. The steam you see coming from the top of a power station's cooling towers is part of that water use.

The *Scientific American* article "Energy versus water: solving both crises together" states: "water is needed to generate energy. Energy is needed to deliver water. Both resources are limiting the other – and both may be running short." This energy–water concern throws-out interesting dilemmas, such as whether electric vehicles as an energy-conscious alternative to current gasoline vehicles really would be a viable alternative. According to studies done at the University of Texas at Austin, generating electricity for widespread plug-in hybrid or all-electric vehicles would require as much as three times the water per mile as gasoline powered vehicles, given current energy mix and efficiency levels.[14] (Energy implications are considered more in Global Trend 9.)

What is very obvious is that some use water in more efficient ways than others. "Industrial water productivity" is a general indicator of performance in water use and varies greatly across countries. Somehow, Denmark manages to generate $138 worth of industrial output per cubic meter of water used per year while the USA only manages to generate $10 worth of industrial output with the same amount of water. The likes of Lithuania, Latvia and the Czech Republic also have relatively high levels of industrial water productivity – and hence perhaps have something to teach many Western countries.

Of course, beyond agriculture and industry, water has a key role in domestic routines, healthy lifestyles and standard of living. To address such challenges, a 2008 joint pilot project of the UN FAO and the International Fund for Agricultural Development proposed a "water livelihoods index" and a draft framework for assessing the performance of water-related interventions for reducing poverty. The index considers four water-related components that influence livelihoods: access to basic water services; crop and livestock water security; a clean and healthy water environment; and a secure and equitable water entitlement. Not surprisingly, many poor countries score low on this index. Thus the highest returns to water investment in order to improve are to be found where income and livelihoods are the lowest, mostly in sub-Saharan Africa, but also parts of Asia and Latin America.

In Africa alone, about 340 million people lack access to safe drinking water, and almost 500 million lack access to adequate sanitation.

According to the 2009 UNESCO *World Water Development Report*, for use in such activities countries in sub-Saharan Africa store only about 4 percent of their annual renewable flows, compared with 70–90 percent in many developed countries, and are therefore far more exposed to the vagaries of nature. In addition, water storage is essential to ensure reliable sources of water for irrigation, water supply and hydropower and to provide a buffer for flood management.

Yet it is not *just* the poor that are likely to suffer from lack of clean water: human beings and natural ecosystems in many river basins around the world are being affected. In a study of the impact of climate change upon freshwater systems, the IPCC* estimated the number of people living along "severely stressed" water basins – with high levels of water withdrawals compared to actual availability – as being in the range of 1.4 billion to 2.1 billion. Many of these areas are outside the poorest areas of Africa, Asia and Latin America – and many are in rich areas of North America, the Middle East and Europe. Just some of the recent water-stress problems include: multi-year droughts in the USA and Canada; damage to ecosystems along Europe's fourth largest river, the Elbe; shrinking glaciers in the Andes; reduced water supply due to erosion in reservoirs in Brazil; health problems due to arsenic in groundwater in India; the Huanghe river in China has run dry due to over-irrigation combined with less precipitation; and damage to ecosystems due to decreased stream flow and increased salinity in the Murray–Darling basin, Australia.[15]

Another important potential driver of future water stress is the reduction in groundwater, which has been used for millennia for human consumption and agriculture. It is estimated that around 20 percent of total water currently used globally is from groundwater sources – some of which is renewable and some not. This proportion is rising rapidly, particularly in dry areas. The intensity of groundwater use with the widespread arrival of the electric pump (partly encouraged by subsidized rural electrification) has led to the emergence of many groundwater-dependent societies since the 1950s. However, the futures of such societies are now threatened as their consumption exceeds the renewable supplies and depletes the finite water resources stored in aquifers.

UNESCO report that groundwater tables and river levels are receding in many parts of the world due to over-exploitation of these finite supplies. In India, the country that extracts most groundwater (around 150 to 200 cubic kilometers per year), farmers are now using nearly 80 percent of the country's available water – largely from receding groundwater wells. An additional problem to the depletion of these nonrenewable water resources is that human activities are often to blame for their pollution. Widespread industrial and agricultural contamination in the form of toxic waste chemicals, fertilizers and pesticides often seep into underground rock layers and water containing aquifers. Scientists have realized that once an aquifer becomes polluted

---

* Climate Change: see Global Trend 4. IPCC: International Panel on Climate Change.

it is virtually impossible to clean and can take decades or more to return to being potable.

> **At current rates, the World Bank estimates that India will have exhausted nonrenewable water supplies, upon which the country currently depends, by 2050.**

The USA is the second-highest groundwater user, followed closely by China. Both extract over 100 cubic kilometers of groundwater per year. But there are many other groundwater-dependent nations, including Bangladesh, Pakistan, Iran, Mexico, Saudi Arabia, Russia, Japan and France to name but a few.[16]

A lot of the increases in water stress in coming years will be due to population growth. From just under 7 billion people currently living on our planet, the population is forecast to grow dramatically to more than 9 billion by 2050. (See Global Trend 7: Demographic Changes.) This growth will mainly occur in developing countries and will put current water levels and infrastructures under great pressure. It will also put agricultural food production under considerable stress.

So now to the associated issue: Food.

Food

From a map created by the UN Food and Agriculture Organization showing calorie dietary consumption per capita per day, it is plain to see that the world is divided into the starving, the hungry, the healthy and the stuffed. And you can probably guess more or less which geographic regions fit into each category. Several African countries and Afghanistan are starving – with less than 2,000 calories eaten per person per day. Several other African, Asian and Latin American countries are hungry – consuming less than 2,400 calories per person per day. Then come the well-fed Russians, North Africans, Middle East citizens, Latin Americans, and Australians – eating under 3,200 calories per day. And finally come the majority of the Europeans and North Americans wolfing down over 3,400 calories on average per man, woman and child per day. Such high calorie intake is more than dieticians would recommend for a healthy life.[17]

Let's look at the starving and hungry first. By the FAO definition:

> Undernourishment exists when caloric intake is below the minimum dietary energy requirement (MDER). The MDER is the amount of energy

needed for light activity and a minimum acceptable weight for attained height, and it varies by country and from year to year depending on the gender and age structure of the population.

During the 1980s and early 1990s, good progress was made in reducing global chronic hunger.* And at the World Food Summit (WFS) in 1996, the Heads of State and Government stated:

> We pledge our political will and our common and national commitment to achieving food security for all and to an ongoing effort to eradicate hunger in all countries, with an immediate view to reducing the number of under-nourished people to half their present level no later than 2015.

Yet, clearly the world is not on track in achieving this goal – and in fact things are getting worse. A lot worse. Even before the current consecutive food and economic crises, the 2009 FAO report *The State of Food Insecurity in the World* warned that the number of undernourished people in the world had been increasing slowly but steadily for the last decade.

While the number of undernourished in the world had been in decline since the 1960s, it has been on the increase again in the 21st century, increasing from about 820 million in 1997 to over 1 billion undernourished in 2009. That is nearly 200 million more hungry within 12 years.

Of these undernourished, 642 million are in Asia and the Pacific; 265 million in sub-Saharan Africa; 53 million in Latin America and the Caribbean; 42 million in the Near East and North Africa; and 15 million in developed countries. That is a lot of hungry people, and the projections are for more increases in the numbers of hungry. Nor can such increases be entirely blamed upon population growth, since the number of undernourished as a percentage of the total has also increased in recent years.

This is where food prices come in. At the end of 2008, staple food prices were 17 percent higher in real terms than two years earlier, and this was true across a range of important foodstuffs. Over this period the price of rice,

---

* "Hunger" and "undernourishment" are used interchangeably by the UN Food and Agriculture Organization.

considered by a large percentage of the world's population to be the most essential food, had increased by nearly 30 percent. Wheat, another essential food, had increased in price by almost 20 percent. Higher food prices have hurt the poorest, especially the landless poor and female-headed households in both urban and rural areas. Families are being forced to choose which type of asset to sell first, and which family member should pay the price in terms of reduced healthcare, education or food consumption.

At the start of 2011 the food industry is again in crisis. World food prices have risen above the peak they reached in 2008, when hundreds of millions of people fell into poverty and "land grabs" carried out by rich grain-importing nations in poor agricultural ones raised awkward questions about how best to help the poor. And just as in 2007–08, food riots have shaken governments in developing countries, exporters have banned grain sales abroad, and there has been panic buying and emergency price controls. Fears that drought might ruin the current wheat crop in China, the world's largest, are sending shock waves through world markets. Discontent over rising bread prices has played a part in the popular uprisings throughout the Middle East. As *The Economist* special report on feeding the world remarks: "… the fact that agriculture has experienced two big price spikes in under four years suggests that something serious is rattling the world's food chain…"[18]

Apparently, this has come as something of a surprise, given that most agricultural problems were considered solved by the 1990s – with fertilizers boosting yields and pests under control. With this shock the world has woken up to the fact that an era of falling food prices has come to an end. This has been as a result of a combination of factors, including rising demand in emerging economies, the increasing use of maize as a source for biofuel, the increasing problems of water supply, unfavorable weather events (possibly driven by climate change), and the inherent link between modern intensive food-production methods and volatile energy costs.

Since the arrival of the "green revolution" after World War II, one of the key factors in the price of foodstuffs has been the cost of energy. After all, energy is a crucial component of modern agriculture – from the water pumps, to the oil-guzzling tractors and enormous combine harvesters, to the oil-based fertilizers. In addition, the oil-price-dependent transport costs of maintaining the modern food supply chain are immense: just imagine the thousands of air-, sea- and truck-miles required to get out-of-season fruit from the southern hemisphere (notably Chile, Argentina, New Zealand, South Africa) to storage and artificial ripening centers in developed nations and then into supermarket logistics systems.[19]

Improvements in irrigation and agricultural technology have enabled growth of over 20 percent in agricultural production in certain parts of Asia, Africa and Latin America between 1997 and 2007. However, interestingly, and somewhat surprisingly, the growth in Russia, North America and Europe appear to have slowed or even stagnated in comparison.

Despite technological improvements, countries such as Australia, France, UK, Italy and Scandinavian nations recorded a drop of up to 20 percent in agricultural output in the decade up to 2007.[20]

This certainly will not have helped to contain increases in food prices overall, and possibly raises the question as to whether it is reasonable to expect ever-increasing levels of agricultural productivity based purely upon petrochemicals and tractors. Certainly growth in investment in agricultural research and development (R&D) has slowed. Although investment in R&D has been shown to generate higher rates of return, underinvestment has remained an issue, specifically for emerging countries. Most private-sector research has been carried out in developed countries and has tended to be focused on the requirements of commercial farmers in those well-developed regions. Low levels of investment in research for developing nations are sometimes explained by market failure to appropriate the benefits from private investment in small markets.[21]

Another major issue affecting food supply is that imported foods, including basic staples such as grains and vegetable oils, now constitute an important component of diets in most countries. From 1970 to 2003, import dependency grew most among the least-developed countries: the proportion of imports to total grain consumption in poorer nations rose from 8 percent in 1970 to 17 percent in 2003; for sugar and sweeteners imports rose from 18 percent in 1970 to 45 percent in 2003; and vegetable oils from 9 percent to 55 percent. For a sample of 70 developing countries the total level of food imports nearly trebled between 1990 (approximately 40 million tonnes) and 2007 (nearly 120 million tonnes). This reliance on food imports was spurred by trade liberalization policies and the expansion and improvement of the global transportation system. On the one hand, increased reliance on grain imports helped reduce prices in general for consumers, on the other, cheaper imports have undermined domestic agricultural growth and exposed many countries to volatility on international markets. This at the same time as an overall reduction of food aid.

During the 2006–2008 global food crises, many countries started to reconsider their reliance on imports as a main source of their food consumption. However, it is worth noting that it is not only food-importing countries that are vulnerable to higher prices in the world markets. Domestic food prices in many exporting countries rose sharply during the crisis as well – for instance, rice prices in Pakistan, Thailand and Vietnam. In fact, any country that is open to trade can be affected. According to the 2009 FAO report *The State of Food Insecurity in the World*: "domestic price stabilization in the face of world price surges is easier if the quantity of imports or exports is a relatively small share of consumption or production, because it can be buffered more easily by reasonable levels of stockholdings."

Linked to food imports is the contentious issue of developed countries subsidizing their own agricultural sectors. For example, the US pays around $20 billion per year in direct subsidies to farmers, and the EU pays €48 billion per year on agricultural subsidies. Globally almost $300bn is spent each year to subsidize agriculture, which is roughly equal to the annual profit of the entire global agricultural trade. While popular with local farmers, the wisdom of such subsidies on a global scale is questionable, since they go against free market principles and effectively hinder agricultural competition and growth in the developing world. When subsidized farmers in developed countries are effectively incentivized to overproduce (perhaps in environmentally nonsustainable ways), crop prices go down and nonsubsidized farmers in developing countries find themselves unable to compete. For example, subsidized maize producers in the US undercut their lower-paid but unsubsidized counterparts in Mexico.[22]

A further subsidy-related concern has been aired about the flood of cheap subsidized food products (such as soya and maize) on to the market, resulting in unhealthy eating habits in certain socioeconomic groups. Such a relative oversupply of cheap refined carbohydrates and vegetable oils has given rise to health concerns relating to a wide range of chronic diseases ranging from obesity to diabetes, heart disease, cancer, and neurological disorders. To compound such complications in food supply, in addition to a tendency towards increased calorie intakes, consumption patterns seem to be changing as emerging nations in particular are developing new tastes. While the share-of-stomach of grains and other staple foods are declining, certain other foods, particularly meat and dairy produce, are increasing. Many emerging societies seem to be turning away from their traditional diet and acquiring an appetite for more Western-style foods – with associated health problems.

Further concerns have been linked to the whole issue of genetically modified (GM) crops and foodstuffs. These are crops with specific changes made to their DNA by genetic engineering to incorporate favorable characteristics, such as higher resistance to heat, droughts, or insects, or a more efficient usage of water. Common GM crops are soybean, corn, canola, and cotton seed oil, with many more in the pipeline. Despite lacking general public support,* the use of biotech crops has been one of the most rapidly adopted new farming technologies. According to the International Service for the Acquisition of Agri-biotech Applications (ISAAA), the amount of land planted with GM crops grew by 10 percent in 2010 to 148m hectares. The USA is by far the largest GM grower, with almost half the total number of hectares, followed by Brazil (which increased its GM area the most) and Argentina. Rates of growth are much higher in developing countries (up 17 percent in 2010) than in developed ones (only 5 percent up). Over 15m farmers planted GM crops in 2010; 94 percent of them come from developing countries, which include 19 of the 29 countries where GM technology is used.[23]

As you would expect there are reports of benefits and increased crop yields with GM crops.[24] Yet the whole area of "Frankenfoods" is still struggling to free itself of the profound worries over potentially serious negative impacts. Critics have strongly objected to GM foods on several grounds, including: health concerns relating to long-term effects of consumption of foodstuffs that have not undergone the same symbiotic evolution over millennia with mankind's digestive system; ecological concerns relating to the unknown impact of cross-fertilization of GM crops with natural species; and economic concerns raised by the fact that GM crops are synthesized and patented products emanating from very few business concerns and subject to intellectual property law.[25] Such serious concerns may, or may not, be justified in the medium and long-term. Ultimately, though, GM crops are still a relatively new technology and the concerns are sufficiently grave to warrant a good deal of caution. While they offer the potential for increasing agricultural

---

* A survey last year by Deloitte found that 34 percent of Americans were either "extremely" or "very" concerned about eating GM foods and a further 36 percent were "somewhat concerned."

productivity in the short term, societies and businesses should beware of widespread roll-out of such technologies without fully understanding the medium and longer-term consequences.[26] (See Global Trend 3 for similar examples of negative effects of widespread technology implementation before being fully understood.)

A related concern is the over-dependence of the human food chain upon an increasingly limited number of crops and species. As the UN FAO report *State of the World's Plant Genetic Resources* states:

"Only 30 crops 'feed the world'... Wheat, rice and maize alone provide more than half of the global plant-derived energy intake... Given the importance of a relatively small number of crops for global food security, it is particularly important that the diversity within major crops is conserved effectively, available for use, and managed wisely."[27]

Yet, the search for the most productive species for agricultural production has resulted in many somewhat less productive – but still genetically useful – species being discarded from commercial farming over the years. As a result during the 20th century there has been gradual whittling-down of commercial animal and crop varieties. For example, India's current rice crop is planted with only a dozen varieties, when there used to be 30,000; since the 1930s, 75 percent of Mexico's maize varieties have disappeared; 90 percent of fruit and vegetable varieties in the USA have been lost in the 20th century.[28]

In total, 75 percent of crop genetic diversity has been lost, with 2 percent disappearing every year.

Crop genetic diversity has reduced in parallel with the concentration of the commercial seed market into a few *"life science"* companies. The top three commercial seed companies (Monsanto, DuPont and Syngenta) account for almost half of patented seeds, which account for 82 percent of the world commercial seed market. To expect a few agricultural species to do well in the long-run against changing climates and in all the diverse conditions in the world is perhaps overly optimistic. At the very least it reduces the robustness of our food chain in the face of possible systemic risks, since genetic uniformity increases crop vulnerability to pests, disease or climate change. The UN FAO identifies about 60 countries in which genetic vulnerability is considered a potential threat to agricultural output. Historical events such as the Irish potato famine indicate the risks of over-reliance upon few, genetically uniform foodstuffs in a changing world.[29]

Beyond GM foods, ecology issues and the environmental impact of intensive food production and the agro-industry have also gained attention. Agribusinesses have been receiving criticism due to their impact on natural resources for several reasons that include:[30]

- Pollution caused by the run-off of fertilizer chemicals into the water supply. The application of inorganic nitrogen fertilizers worldwide has risen more than nine times in the past 50 years. According to the World Resources Institute, this practice is dramatically increasing the amount of harmful nitrates entering soils, freshwater and marine ecosystems.

- The emission of carbon dioxide and methane (a powerful greenhouse gas produced by livestock). With a share of 14–18 percent of greenhouse gas emissions, livestock generate more greenhouse gases than is generated by transport. (See Global Trend 4: Climate Change.)

Another major area of food concern is the rapid increase in obesity and related health problems such as heart attacks and diabetes, particularly in developed nations. The World Health Organization considers obesity an epidemic. According to the International Association for the Study of Obesity (IASO), adult obesity is now more common globally than undernutrition and is the third-biggest cause of premature death and disability in the affluent world after smoking and high blood pressure. Obesity problems have spread to less wealthy nations such as Mexico, which has the second highest obesity rate after the USA, and Guatemala, where obesity has quadrupled in 30 years. With the rise of obesity fast food companies and others in the food industry are coming under growing scrutiny from consumers. Food companies today are more willing than before to admit the need to share responsibility for tackling such health concerns: companies like PepsiCo and Kraft have changed the ingredients of some of their products to include less saturated fat and salt and have also launched healthier choices.

Both developed and emerging nations are facing problems beyond a simple calorie intake. As *The Economist* article "Not just calories: People also need the right nutrients" outlines, it is about nutrition, not just food. Many in rich and poor countries suffer from nutritional deficiencies, with the modern diet of processed and transported foodstuffs often lacking adequate levels of nutrients. As a result: 1.5 billion people suffer from iron deficiency induced anemia, including half of all women of child-bearing age in poor countries; insufficient levels of vitamin A result in half a million children becoming blind each year, and half of those dying; and inadequate zinc levels are believed to cause about 400,000 deaths a year.[31]

Particularly disturbing are the problems of food waste. Squandered food is a waste of resources and a contributor to shortages and higher food prices particularly in developing countries. The problems of wasting food are economic, ethical and environmental. For example, in the UK, at least 8.3 million tonnes of food are thrown out each year, of which 5 million tonnes are perfectly edible. According to the Environmental Protection Agency, the US spends more than $1 billion on the disposal of food waste. According to *The Economist*:

> *"Both in rich countries and poor, a staggering 30–50 percent of all food produced rots away uneaten."*[32]

This is scandalous, and would indicate that a good deal of the global food crisis derives not from underproduction but from failing to ensure that food which is produced actually arrives at peoples' tables, plates, forks, mouths and stomachs. Any system with such losses would be difficult to sustain. What's more, if the world's population is to increase from almost 7 billion now to over 9 billion in 2050 (for more details see Global Trend 7: Demographic Changes) then it would appear that the question of how to feed so many people has a relatively simple answer – waste less! As is often the case in business, it may not be the production side that is at fault, rather the managing of the supply chain and end consumption.

Threats and opportunities

All of the above trends in water and food give some idea of the extent of threats posed by these issues to societies, businesses and individuals. Without a doubt, many of the trends could lead to catastrophic global impacts if they remain unchecked. Drought, famine, starvation are not words that humans like to see, especially not at the global level. Tremendous efforts will clearly be needed to mitigate such fundamental life-threatening issues in the years to come, and pessimists certainly have plenty of evidence to back up their nightmare scenarios of a world without sufficient clean water or nutritious food.

In addition, climate change will play a key role in the years to come – with a mixed bag of negative and positive impacts upon water and food supply. Water and food threats and opportunities will arise from climatic changes, largely depending upon geographic position. According to the Intergovernmental Panel on Climate Change,[33] by 2050 the annual average river runoff and water availability are projected to:

- increase by 10–40 percent at high latitudes and in some wet tropical areas;

- decrease by 10–30 percent over some dry regions at mid-latitudes and in the dry topics, some of which are already water-stressed areas.

As a result, drought-affected areas will likely increase in extent and agriculture may become unsustainable in such regions. On the other hand, heavy precipitation events, which are likely to increase in frequency, will augment flood risk in those areas lucky enough to have water.

During the 21st century, water stored in glaciers and snow cover is projected to decline, reducing water availability in regions supplied by meltwater from major mountain ranges (where more than one-sixth of the world population currently lives.) As a result of these changing water supply patterns, crop productivity is projected to:

- increase slightly at mid to high latitudes for local mean temperature increases of up to 1–3°C;

- decrease at lower latitudes, especially seasonally dry and tropical regions, for even small local temperature increases (1–2°C), which would increase the risk of hunger.

Increases in the frequency of droughts and floods are projected to affect local crop production negatively, especially in subsistence sectors at low latitudes. Adaptations such as altered cultivars and planting times should allow low – and mid – to high-latitude cereal yields to be maintained at or above baseline yields for modest warming.

Nevertheless, while current trends are towards an uncertain – even precarious – future for those in certain global regions, there are also some reasons for optimism – not least the historically proven human ingenuity in adverse situations and against all the odds. The following are four areas that represent potential opportunities for societies, businesses and individuals to prevail:

Firstly, there is plenty of scope for innovations that help reduce water use and increase food production. As scarcity-induced regulations and increased water prices make using large amounts of water more costly, there will be a need to develop technologies that help reduce water use at all levels of life. Finding ways to use water more efficiently in agriculture is, perhaps, especially critical. Agricultural companies are already looking for ways to improve water management through: designing better drip irrigation technologies that will keep farmers from overwatering; improving seeds (not just GM) that flourish with minimal water and that can withstand lower quality "grey" water; and creating crop management systems, fertilizers and pesticides that use less water, as well as reducing contamination of existing water supplies. In terms of food production this should not come down to a petty "organic versus inorganic" argument. *The Economist* special report on feeding the world indicates that best practices in both organic and conventional farming practices seem capable of producing similarly high levels of tonnage per hectare. Therefore both systems probably have their place in providing sufficient levels of nutritious food for the world's populations in the coming years.

Secondly, there are large opportunities for improving water and food infrastructure. Poor infrastructure may cause much of the current undernourishment of the world. An increase in yields alone is not of much help to farmers if their additional harvest rots in the fields because of difficulties in transporting the harvest to market places in an efficient and timely manner. Most developing countries lack reliable infrastructure for local agricultural products to gain access to regional and global food markets. Investments could be made into education, roads and transport, production facilities, and efficient supply chain operations in order to bring more food to the global plate. Particular areas of focus should include avoidance of pollution of existing finite water resources and the ridiculous levels of waste throughout the food chain.

Thirdly, there will be opportunities for breaking the link between water, food and volatile energy costs. It may make some short term sense in terms of quick profits to stop local production while energy costs are low and to transport foodstuffs from far-flung places, but in the medium and long term this is unlikely to be sustainable – either on social, business or individual levels. While the cheap energy requirements of modern agriculture are enormous there are other related concerns too. Concentrating the worlds food basket into a limited selection of foodstuffs that are able to survive long-distance transport, picking it green to subsequently ripen under energy intensive artificial lighting, and then throwing a significant proportion away into landfill sites does not seem very sensible on any level. If there are plots of land lying idle right next to the local supermarket it does not seem to make sense to be plowing up irreplaceable tracts of Amazonian rainforest. Surely modern supply-chain methods can cope with bringing more locally produced items to the plates of the many rather than the privileged few.

And last, but by no means least, are the opportunities surrounding moderation of consumption. Public and private education programs have proved to be successful at society, business and individual levels in changing behaviors in terms of using less high-quality water and consuming less, more healthy food. Such projects represent an opportunity not only in terms of redressing the balance of food consumption between rich and poor nations, but also a cost-effective way of preventing epidemics of water – and diet-related diseases. Ultimately, we all have the ability to reduce and improve our water and food consumption and act more responsibly in light of the profound problems facing the very stuff that sustains human life. At the national level, certain countries have found ways to manage the demand side: Singapore for example stands out as a country that could serve as an example for others to follow.[34]

With the above opportunities in mind, one of the key areas for effort in improving the current gloomy outlook for global water and food trends – on both supply and demand sides – lies in education; the topic of the next Global Trend chapter.

Global Trend 6

Education

"If you look at the economy, it is really only providing opportunities now to people with a better education... Yet if you're [from a] low income [background] you have less than a 25 percent chance of ever completing a college degree... if you're low income in the United States you have a higher chance of going to jail than you do of getting a 4-year degree."

Bill Gates, Founder, Ex-CEO and
current Chairman of Microsoft[1]

nteresting that Bill Gates should have such an interest in education – especially since much is made by the media of him being a college drop-out. Apparently, though, this college drop-out thing is a bit of an urban myth. He didn't actually drop out but rather took a leave of absence... from Harvard University... To found Microsoft. And things went so well that he didn't return to complete the degree.[2] Very probably neither would you if you were declared a billionaire by the age of 32 and subsequently listed as number one on the *Forbes* list of The World's Richest People from 1995 to 2009 (with a slight slip to number three in 2008). Actually, Bill Gates is very well educated, having attended the private, prestigious and successful* Lakeside School[3] in Seattle, achieving 1590 out of 1600 in the standardized SAT college entrance test, and gaining entry to Harvard. His father was a lawyer and his mother on the board of directors of a bank. His grandfather was a national bank president. Clearly William Henry "Bill" Gates III is no average college drop-out, and nor are most of the other millionaires that the media likes to portray as educational failures.

---

* Lakeside School regularly sends 25 percent of its graduating class to Ivy League universities, and 99 percent go on to college.

Look at a list of the world's most phenomenally wealthy and you invariably see a story of educational success behind them. Carlos Slim, Warren Buffett, Mukesh Ambani, Kakshmi Mittal, Lawrence Ellison, Bernard Arnault, Eike Batista, Amancia Ortega, Karl Albrecht, Ingvar Kamprad, Stefan Persson all apparently made it through high school. Several went on to get a bachelor degree at university and some have masters. It is true that some left university – probably having decided that they already had sufficient skills for their chosen life path. It is also true that few of these economic winners have a PhD – again probably because they felt they didn't need such a high degree of educational specialization. Even if they didn't make it *all* the way through the education system, they left their respective education systems at an appropriate level with adequate life skills to succeed in their field. At least they received a solid enough basic education to communicate effectively and understand their bank balance.

The same cannot be said though of millions of the world's educational losers. Children who do not get access to a decent education go on to consistently underachieve in the workplace and life in general. In the USA and other developed nations such children come in the main from ethnic minority and low income backgrounds. And things get worse moving to poorer nations – as we shall see in a moment. No, there is a link between a good education and moving up in the world – both at individual and national levels.

As the United Nations Educational, Scientific and Cultural Organization (UNESCO) Education for All (EFA) Global Monitoring report states:

> In 2000, world leaders made two sets of major development commitments. The first was the Dakar Framework for Action, where governments from 164 countries adopted six ambitious targets for education for all children, youth and adults for 2015. The second, also for 2015, was the Millennium Development Goals (MDGs): eight wide-ranging commitments for areas including education, child and maternal health, nutrition, disease and poverty. The EFA goals and the MDGs are mutually interdependent. Not only a right in itself, education plays a crucial role in reducing poverty and inequality, improving child and maternal health, and strengthening democracy. Conversely, progress in education depends on gains in other areas, such as the reduction of poverty and disadvantages, and increased gender equality.[4]

First though, what is education? And what is it for and how do we go about it? As Sir Ken Robinson asked at his lecture to the Royal Society for the encouragement of Arts, Manufactures and Commerce (RSA):[5]

"How do we educate our children to take their place in the economies of the 21st century… given that we can't anticipate what the economy will look like at the end of next week!"

Certainly education is a complex issue – and becoming more complex given the pace of change, economic limitations, cultural variety and the global nature in which education takes place and how the consumers are subsequently expected to apply their knowledge. Yet within these constraints, some core processes need to work well, given that education is the process by which society deliberately transmits its accumulated knowledge, skills and values from one generation to another, and that it can be an excellent agent for improving things. Theodore Schultz argued that population quality and knowledge constitute the principal determinants of the future welfare of mankind.[6] Conversely, according to some, a country which is unable to develop the skills and knowledge of its people and to utilize them effectively in the national economy, would be unable to develop anything else.[7] In summary, education is widely regarded as the route to economic prosperity, the key to scientific and technological advancement, the means to combat unemployment, the foundation of social equity, and the spread of political stability and cultural vitality.[8]

Quite an important Global Trend to consider then.

Article 26 of the 1948 UN universal declaration of human rights states that everyone has a right to education and that this education shall be free and compulsory. But the world is still a long way from reaching this goal – with huge disparities between developed and emerging economy countries, between rich and poor within countries, and between boys and girls. The UN charter remains a huge challenge.

Let's get some definitions out of the way to help work our way through the complex maze of differing educational systems around the globe. The world's education systems vary widely in terms of structure and curricular content. Consequently, it can be difficult for national policy-makers to compare their own education systems with those of other countries in order to learn from their experiences, so UNESCO formulated an International Standard

Classification of Education (ISCED) comprising seven levels – 0 to 6 as outlined and summarized below:[9]

- **Pre-primary education (ISCED level 0):** Programs at the initial stage
  of organized instruction, primarily designed to introduce very young
  children, aged at least 3, to a school type environment. (US Preschool)

- **Primary education (ISCED level 1):** Programs normally designed
  to give pupils a basic education in reading, writing and mathematics
  (plus possibly an elementary understanding of subjects such as history,
  geography, natural sciences, social sciences, art and music). Entrance
  between 5 and 7 years old and comprising, in principle, 6 years of full-time
  schooling. (Approximately: US First to Sixth Grade; UK Primary School)

- **Lower secondary education (ISCED level 2):** Generally designed to
  continue the basic programs of the primary level, but the teaching is
  typically more subject-focused, requiring more specialized teachers
  for each subject area. Entry is after 6 years of primary education.
  (Approximately: US Seventh to Ninth Grade; UK Secondary School)

- **Upper secondary education (ISCED level 3):** Further specialization than
  ISCED level 2. with yet more qualified/ specialized teachers. Entrance
  after 9 years of schooling, typically at 15 or 16 years old. (Approximately
  US Tenth to Twelfth Grade; UK Years 12 and 13 (Sixth Form).)

- **Post-Secondary Non-Tertiary (ISCED level 4):** Not significantly more
  advanced than ISCED level 3, but serves to broaden knowledge and
  prepare those students that need it for tertiary education. This level
  usually constitutes pre-degree foundation or short vocational programs.
  The typical duration is 6 months to 2 years.

- **Tertiary or higher education (ISCED levels 5 and 6):** Programs with an
  educational content more advanced than what is offered at ISCED levels
  3 and 4. It is composed of largely theoretically based programs intended
  to provide sufficient qualifications for gaining entry to advanced research
  programs and professions with high skill requirements.

Now that it is possible to conduct cross-country comparisons using the
above ISCED framework, it becomes clear that education opportunity for

children is highly polarized. By age 7, almost all children in Organization for Economic Co-operation and Development (OECD)* countries are in primary school, and the vast majority will complete this primary schooling.[10] By contrast, only 40 percent of sub-Saharan African children are in primary school at this age and half the children in poor countries such as Bangladesh and Guatemala will not complete primary school. At age 20, in OECD countries 30 percent are in post-secondary education compared with 2 percent in sub-Saharan Africa. In rich countries such as Canada and Japan, over half the population aged 25 to 34 has reached tertiary level – while this level is almost nonexistent in poor countries, and the majority of students still in education in sub-Saharan Africa by 24 are still completing a lower secondary level.

The starkest contrasts are between OECD nations and sub-Saharan Africa. Think of the abdominal profiles of two healthy 4-year old children. One that has just had a jolly good Sunday meal and physically couldn't manage another spoon of ice-cream, and another that is still ok but hasn't eaten since last night. The difference in these profiles roughly translates to the difference in shape of the distributions of ages of children in school in OECD versus sub-Saharan African nations. Take a look at Figure 6.1. This graphically illustrates the contrast in average life-chances for education associated with being born in the OECD countries or in sub-Saharan Africa.

For example, starting around the lower waistline: At 6 years old, 80 percent are in primary school in OECD versus only 20 percent in sub-Saharan Africa. Moving to the belly-button area, at 9 years old virtually 100 percent are in primary school in OECD versus about 70 percent in sub-Saharan Africa. This plump belly continues in OECD countries right up to the rib-cage: with nearly 80 percent of 17 years old still in education compared to barely 50 percent in sub-Saharan African nations.

However, perhaps the most startling thing is not the pure difference in the waistlines, but what is actually going on inside these educational "stomachs." The sub-Saharan African countries not only have less inside, but what is there is less educationally nutritious. By 12 years old, the vast majority – about 70 percent – of OECD kids have finished their primary (ISCED level 1)

---

* Organization for Economic Co-operation and Development (OECD) is an international economic organisation of 34 countries founded in 1961 to stimulate economic progress and world trade. It defines itself as a forum of countries committed to democracy and the market economy, providing a platform to compare policy experiences, seeking answers to common problems, identifying good practices, and co-ordinating domestic and international policies of its members.

Figure 6.1: Proportion in education in OECD countries and sub-Saharan Africa

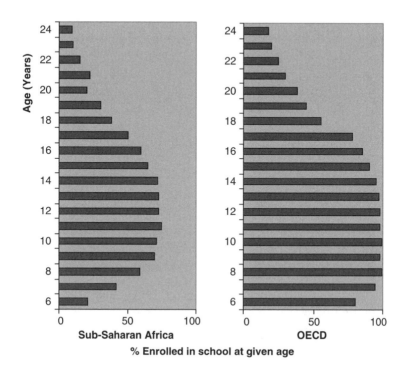

% Enrolled in school at given age

Source: Based upon approximate figures obtained from the *UNESCO EFA Global Monitoring Report, 2009*

education and are learning more advanced stuff in secondary (ISCED level 2 and 3). The overwhelming majority of those 12-year-olds lucky enough to be in education sub-Saharan Africa are still in primary learning how to write their name and add-up. This laggard trend continues with the African nations right the way through – those fortunate enough to be in education at all are way behind their developed nation counterparts.

At 15, virtually 90 percent of OECD kids are doing fairly complex things in school across a broad variety of subjects. In contrast, of the lucky 60 percent or so to be in school in the poorer African nations, well over half are still struggling to grasp the basics.

While the developed nations have nice full "lungs" of students going on to tertiary education from 18 onwards, the poor few sub-Saharan Africans that are still in any form of education at 24 are still struggling to complete a secondary education. It is a sad story, because they just never catch-up. A tertiary education is a thing of dreams for sub-Saharan Africans, with only a tiny proportion having any chance of going to further education colleges. Most that do will probably go overseas to developed nations. In contrast, by 20, most developed nation children have finished secondary schooling and over 30 percent of youngsters are in some form of tertiary education learning complex things.

In fact, it may be that many students in developed nations are learning (or being stuffed with) too-complex things, given where their lives are likely to go. Being "overqualified" has become an issue in many countries, and getting a university degree is no longer any guarantee of career success, of a secure job, or even of any job at all. To continue with the stomach metaphor, it does sometimes seem as though education follows the same trends as food intake (see Global Trend 5). While the rich populations of the West are perhaps gorging on education, the poorer nations are close to educational starvation.

Something similar happens at the younger end of the scale in pre-primary education (ISCED level 0). In 2006, pre-primary gross enrolment ratios* averaged 79 percent in developed countries and 36 percent in developing economy countries, falling as low as 14 percent in sub-Saharan Africa. On the surface this looks bad for the African nations, yet it might become a concern for developed nations. Why? Because, while both developed nation parents are (very probably necessarily) at work, their 3-year old children may be becoming institutionalized – and possibly missing out on important one-to-one family bonding that endows confidence and well-grounded human beings in the longer term. The trend is towards leaving younger and younger children in pre-primary kindergarten, crèche and day care for longer and longer periods of time – the drivers of which are more economic and social pressures than purely educational benefits.

Developing economy countries are not alone in struggling to make Early Childhood Care and Education (ECCE) more equitable. There are large disparities in preschool provision even among OECD countries. The United States currently has no national standard or regulatory structure for early childhood education, resulting in large variations in quality and coverage.

---

* Gross enrolment ratio is the ratio of total enrolment, regardless of age, to the population that officially corresponds to that level of education.

Beyond the inequalities between rich and poor countries, inequalities *within* countries also create a stark picture of disparities in opportunity. Data on national *average* life chances in education have the effect of masking the distribution of life chances across different groups in society. When within-country distribution is superimposed on cross-national disparity, the effect is to magnify the scale of inequality even further.

For example, comparing the richest and poorest 20 percent of populations across developing regions such as Latin America, South and West Asia and sub-Saharan Africa quickly reveals that this is primarily a rich–poor problem. Between 90 and 100 percent of the rich in Latin American, Asian and sub-Saharan countries enter education at 6. In Latin America and Asia most of these stay on until at least 15 years old (i.e. finish ISCED level 3). In sub-Saharan countries 70-odd percent of the richest 20 percent also stay on to about 15 years old (US equivalent grade 9).

Looking at the poorest 20 percent in these regions is quite revealing. Latin America performs reasonably well to start with, with nearly the same percentage of poor kids entering education at age 6 as the rich (about 95 percent) – but by around age 15, this has tailed-off to only 60 percent of the poor still at school. For the poor in South and West Asia and sub-Saharan Africa the situation is nothing short of abysmal. Only 60 to 70 percent of poor 6-year-olds go to any form of school, and this rapidly drops-off to around 30 percent by the time they are 15.

In other words, being born into the poorest 20 percent of the wealth distribution in certain African and Asian nations more than halves the chance of school attendance at age 15.

And it is not just that fewer kids go to school in the poorer nations – those that do go stay there for less time than in rich countries. "School life expectancy" varies widely across the globe. An average child that goes to school in sub-Saharan Africa and South and West Asia, will stay in education for around 9 years – to about age 15. This compares with an average total school life expectancy – from primary to tertiary – of 16 years for a child in North America and western Europe.

As a result, sub-Saharan and South West Asian nations suffer from high levels of out-of-school adolescents. A recent UNESCO data analysis suggests that nearly 71 million adolescents were out of school in 2007 – almost one in five of the total age group. The out-of-school problem is twice as large as it is typically reported to be. Shockingly, in sub-Saharan Africa only 23 percent of children of lower secondary-school age are actually in secondary education – while a full 39 percent are still in primary school, and a further 38 percent are out of school. South and West Asia is not much better with 28 percent of lower secondary school age youngsters on the streets.[11]

Yet while things may be bad now, they were a lot worse before: things have improved. The average net enrolment ratio* for primary education in developing countries as a group has increased since 1999 at twice the rate registered in the 1990s, reaching 85 percent in 2006. On the whole, global trends for primary enrolment ratios have moved in the right direction between 1999 and 2006. In fact, of those in transition on a global level it was the developed nations that let the side down and slipped a bit from the high-90 to the mid-90 percents – and as a result are only just above aggregate enrolment rates for countries in transition (now approximately 90 percent).

More good news is that enrolment in secondary education is also rising. The world average secondary net enrolment ratio increased from 52 percent to 58 percent. Developed countries and most transition countries are moving closer to universal enrolment, but, unsurprisingly, the situation is much more mixed for developing economy regions.

A lot of the biggest growth though has been in tertiary education – and with the majority of new tertiary educational institutions being set-up in developing countries. However, global disparities remain large. Tertiary Gross Enrolment Ratios range from 70 percent in North America and Western Europe, to 32 percent in Latin America, 22 percent in the Arab States and 5 percent in sub-Saharan Africa.

An increase in tertiary education has not translated into improved access to learning for adults. In fact, previous improvements in adult literacy have apparently stagnated in recent years. Now, over 775 million adults worldwide lack basic literacy skills, and, what is possibly even worse, have little or no access to lifelong learning or skills training. Let's just repeat that statistic:

Over 775 million adults worldwide cannot read health advice, manage a bank account, read an advertisement or write a Christmas card. That is 16 percent of the world's adult population.

---

* The net enrolment ratio (NER) shows the extent to which children in the official age group are enrolled.

Of further concern is that two-thirds of these illiterate adults are women.

The vast majority of illiterate adults live in South and West Asia, East Asia and sub-Saharan Africa. Eighty percent of adult illiterates worldwide live in only twenty countries and half live in Bangladesh, China and India. Between 2000 and 2006, India alone had 270 million adult illiterates (over 15 years old); China over 73 million; Bangladesh over 48 million; and Pakistan over 47 million. This is a dreadful wasted opportunity on political, social and personal levels. Clearly, reading and understanding a democratic political manifesto would most likely be beyond these adults. Yet, many governments do not prioritize nonformal education in strategies and policies to promote adult learning programs.

As for youth aged 15 to 24, at least the figure for those lacking literacy skills has declined from 167 million in 1985–1994 to *only* 130 million in 2000–2006. Absolute numbers dropped in most regions except sub-Saharan Africa.

As you'd expect, the share of national income devoted to education as a whole differs substantially among regions and income groups. Low-income countries in sub-Saharan Africa and South and West of Asia, where some 80 percent of the out-of-school population lives, tend to invest the smallest shares of Gross National Product on education – 4.4 percent and 3.3 percent of GNP respectively, versus 5.5 percent in North America and western Europe for example. A contradictory statistic, however, indicates that sub-Saharan and South and West Asian countries actually spend a higher proportion of total government expenditure on public education – 18 percent and 15 percent respectively compared to only 12 percent in North America and western Europe. Yet this is somewhat deceiving, since general government spending in these poorer countries is apparently lower overall.

Of the total global public education expenditure, 55 percent is spent in North America and western Europe, 18 percent in East Asia and the Pacific, 8 percent in Latin America/ Caribbean, 7 percent South and West Asia, 7 percent in Central and Eastern Europe, 3 percent in Arab States, 2 percent in sub-Saharan Africa and 0.3 percent in Central Asia. In many senses this is the opposite to what it should be, considering that the most populous countries with most youth requiring education are precisely the poorer nations. But the statistic that more faithfully represents on-the-ground conditions is probably per-student education expenditure:

In 2006, per-student expenditure at primary level varied from less than US$300 in much of the sub-Saharan Africa to over US$5,000 in most developed countries.

Of course, it is not just a question of how much is spent, but also how *well* it is spent. Increases in funding must be complemented by improvements in financial efficiency and strengthened governance of spending. One suspects that in this aspect, certain poorer nations also lose out.

A recourse often promoted to improve basic education standards across all nations has been private, fee-paying schools. Yet, according to the UNESCO Education for All Global Monitoring report, the rapid emergence of low-fee private schools may be a response to real demand, but there is little evidence to suggest that they offer a genuine choice of affordable, accessible, high quality education. Apparently, in the poorest countries, private finance and provision in basic education are no substitutes for good public systems.

Of primary concern in the quality of education is the supply and quality of teachers. There is broad consensus that classes should have no more than forty students per teacher (Pupil/Teacher Ratio of 40:1) for a good-learning environment. In Afghanistan, Chad, Mozambique, Rwanda, and other sub-Saharan countries, national pupil/ teacher ratios in primary school exceed 60:1. This is despite some 80 percent of the 27 million or so teachers worldwide working in developing countries. Their numbers increased by 5 percent between 1999 and 2006, with the largest increases occurring in sub-Saharan Africa. The question is, though, whether such increases can keep pace with increasing youth populations (see Global Trend 7).

With increased quality of education, comes improved results in more complex fields such as scientific literacy – which is measured by initiatives such as the Program for International Student Assessment (PISA). And as you would possibly expect, 15-year-old students in countries such as Finland, Canada, Japan, Australia, Netherlands, New Zealand, Germany, Ireland, Switzerland, Austria, Sweden, United Kingdom and Belgium score pretty highly in scientific literacy (and in this order). After all, the economies of these countries depend upon scientific and engineering innovation. Also within the top 20 are the ex-Eastern bloc European countries such as such as Estonia, Slovenia, Hungary, the Czech Republic, Croatia and Poland; as well as certain "points-of-excellence" in Asia such as Macao (China) and South Korea. The United States is behind Russia and Greece and just better than Portugal. At the other end of the scale are Kyrgyzstan, Qatar, Azerbaijan, Tunisia and Indonesia – but at least they are still rated.

No sub-Saharan or Asian country (except Japan, Macao and South Korea) even makes it onto this achievement scale.

> **Yet, as the likes of Bill Gates would point out, do not make the mistake of assuming illiteracy and low literacy problems are confined to poor countries.**

For example, even in a high performing country such as the Netherlands, some 1.5 million adults are classified as functionally illiterate. Also, according to an assessment in 2004–2005, in Metropolitan France, 9 percent of adults of working age (18 to 65) – more than 3 million people – had attended school but had literacy problems. The majority of people in France with literacy problems were over 45, and half of them lived in rural or sparsely populated areas. Yet France is often held-up as being one of the countries with the highest educational standards.

Another big issue in education is that of gender parity – or equal access to education for both boys and girls. While clearly girls come-off second best in many countries for a whole host of social and cultural reasons, by 2006, about two-thirds of 187 countries with data had achieved gender parity at the primary level, and most of the remaining 71 countries had made progress towards classroom equality since 1999. Nevertheless:

> **Only 37 percent of countries worldwide had achieved gender parity at secondary level.**

In fact, when given the opportunity, girls in school tend to perform better than boys: they are less likely to repeat grades, more likely to reach the final grade and more likely to complete primary school.

Much of the improvements in basic education in developing countries have come as a result of aid commitments which showed a trend of significant increasing from 1999 to 2004 to $5.2 billion, before dropping off again in 2005 to $3.7 billion. Total aid for basic education in low income countries has been dominated by a small core of donors in the following order: the Netherlands, the United Kingdom, the World Bank's International Development Association (IDA), the European Commission, the United States, France, Canada, Japan, Norway, and Sweden.

Threats and opportunities

Possibly the single biggest threat comes from the major national and global disparities in education provision dividing the world's richest and poorest children. Lack of education leads to lack of opportunities for young people to make their way in the modern world. While global enrolment ratios have been increasing on the whole over the last decades, the danger is that the number of children entering basic education could stagnate – especially as other global challenges take the limelight away from such an apparently mundane issue. As long as children from poor households, rural areas, slums and other disadvantaged groups face major obstacles in access to a good quality education there is likely to be continuing social problems, limited economic growth and untapped potential.

It is sometimes questioned in my business school courses whether education warrants the Global Trend label. Perhaps because I am a teacher I strongly believe it does. This belief is supported by the fact that education is apparently a driver or limiter of most other Global Trends. Without education economic growth and innovation is limited; geopolitical communication is more challenging and global relationships are distorted and less stable; global responses to issues such as climate change, pollution and resource consumption are more challenging; adopting healthy living habits and addressing demographic issues is less likely… and so on. As UNESCO's EFA Global Monitoring Report indicates, the large disparities between students across rich and poor countries and inequalities between regions, communities, schools and classrooms have profound implications for the wider distribution of opportunities in society.

There are clear educational challenges in all corners of the globe, but one geographic area continues to be a relative "black hole": sub-Saharan Africa. Many of the challenges this region faces are likely to remain unsolvable whilst enrolment levels and school life expectancy figures stay at such paltry levels. When the majority of the youth of an entire region do not receive a good-quality basic-level education there are severe causes for concern. The world as a whole is likely to need the African region's natural and human resources in future years to sustain global economic growth – but without populations that can read and write this potentially positive contribution will be lost.

Another global educational black-hole is that girls have less access to education than boys – especially at the secondary level. This seems ridiculous on a couple of levels: firstly it seems just plain unfair; but secondly, and perhaps more pragmatically, it is just plain stupid. Girls do better than boys in primary education and are more likely to finish school if they are given the chance to enter in the first place. So it would appear that by under-representing half of the population of secondary-school age in 63 percent of countries, we are overlooking some considerable untapped brainpower resources.

Beyond children, the fact that 16 percent of the world's adults are illiterate and that they have no access to measures to correct this is simply outrageous. As with the youth of African nations, these people represent a drag on the world's progress when they could be making a valuable contribution. It is virtually impossible to tap into the creative (or consuming) potential of a human being if they are unable to read, write or add up. Yet, apparently, many governments are not giving priority to youth and adult lifelong learning needs in their education policies. And this represents a huge loss of productive potential at a time when most politicians seem to be talking of improving productivity to exit the woes of the economic crisis (see Global Trend 1).

Below-par education, stagnating literacy rates and exclusion of girls from education have profound impacts across various levels. With high illiteracy rates, societies are less able to learn about and cope with inevitable challenges. In addition, poor countries with perpetually inadequate education levels are likely to have correspondingly low economic activity into the future. This in turn is likely to continue breeding poor social conditions and widespread discontent in these nations. Girls who are not permitted access to a decent education are also unable to contribute to societal progress, and there is a knock-on effect to following generations, given that it is often mothers that form the basis of family education. Simply put, an uneducated mother is less likely to create the home conditions necessary for a child – girl or boy – to do a good job of homework.

For businesses, low education levels create certain sectors of the workforce that are inflexible and unattractive at best, and at worst potentially unemployable. Furthermore, a population's inability to read or write translates into a big challenge for firms aspiring to tap into the potential of that population and the new markets that it represents.

Of course at the personal level, beyond an inability to cope with emerging challenges, illiteracy also potentially translates into lifelong frustration with limited possibilities and social stigmatization.

While the main challenges do seem to be in the developing world, developed nations are certainly not exempt from educational risks. Beyond the widespread rich–poor educational disparities present in the Western world, there are also concerns within those socio-economic groups lucky enough to get an education. We may be entering a phase when perhaps, just perhaps, education is starting too young, and going on for too long. Children of less than three are increasingly routinely put into "full-time" kindergarten, crèche and day care on grounds of "education" – when in fact the drivers are more social and economic pressures (on the parents) than educational benefits (for the children). Such potential institutionalization at such an early age, to the exclusion of learning other fundamental human and family attributes, could come back to haunt the populations of rich countries in the future. In addition, having youngsters study and specialize in higher education is generally a good thing... as long as there are opportunities to put this education into practice. After all, formal education should be for a purpose; otherwise it might just be a waste of time and resources that could be better employed doing something else.

Related to this threat is the concern that education systems are not aligned with the labor market – resulting in the potential for systemic unemployment and lack of attractiveness of specific countries to new venture investment. Businesses that cannot find the required skill-set locally might prefer to hire people from abroad or simply move elsewhere. On the individual level, although jobs might be available, individuals without the appropriate education or training are unlikely to possess the required skill-set. To mitigate this threat, governments should, perhaps, engage with business to determine requirements and incorporate them into the educational system.

So, on to the opportunities in education. In the light of the above, it goes without saying that there are tremendous opportunities at society, business and individual levels to improve education at national and global levels. Education will remain a huge challenge, especially for developing countries which are in great need of quality education as a basis for their much needed economic development. Nevertheless, politicians and policy-makers have a very real opportunity to raise the bar at all levels of both developed and emerging nations. Rich countries should probably continue to help those poorer countries with lower education levels to raise their game. Investing in education at a society level is just that – an investment that is highly likely to yield future benefits of increased social stability and ability to overcome 21st-century challenges presented by other Global Trends. Governments of all denominations have the opportunity to work at reducing the gap between private and public schooling and improving overall levels. This should not translate simply into more time spent in education, but into improved quality education that meets the needs of society at large and the businesses and organizations that drive the economy. Leaving behind whole sectors of the community will inevitably be a drag on progress. Furthermore, public policy could perhaps reduce an emphasis upon purely achieving "empty" grades and refocus upon preparing young people for an enriching and rewarding life in which they can play a continuing active part in society and face-up to the inevitable trials along the way. This is easier said than done, but represents one of the biggest opportunities for politicians to "make a difference." This does not necessarily mean spending more – but rather a more thoughtful allocation of available resources. After all, it is apparent that the best-performing education systems are not necessarily the most expensive.

As one of the main beneficiaries, business clearly has an important role to play in improving education by making investments at local and national levels to develop workforce knowledge and skills and to tap into new market opportunities. The business community should work with governments of developed and developing nations to ensure the education given meets the needs of modern businesses by molding innovative, flexible people, with appropriate problem-solving skills and the confidence to overcome inevitable business hurdles. Currently, many poor countries and low socioeconomic groups within rich countries are caught in a trap of inadequate education, leading them to make little or no contribution to society and to become a constraint on businesses in general. Direct investment in education as a for-profit business is one potential way to go, but care should probably be taken not to exclude the lower levels of society yet again. Perhaps a better way would be greater contribution to public education systems. Businesses should be aware that, in the longer-term, education systems based upon over-preparing an elite and largely ignoring larger portions of society is unlikely to provide the conditions for sustainable business growth. Corporate Social Responsibility (CSR) has a potentially important role to play under the motto of "Doing good and doing well." Yet, unlike some other forms of charity, contributing to education has very real potential for future business returns. While most current business involvement is focused upon the latter stages of education (in university curriculums for example), there is an opportunity to become involved in promoting excellent standards of basic education across all levels of society and equality for boys and girls. Similarly, there is the opportunity to improve continued adult learning through in-company and sponsored education and training initiatives. Such initiatives, undertaken thoughtfully by well-educated business leaders, are highly likely to yield significant commercial benefits in the short, medium and longer term.

Beyond the tremendous scope for entrepreneurial initiatives in delivering conventional education, at the individual level there is a clear need for continued lifelong learning. The modern world is a complex place that does not allow for stagnation of thinking upon graduation from school, college or university. There is always more knowledge to be gained, both theoretical and practical, and those with a more solid education are simply less vulnerable to negative influences or shocks. For parents, there is strong evidence that such educational success starts at home through parental encouragement of reading, writing and mathematics skills. Parental emotional support is perhaps something that cannot be outsourced entirely to an institutional education system. Conversely, the "pushing" of individual children to achieve high grades from an early age is unlikely to result in confident, well balanced and happy human beings in the longer term. Another point to remember in modern societies is that schools and colleges were not originally intended for "parking" children during working hours – but rather to transfer knowledge to upcoming generations, and engender within them the ability to further develop this knowledge for the progress of mankind. All of us will at some point be dependent upon the next generations in some form or other. As such, the time-serving approach to fit in with adult work routines should perhaps be rejected in favor of an education that genuinely adds appropriate and useful theoretical knowledge, practical skills and social values. In line with this point is the need for collaboration between individual parents and their child's school. Instead of using schools as an outsourcing service, parents should consider ways of serving the school. After all, it would seem that the best performing schools invariably have high levels of parent involvement.

There is a final twist in the education Global Trend. The worst education happens to coincide with the areas of the world where the youth population is growing the fastest. This presents a double whammy of threats and/ or opportunities when it comes to dealing with challenges relating to demographic changes – the topic of the next Global Trend.

Global Trend 7

Demographic Changes*

> *"The old mindset is one of 'us' and 'them'... the Western*
> *world as a long life in a small family and the developing*
> *world as a short life in a large family...Size of family is*
> *really about the bedroom; whether a man and woman*
> *decide to have a small family... Length of life is about the*
> *bathroom and the kitchen – if you have soap, water and*
> *food you can live long."*

Hans Rosling, Professor of International Health, Karolinska
Institute, and Chairman of the Gapminder Foundation[1]

According to Professor Rosling,[†] in the 1950s the world did indeed consist of two broad sets of countries: the developing countries where families tended to be larger with between five and eight children per woman and life expectancies at birth of between 30 to 50 years; and the developed nations with between two to four children per woman and longer life expectancies of 55 to 75 years old. The world was very much us and them.

Yet from the 1950s onwards amazing things happened in the world. Soap, clean water, reliable food and medicine arrived in the developing world and life expectancies started to catch up fast with those in the Western world. Now, instead of two distinct clusters on a *"Life Expectancy versus Family Size"* graph, there is one big blob incorporating the majority of the world's countries. Both developed and developing[‡] nations now form this bigger group

---

* Demography is the study of size, structure and distribution of populations, and changes in them in response to birth, migration, aging and death. Social demography also analyzes the relationships between economic, social, cultural and biological processes influencing a population.
† By the way, if you get the chance to see Professor Rosling speak, I would recommend it. In fact there are some good videos of him in action online at the likes of TED Talks and YouTube.
‡ As the United Nations Statistics Division states: "The designations 'developed' and 'developing' are intended for statistical convenience and do not necessarily express a judgment about the stage reached by a particular country or area in the development process."

where life expectancies are between 60 and 90 years and family sizes have generally reduced to between one and three children. Sadly, many cases are still back at the starting line on the world's life expectancy race to the top – theirs still hover in the 40 to 50 years range. Apart from obvious cases such as Afghanistan, many of these unfortunates are in sub-Saharan Africa, for example Liberia and the Congo.

Clearly, notwithstanding these laggard countries, a lot of things have changed in the world that require a resetting of this "us versus them" mindset. In fact, many otherwise well-educated Westerners are ignorant of these huge leaps in life expectancy in developing economy countries. As Hans Rosling states:

> The world view of my students corresponded with the reality the year their teachers were born!... Mexico and China have caught up with the United States in these social dimensions yet less than 5 percent of specialists in global health were aware of this.

This progress of the developing countries towards greater health should be of no great surprise – after all, the Western nations had made similar health leaps, albeit somewhat earlier. In fact, at the beginning of the 1800s the life expectancy in the United States and western Europe was approximately 35 to 40 years – on par with Afghanistan today. Yet throughout the 19th century and first part of the 20th, the USA and Western European countries got richer and their health improved generally for the same reasons: education, soap, water, food and medicine. In the case of developing and emerging countries, an interesting point seems to be that the massive improvements in health over the last 50 years have not necessarily followed correspondingly high levels of wealth. While the life expectancy in developing and emerging economies is often very close to that in developed nations, their absolute wealth levels may have improved but they still lag relatively further behind on GDP income per capita than their health levels would suggest. In other words, developing world countries have been able to apply the healthcare knowledge to reduce infant mortality and increase life expectancy without needing to get rich first – simply by improving the conditions in kitchens and bathrooms around the world.

Thus, although there are lots of "ifs and buts" (in terms of the poorest nations being left behind, and the sustainability of improvements if they are not also accompanied by economic development) the world has moved away from a simplistic us and them towards some convergence of most nations – at least in health terms such as increasing life expectancy and decreasing child mortality.

This is clearly good news and is a genuine human success story. Yet this good news has left the world as a whole with a couple of new problems. Firstly, as a result of a rapid decline in premature deaths in developing countries over the last 50 years their populations are increasing fast and there are more mouths to feed on a global level. Secondly, the developed world has got itself into an awkward corner as a result of consistently high life-expectancy combined with ever-declining fertility rates: the tricky issue of just how to sustain so many aging people with a declining number of young people.

With the combined changes across both developed and emerging economies of continually increasing life expectancy, lower child mortality and decreasing fertility, come new demographic challenges for the 21st century.

In fact, the World Economic Forum Global Risks Landscape report identifies demographic challenges as very likely to occur in the next ten years, and attributes a financial impact of approximately \$400 billion.[2] Industrialization and shifting cultural norms and values have resulted in tremendous social change across the world during the 20th century and this is likely to continue impacting upon everything from how we do business to how we live our lives.[3]

The world will have to respond to a new demographic landscape with a better-informed mindset because a lot is at stake. In richer countries demographic trends such as an increasingly elderly population are behind the heated debates over social security and pension reform and immigration controls. On the other hand, in developing and emerging nations, growing youth populations without sufficient opportunities have been blamed for recent social unrest and ultimate overthrow of Middle East and North African regimes.

The ideal capacity of the planet is another underlying issue that is vigorously discussed across various scientific, economic, political, religious and moral opinions. Are there too many or too few people in the world today? Those who feel that there are too many argue that the world hasn't developed sufficient infrastructure to support this many people, especially in developed countries. The environmental impacts of actions needed to obtain the resources to support population growth are apparently damaging the planet. On the other hand, those who feel that further population growth is necessary argue that a young population is needed to support the elderly economically, and that there is still a lot of potential for growth – especially in developing countries.

For the time being, though, let's put such debate to one side and look at some numbers.

In 2009, the world population was 6.8 billion. On current trends, by 2050 this will have risen to 9.2 billion.[4]

In the last 50 years, we have seen massive growth in the populations of developing countries while seeing limited – or stagnating – growth in developed countries. In the next 40 years, this trend is expected to continue. Birth rates in developing countries are still more than double those in developed countries. This, combined with decreasing death, results in accelerating population growth in developing countries.[5] According to the United Nations *World Economic and Social Survey 2010*,[6] 80 percent of the world's population currently live in emerging and developing-economy countries, that is, around 1.2 billion in developed countries and about 5.6 billion in developing countries. This percentage is expected to increase through to 2050 – with population in developed countries remaining at around 1 billion, and the population in developing countries is set to rise to over 8 billion.

Currently there are nearly 140 million births per year worldwide: about 14 million in more developed countries and nearly 125 million in developing nations. Compare this with the current death rates of approximately 56 million per year worldwide: over 12 million in developed countries versus 43 million in developing countries. You clearly see why the world's population is increasing at over 82 million people per year. With the number of births in developing countries being around nine times higher than in developed countries, and with deaths *only*(!) around three times higher – the result is higher population growth in developing countries.

The current top ten most populous countries in the world are: 1. China (1,331 million), 2. India (1,171 million), 3. USA (307 million), 4. Indonesia (243 million), 5. Brazil (191 million), 6. Pakistan (181 million), 7. Bangladesh

(162 million), 8. Nigeria (153 million), 9. Russia (142 million) and 10. Japan (128 million).

By 2050 this top-ten list is projected to transform into: 1. India (1,748 million), 2. China (1,437 million), 3. USA (439 million), 4. Indonesia (343 million), 5. Pakistan (335 million), 6. Nigeria (285 million), 7. Bangladesh (222 million), 8. Brazil (215 million), 9. Congo (189 million), and 10. Philippines (150 million).

Of course, within the subset of developing countries, population growth is not homogenous. The populations of less-developed countries, mainly in Africa, Asia and Latin America, are expected to increase by 50 percent between 2009 and 2050. Moreover, the populations of the poorest of these nations are expected to double in the same period.

> **As the populations in developing countries will continue to grow, by 2050 nine of the top ten most populous nations in the world will be developing and emerging economy countries.**

Yet, there is another undercurrent to this population growth story: fertility rates* are dropping across the world – and fast. According to the United Nations data, in the 1950s the worldwide average fertility rate was 5.0 children per mother: 6.2 children per mother in developing nations and 2.6 in developed nations. By the first part of the new millennium, worldwide fertility rates had dropped to 2.6 children per mother (that is a drop of nearly 50 percent in 50 years): 2.9 in developing nations and 1.6 in developed countries. These trends of lower fertility rates are predicted to continue for the coming decades.

What is interesting is to compare these fertility rates with another statistic – the *replacement rate*: the number of children each woman needs to have in order to maintain the same population. So, if fertility rates are higher than replacement rates then the population increases – if not the population decreases. In a perfect world with no "population inconveniences" such as premature mortality or gender inequalities (apparently more males are born than females), then the replacement rate would be 2.0 children per woman – one for each parent. However, the actual real-world replacement rates are

---

* Total fertility rate is defined as the number of children an average woman would have if she were to survive throughout her reproductive life – conventionally taken to be between the ages of 15 and 49.

higher. In the developed world, replacement rate is about 2.1 children per woman. The rate in the developing world is higher at 2.33 largely because of higher child mortality rates.

Thus the developed world already has a fertility rate which averages below the replacement rate of 2.1. In other words the developed country populations are already in decline. In the future, more developing countries will be joining them. As healthcare is developed and economies prosper there is apparently less need and/ or desire to have so many children and fertility rates drop down close to, or below replacement rates. By 2050 the developing world average fertility rate is predicted to be 2.1 – which would imply a *falling* global population.

As *The Economist* remarks in the article "Fertility and Living Standards: Go forth and multiply a lot less," within the next few years the world will reach a milestone: "half of humanity will be having only enough children to replace itself." According to the United Nations population division, between 2000 and 2005, 2.9 billion people out of a total of 6.5 billion were living in countries with fertility rate of 2.1 or below. Within the current decade this proportion is predicted to increase to 3.4 billion out of 7 billion, and rise to over 50 percent during the next decade. The countries affected will include the likes of Russia, Brazil, Indonesia, China and southern parts of India.

Apparently this trend of falling fertility will be "one of the most dramatic social changes in history" and will result in the slowing down of global world population growth, with a predicted flattening-off, or stabilizing, of global population around 2050.

> **So, the world population will rise from 6.8 billion to 9.2 billion in 2050… but will then level-off.**

While this may be received as good news in certain quarters, it will undoubtedly present challenges as well. There are profound consequences to a shrinking – or at least non-growing – population, especially for younger generations who are expected to become future contributing members of society and carers of the elderly.

A specific issue in global demographics is that of youth populations. Globally, the number of youths between the ages of 15 and 24 years old, will have risen from just under half a billion in 1950 to 1.2 billion in 2050 – a threefold increase in 100 years. Yet, as a result of decreasing fertility rates in the developed world these increases in youth population will consist almost entirely of growth in developing countries. The geographical distribution of this population is also noteworthy, as 90 percent of the world's youth will be living in developing countries in 2050 – with Africa's population of youth growing by almost nine times the global average. Only time will tell if the economies and infrastructure of African nations will be able to cope with the needs of this population.

By 2050, nine out of ten of youths will be in developing countries.

This raises two concerns with differing implications for developing and developed nations. Firstly, there is a mismatch between the economic opportunities available in many of the developing countries with highest youth populations – leading to potential youth frustration and social insecurity in these countries if the expectations of youth are not met. Secondly, in developed countries the question will emerge as to how to sustain aging populations with ever increasing life expectancy with only one-in-ten worldwide youths entering the developed nation workforce.

This brings us to the issue of population distributions – or what is commonly referred to as "population pyramids." As we have seen. several trends within developed and developing countries are contributing to significant changes in global population distributions. In observing these changes in population distributions, it should be remembered that there are some "ideal" characteristics that a human population should have, including average age within certain ranges, and appropriate age and male/female distributions. For example, too many children or elderly as a percentage of total population means that there may be insufficient people of working age to support them and for the population to be of questionable sustainability given existing frameworks. In the long-term, distortions in a population pyramid – such as an aging population or a lop-sided male/female distribution – would put pressure on the population in social and economic terms. As in architecture, for populations a pyramid is a very stable – if somewhat brutal – form.

The population pyramid evolution of the last fifty years, and forecasts for the next 40 years, are indicated in Figures 7.1and 7.2.[7]

Sixty years ago, a substantial population of developing countries was made up of children. Lifespans were shorter and birth rates higher – possibly with the aim of ensuring survival of a minimum number of offspring. As countries prospered, soap, clean water and good food were more widely available, life

Figure 7.1: Population pyramid evolution for a typical developing country

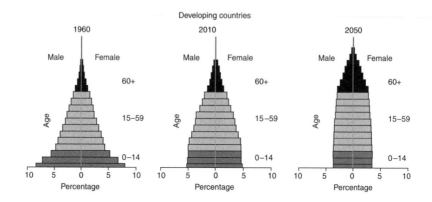

Source: Based upon data from the *United Nations World Economic and Social Survey*

Figure 7.2: Population pyramid evolution for a typical developed country

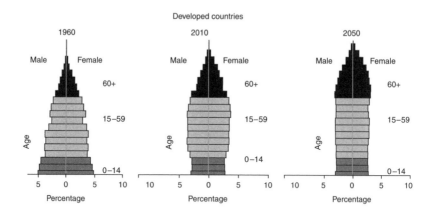

Source: Based upon data from the *United Nations World Economic and Social Survey*

expectancy increased and many families felt somewhat less inclined to have larger families. This all resulted in an upward "*bulging*" of the population pyramid. This overall trend towards decreasing size of youth segments and a corresponding increase in size of elderly segments of population is expected to continue through to 2050. The evolution of the population distribution in developing and emerging countries can be described as moving from a population pyramid to a "*skyscraper*" – moving from being less bottom heavy but still comparatively stable.

Developed countries are a step further in this population evolution.

From a more-or-less pyramidal form 60 years ago, the majority of the population is already between the ages of 15 and 59, and the number of elderly has already surpassed the number of children. Lower birth rates and longer life expectancies have resulted in the bulge moving up the scale. With a view towards 2050, this trend shows no signs of abating. Some have described this evolution as a move from a population pyramid towards a population "*coffin*" – a metaphor which is not entirely inappropriate, given the potentially serious consequences for the dynamics of these "top-heavy" societies.

With increased healthcare and lifespan, the population of elderly in society has been increasing steadily in both developed and developing countries. With continuous reduction of adult mortality, the age-group with the strongest growth in the next 40 years will be the elderly. In fact, the number of elderly is expected to exceed the number of children in the world for the first time ever in 2047 – and for developed nations this point was passed in 1998. Such population aging is without parallel in the history of humanity.[8] The proportion of people aged over 60 has been rising steadily on a global level from 8 percent of the total world population in 1950, to 11 percent in 2007 and is expected to reach 22 percent by 2050. While those aged 65 and over currently represent about 7 percent of the total population in developing countries, this is predicted to double to around 15 percent by 2050. Meanwhile, in developed nations the elderly (65+) already represent 15 percent of the population and this is expected to rise to over 25 percent by 2050.

Perhaps the easiest-to-grasp indication of an aging population is the median age. The United Nations estimated the world median age to be 28.9 years old in 2009. By 2050 this is projected to increase nearly a full 10 years to 38.4 years old.

> **The current worldwide median age of nearly 29 will increase to over 38 by 2050.**

The combined lowering of fertility rates, extending of life expectancy and resulting aging of populations is likely to have deep and lasting impact in transforming societies. On the social level, population aging influences family composition and living arrangements, housing demand, migration trends, epidemiology and the need for healthcare services. On the economic level, population aging will have an impact on economic growth, savings, investment, consumption, labor markets, pensions, taxation and intergenerational transfers. In the political arena, population aging may affect voting behaviors and political representation.

One indication of this overall impact is the "potential support ratio" – or how many potential workers there are (aged 15 to 64) per older person aged 65 or over. As a population ages, the potential support ratio diminishes. For the world as a whole, this ratio has dropped from 12 potential workers per elderly person in 1950, to 9 in 2007, and is predicted to fall to only 4 workers per elderly person by 2050.

Worldwide, there will only be 4 potential workers per 65+ year-old by 2050.

Yet this ratio is predicted to get much worse for certain countries. According to International Monetary Fund and UN data, several countries including Japan, UK and Spain are already at this level of 25 people aged 65+ for every hundred 15–64-year-olds. By 2050 the USA is likely to have 33 elderly (age 65+) per 100 working age population; China 36; UK 40; Spain 52; and Japan a full 65 people aged 65 and over for every 100 of working age between 15 and 64.[9] Clearly, this is going to present considerable challenges with the way developed and developing countries are currently set-up.

On a human level, the percentage of elderly living alone indicates the scale of the problem. Worldwide, 8 percent of men and 19 percent of women aged over 60 years-old live alone (women live longer.) As you'd expect given falling fertility rates and increasing life expectancy, this tends to be worse in the developed countries – rising to 14 percent of elderly men and 34 percent of elderly women living alone in North America. And in Europe, 16 percent of elderly men and a full 37 percent of elderly women living alone.

In Europe in 2005, 37 percent of women aged 60 or over were living alone.

In developed countries, with increasing life expectancy and decreasing numbers of younger generations coming up, will there be enough people of a working age to care for this growing elderly population – both in terms of personal and infrastructure support and on a pension funding level?

To date, one of the key ways of coping with the dual demographic challenges of a shortfall in younger working-age generations in developed nations, as well as an "excess" of younger generations in developing nations, has been through migration. Moving to another region or country is a phenomenon that has taken place since the dawn of mankind and, although life today may be more complex, the underlying motivation for migrating has always been the same: the search for a better life.

Today, international migration is crucial to compensate for labor shortages and to support aging populations – especially in developed countries.[10] Between 2000 and 2008, the number of international migrants increased from 150 million to 214 million, comprising about 3.1 percent of the world's population at the time.[11] Of these, perhaps unsurprisingly, approximately 60 percent went to more developed regions. According to the International Organization for Migration, since 1960 the average annual net number of migrants moving to the more developed countries has generally been increasing, reaching the highest value of 3.3 million persons per year in the period 2000–2005.[12]

Of all international migrants in 2005, over 20 percent went to the USA (38 million), 6 percent to the Russian Federation (12 million), 5.3 percent to Germany (10 million), 3.6 percent to Ukraine (7 million), 3.4 percent to France and 3.3 percent to Saudi Arabia (6.4 million).[13] As you would expect, most opportunities for moving to seek a better life fall to the highly educated and skilled, and many of these choose to move to richer countries – such as the OECD nations. This sector of migrants potentially offers more "value-adding" skills for the hosting nation's economic activity – and it is interesting that the list of top-destinations for these "smarter" migrants differs somewhat to those attracting large numbers of migrants in general. 8.2 million highly skilled immigrants were working in the USA alone. In Canada there were just over 2 million; in Australia nearly 1.5 million; Germany and UK about 1.4 million each; and France just over 1 million highly skilled foreign workers.[14]

A downside for those nations losing such highly educated or skilled emigrants is the effect commonly referred to as "brain drain."

To give-up the smartest most dynamic sectors of society – albeit temporarily – can result in a severe drag on the emigrants' home country. Effects can include the slowing down of potential economic development and the widening of the gap between the developing and the developed world. In certain parts of the developing world, the emigration of educated people can be quite staggering. While large parts of Latin America, Asia, North Africa and the Middle-East regularly see 5 to 10 percent of their smartest people emigrating for better opportunities elsewhere, this translates to over 15 percent across most of Central Africa. In fact, several African countries see between 33 and 55 percent of their highly-educated people migrate to developed nations. In countries such as Fiji, Haiti, Jamaica, and Trinidad and Tobago, this figure rises as high as 60 percent.

Nevertheless, failing better opportunities at home, developing countries that lose some of their brightest and best to emigration perhaps don't lose out altogether – and may even do quite well out of the deal. Even though some of a nation's workforce is contributing to economies elsewhere, the home country may still stand to benefit from remittances sent back from overseas. In 2008, according to the World Bank, foreign workers sent $328 billion from richer to poorer countries – more than double the $120 billion in official aid flows from OECD nations. Such money flows represented 76 percent of total remittances worldwide. These remittances are important to GDP in developing countries, and in some cases contribute almost 50 percent of GDP.[15] China and India, with large numbers of migrant workers abroad, receive large remittance levels. In 2008, India received nearly $52 billion from its diaspora, more than it took in foreign direct investment.[16]

However, as a result of the successes of emerging economies, the patterns of migration are changing. While traditionally there were specific developed-region destinations for migration, led by the United States, over time the proportions of migrants have spread out over a larger number of countries. The top ten countries actually attracted a smaller percentage of migrants in 2008 than in 2000.[17] Furthermore, net migrants to developed countries are expected to drop. As developing countries continue to prosper economically, developed countries may become less attractive for migrants, and as a result, net migration to developed countries is expected to reduce and stabilize to 2.3 million migrants per year by 2050. While this may be good news for those developing countries to reverse the brain drain and maintain their highly educated and younger generations as an economic boost – the reverse could be true for developing nations. If immigration declines – particularly amongst the "value adding" highly educated and skilled – developed nations will need to look for ways to encourage migrants to come, or seek other models of economic and social sustainability.

Yet, even with the potential benefits of migration there are considerable social challenges associated with the issue – even during "good" times. The many sensitive topics such as displacement of existing workforces, illegal immigration and the black economies that benefit from related operations are perpetually bubbling under the surface tension of most societies. Even so, it does seem strange that one of the immediate "knee jerk" reactions of many developed country populations to the economic crisis was to suddenly clamp down on immigration – both officially and in terms of anti-immigrant sentiment – at a time when, demographically speaking, immigrants are apparently so important to prevent the top-heavy population coffins from toppling over.

Threats and opportunities

Different countries will face different challenges as a result of demographic changes. One thing is certain though, societies, businesses and individuals around the globe will have to adapt to cope with the social and economic transformations resulting from: firstly, an increasing global population between now and 2050, and then a stabilization around 9.2 billion; and secondly, an aging of the global population as a result of decreasing fertility rates and longer life expectancy.

Clearly, global population increasing by over a third from 6.8 to 9.2 billion within the next 40 years is going to represent a challenge – to put it mildly. For every two people currently on earth, there will be an extra one to feed, house and consider within the social and economic fabric. Whether you believe this to be a threat or an opportunity for the planet depends very much on your own ideology and beliefs – but at the very least it will imply considerable upheaval in the way the world looks and works. Developing countries will bear the brunt of the population growth and will have to find ways of feeding, housing and educating the upcoming youngsters, while also looking after the ever-growing numbers of elderly. On a global level, with so many extra mouths to feed there will be increased competition for resources. And in developing countries, if the expectations of young and growing populations are not met there is huge potential for political upheaval and insecurity – just look at what is happening (or by the time you read this – what *has* happened) across the Middle East and North Africa. The 2010 "Jasmine Revolution" in Tunisia has served as a catalyst for regime change across the region, largely as a result of a youth "bulge" in a context of high unemployment, increasing food prices and unfulfilled expectations. Given the direction of global demo-graphic trends, we can possibly expect more of such events in the coming decades across developing and emerging regions. This is the demographic threat posed by too many unfulfilled young.

Yet the developed world suffers the opposite threat – not enough young (to be fulfilled or otherwise). While lower child mortality and longer lifespans are clearly a good thing, they have been in place for many decades in developed countries and are now causing new problems for them. "Population coffins" are likely to be socially and economically unsustainable without profound alterations to the way things are done. In developed countries there is already a worrying trend in decreasing worker-to-elderly sup-port ratios, and a somewhat alarming number of elderly who live alone. And these percentages are predicted to increase, perhaps even more rapidly, in the coming years.

While dealing with the demands of young populations will be the immedi-ate priorities of developing and emerging nations, they are not that far behind in terms of increasing lifespans and reducing fertility rates. Hence, moving towards 2050 they will also have to address the issue of supporting an ever larger maturity "bulge" as their population skyscrapers continue to swell upwards. To date, perhaps, developing nation family units have been able to span several generations and live under the same roof. But will this continue when there are fewer income-generators and carers under that roof?

Overall, while the drivers may be the results of positive developments in human history (soap, water, food etc.), an aging population can be seen as a long-term local and global problem at least until new social and economic frameworks are in place to sustain such new population structures. Such sus-tainable solutions need to be developed to counter the challenges for both public and private sectors.

One particularly glaring area in need of reform is that of developed-nation social security and pension schemes. The whole concept perhaps needs a rethink. With ever-higher dependency ratios of elderly to an increasingly overloaded working population – and with continuing low fertility rates and the potential of lower future immigration offering little respite – it is a sys-tem potentially edging towards breaking-point. When there are more people aged 65 and over than there are children, perhaps it no longer makes sense to retire people and send them to the beach for the rest of their lives – but rather to encourage a continuing active social and economic contribution. For those currently working, in purely financial terms it is becoming increasingly dubious as to whether contributing to a pay-as-you-go pension scheme will actually result in sufficient funds to secure financial stability for such a long retirement period in the future. With extending lifespans will probably come an inevitable move towards longer working lives as well.

Inextricably linked to supporting an aging population with lowering fertility rates is the tricky-to-manage issue of migration. Developed countries clearly need youthful, educated and skilled immigrants to fill the gap in upcoming new generations in order to hold-up the otherwise unstable, top-heavy population structures. This need will probably become more pressing in the future, with developed-nation fertility rates continuing to decline and expectations for standards of living in the latter years showing no signs of abating. The potential trend towards less migration – as developing and emerging countries become richer, and their own youth populations start to stabilize – will prove to be an extra challenge. Attracting a decreasing pool of appropriately educated and skilled young foreigners will become both increasingly necessary and increasingly difficult for developed nations.

Thus, the interconnected concepts of retirement and immigration – virtually hard-wired into the workings of developed nations – will have to undergo profound metamorphoses. Changes of mindset are likely to be necessary on both counts, though this will be easier said than done given the historically sensitive nature of both issues.

On the issue of retirement, any changes will clearly not sit-easily with the significant sections of society that have contributed to pension schemes throughout their working lives with the expectation of a happy and financially stable holiday for their last 10, 20, 30 years... This is not an issue that has emerged overnight (bulging mature populations take time and there is a high degree of predictability), but many political leaders have taken the popular route of ignoring the problem. While big sections of the voting public are either pensioners, close to retiring or paying into pension schemes with the expectation of retiring comfortably on the proceeds, any talk of pension reform will be politically sensitive. Hence, pension reform is one of the most controversial political topics today throughout the developed world – despite the fact that governments are already having trouble sustaining the current system of social security and pension systems. Several countries have implemented plans to increase retirement ages, and these moves have led to opposition by unions and social unrest. Other governments have increased carrot-and-stick incentives to continue working with favorable terms for late retirement and/or full-scale cutbacks on benefits. This is a battle that is unlikely to end soon.

On the issue of immigration, it would appear that developed nations are likely to have to work harder and harder to attract a decreasing pool of foreign workers – especially highly educated and skilled ones who can add more value to the economy. Yet, in turbulent times the common human sentiment is that immigration causes locals to lose jobs due to replacement by cheaper, less demanding migrant workers. Migrant workers and their families suffer discrimination of all types when in a new country, regardless of whether their status is legal or not. Such sentiments not only cause social unrest, but also could be a cradle for undesirable activist groups to use these undercurrents of discontent to push their agendas. Furthermore, apparently, legal migration is often unable to fulfill the demand of movement of people, creating a niche for smugglers and traffickers to profit from the imbalance. This is another very hard battle to win.

Yet, since the Egyptian pyramids, human beings have managed to invent clever new building construction techniques to escape the natural forces that tend toward stable, bottom-heavy structures. Perhaps human beings will have to be similarly inventive in coping with ways of sustaining top-heavy *population* structures in the future. This is especially true given that developing countries are apparently continuing to follow the past trends of the developed nations and their population pyramids are also evolving skywards.

Clearly, policy-makers need to be creative in inventing systems and incentives to deal with these demographic trends. But businesspeople also have a significant role to play in mitigating such demographic threats. It may be tempting for business to pass these particular hot potatoes into the arena of the politicians and public institutions, but there are potentially negative consequences of doing so. Businesses have considerable interests in the social security and pension systems being appropriately managed in line with business objectives. After all, businesses often bear much of individual worker pension scheme costs. Also, state-imposed retirement ages have long been a type of brain-drain, as experienced and knowledgeable employees are routinely ejected from the workforce at the age of 60 or 65. Similarly, one of the current sources of employer frustration is in working through overly bureaucratic processes in order to tap into the much-needed skills and energy of young foreign workers. As a result of such excessive state paperwork, sometimes it is even easier to employ illegal immigrants than legal ones – with all the social repercussions that entails. Business should play their part in correcting such errors.

Thus there are big opportunities for business leaders to work alongside politicians in making sustainable improvements to systems to facilitate increased *working life expectancy* and encouraging the removal of barriers to migrants seeking a better life. On both counts the more fruitful focus would probably be upon encouraging those – either elderly or foreign – who are willing and able to make valuable contributions to business, economy and society beyond the traditional retirement thresholds or international borders. This seems to be a better and more businesslike approach than continuing to "kick the can down the road."

For politicians, the opportunities lie in setting the right incentives and creating the best infrastructure in education, healthcare and so on to have better chances of attracting the best talent from around the world. Similarly, governments of countries with large numbers emigrating could develop reciprocal ties with target countries to maximize win–win opportunities. In addition, developing- and emerging-nation politicians and businesses probably should work to improve infrastructure to encourage their own best talent to remain in, or at least return to, the country.

Of course, as long as the threats can be successfully mitigated, each of the demographic trends represents big opportunities for businesses across the globe. For example, faced with increasing elderly populations there will be significant business opportunities in meeting higher demand for products and services aimed at these society segments in future. Consumption habits of this increasingly important age segment will also change as the over 65s move from "baby boomers" to "internet kids" – and these new habits can be exploited for new business markets. Specific age-related health spending is highly likely to increase across the world and this will spawn new business. On the operations side, those companies that manage to increase productivity of their diminishing young and extending old workforce – for example through continuous education and training – will gain competitive advantage over those that don't. Similarly those that manage to retain the experience and valuable knowledge of senior workforce while capturing the vitality of the young indigenous and immigrant workforce will triumph.

At the individual level, it is perhaps best to maintain an open mind on expectations in later life. On both the threats and opportunities side, it would appear that we are all in for a longer life (at least in statistical probability terms). The key will be in finding ways to make this long life healthy, contented and fulfilling rather than the opposite. Purely in demographic patterns, social structures and systems are likely to change, and it seems highly likely that individuals in developed and developing countries will have to take a more proactive stance when it comes to preparing for their older years. Outsourcing all financial decisions to pension systems or established social norms that apparently have a built-in shelf-life may not be the best course of action. Clearly this is something that needs to be done with a good deal of anticipation.

It is also worth bearing in mind that the best opportunities will generally go to the well-educated, who can make a valuable contribution to society and business. Such people are likely to be in constant demand everywhere. In particular, given their youthful vigor, developing and emerging economies will represent considerable opportunities in terms of entrepreneurial activities, career development and personal growth for such value-adders, perhaps without the existing burdens and demands of the top-heavy developed-nation societies... yet.

Finally, of particular demographic concern is the historical fact that with increasing populations comes increasing competition for scarce resources. Throughout human history, this has been one of the underlying drivers of war, terrorism and social unrest. These are the issues addressed in the next Global Trend.

Global Trend 8

War, Terrorism and Social Unrest

"I know not with what weapons World War III will be fought,
but World War IV will be fought with sticks and stones."

Albert Einstein, Physicist[1]

Mankind certainly has an amazing capacity for violence against others. Any parent of a young boy will notice the unnerving tendency towards war and fighting games based upon good versus evil.* Unfortunately, though, as these boys grow up, with correspondingly increased adrenaline and testosterone levels, things get more complicated, and adolescent males do not always play the "goody." As a result, dealing with young males seems to be a constant physiological challenge for communities – from combating aggressive, unorganized and sporadic violence to controlling organized hooliganism, crime and gangs. Most societies spend a good deal of their wealth on a police force to combat such social ills. Yet what happens when this destructive capability is not simply between individuals or small groups, but unleashed between societies and nations? The pretexts seem to be similar to those of the young boys: we (the *goodies*) are right and they (the *baddies*) are wrong.

Such apparently intrinsic basic instincts and behaviors are behind several global 21st-century issues such as organized crime, illicit trade, terrorism, corruption, fragile states, and weapons of mass destruction, all of which are identified by the World Economic Forum's *Global Risks 2011* report as either "*likely*" or "*very likely*" within the coming decade and with significant associated economic impacts. Of particular note is the perceived likelihood of *geopolitical conflict* as a consequence of the high probability of *global*

---

* Interestingly, war as a behavioral pattern is not confined to human beings, but can be found among other primate species and also in many ant species.

governance failures resulting from geopolitical power shifts (see Global Trend 2):

> **Geopolitical conflict:** *likely/very likely* **within 10 years.**
> **Estimated economic impact: $1,000,000,000,000.**[2]

The WEF report doesn't graph any potential human suffering from such conflict.

So it would appear that 21st-century humans are not about to break from our turbulent past. Humans after all are tribal beings with a violent history. Table 8.1, a scan through the estimated death tolls of some of the worst wars in history[3] (from a seemingly endless list dating back thousands of years), gives an indication of just how violent a history we humans have had.

The accuracy of this list may be disputed, as there do seem to be some historical reporting discrepancies: nevertheless it does indicate two indisputable things.

1. Human beings have been killing each other, often on massive scales, for a long time. One can only shudder at the scale of violence encountered in the pre-mechanized weapon, hand-to-hand combat eras. For example, just imagine the truly staggering levels of butchery required to put 33 to 36 million people to the sword within 8 years in 8th-century China.

2. The 20th century does crop-up more regularly than one would wish in the lists of all-time most murderous events. Of this list of 22 calamitous wars going back nearly 2,000 years, a full nine were in the hundred years between 1901 and 2000. After all, with the advance of technology killing has become an easier – and frankly a more "hands-off" – exercise than it used to be.

Before addressing issues of global safety and security in the 21st century, it is worth reflecting on both of the above historical points in order to give some foundation for understanding where these Global Trends are likely to go in the coming decades.

Regarding the long history of humans killing humans, the conduct of war extends along a continuum. From the almost universal primitive local tribal warfare that began well before recorded human history, to advanced nuclear warfare between global alliances and the potential for mass extinction. At the

Table 8.1: Estimated death tolls of some of the worst wars in history

Death Toll	Conflict
40–72 million	World War II (1939–1945)
33–36 million	An Shi Rebellion (China, 755–763)
30–60 million	Mongol Conquests (13th century)
25 million	Qing dynasty conquest (1616–1662)
20–30 million	Taiping Rebellion (China, 1851–1864)
15–20 million	World War I (1914–1918)
15–20 million	Conquests of Timur (1369–1405)
8–12 million	Dungan revolt (China, 1862 –1877)
5–9 million	Russian Civil War (1917–1921)
3.8–5.4 million	Second Congo War (1998–2007)
3.5–6.5 million	Napoleonic Wars (1804–1815)
3–11.5 million	Thirty Years' War (1618–1648)
3–7 million	Yellow Turban Rebellion (China, 184–205)
3–4 million	Deluge (1655–1660)[a]
2.5–3.5 million	Korean War (1950–1953)
2.5–6 million	Vietnam War (1955–1975)
2–4 million	French Wars of Religion (1562–1598)
2 million	Shaka Zulu Conquests (1816–1828)
1–2 million	Second Sudanese Civil War (1983–2005)
1–9 million	Crusades (1095–1291)
0.5–2 million	Iran–Iraq War (1980–1988)
0.5–2 million	Mexican Revolution (1911–1920)

Note: [a] The Swedish invasion and occupation of the Polish-Lithuanian Commonwealth.

Source: "List of wars and anthropogenic disasters by death toll" Wikipedia. The Free Encyclopedia.

beginning of human history, war likely consisted of small-scale raiding of resources for survival. One half of the people found in a cemetery dating to as early as 12,000 years ago had died violently. As such, war has been considered to be an inescapable aspect of human nature. In "*A History of Warfare*," John Keegan regards war as a universal phenomenon whose form and scope is defined by the society that wages it.[4] Others argue that war is rare in certain types of societies, such as nomadic forager societies, and becomes more common when humans take up settled living. Certainly since the rise of the state some 5,000 years ago, military activity has occurred over much of the globe.

> **Approximately 90–95 percent of known societies throughout history engaged in at least occasional warfare and many fought constantly.**

Evidence shows that tribal warfare was on average 20 times more deadly than 20th-century warfare.[5] In one battle in 1857 among the Mohave-Yumas, 49.6 percent of combatants were killed; in a great Aztec battle fought in 1478, 87.1 percent of 24,000 combatants were killed; while 100 percent of combatants were killed during the Blackfoot Indian raid which annihilated the Assiniboine in 1849.[6] Such has been the historical acceptance of warfare that Prussian military general and theoretician Carl Von Clausewitz, in his 1832 book *On War*, declared war to be the "continuation of political intercourse, carried on with other means."[7]

> **As for the 20th century, between 69 and 122 million people were killed in major wars.**

That doesn't include all the "minor" wars, battles and skirmishes that also occurred throughout the world during this time. Also the range of uncertainty defies belief. How is it that we do not *know* how many people died? Give or take 53 million or so people does seem to be a rather large margin of error.

The 20th century saw a myriad of technological "advances" – from the widespread use of swords, gunpowder, guns and cannons of traditional warfare to the intercontinental missiles, spy satellites and pilotless drone aircraft of modern warfare. Such developments in the technologies of war – and especially the emergence of nuclear arms – caused widespread public concern. Perhaps such concern and the threat of such massive destruction actually forestalled the outbreak of a World War III – primarily between the communist Soviet Union and the anti-communist West in the years between 1947 and 1991. At the end of each of the last two world wars, concerted and popular efforts were made to reduce or even eliminate war altogether. These efforts ultimately materialized in the form of the United Nations after World War II – which most nations joined as an apparent token of support for the concept of global peace.

Yet, despite such peaceful intentions, the 20th century was violent – to put it mildly – with several major wars being waged. By way of providing some historical perspective, the following is a brief synopsis of just a few of those major wars.

While it had apparently been long in the making, World War I was triggered by the assassination of Archduke Franz Ferdinand, the heir to the throne of Austria-Hungary, in Sarajevo in 1914. Among the long-term causes were the imperialistic foreign policies of several of the great powers of Europe. Several alliances that had been formed over the previous decades were invoked, and within weeks the major powers were at war. There were essentially two sets of belligerent nations along with their associated empires. The Allied Powers included: Russia, Britain, France, Italy, USA, Serbia, Belgium, Romania and Japan. The opposing Central Powers included Austria-Hungary, Germany Empire, Turkey (Ottoman Empire) and Bulgaria. As all of these countries had colonies, the conflict soon spread around the world. World War 1 ended when the Germans agreed to a ceasefire in 1918.

Estimated World War I casualties were 7,996,888 dead, 21,755,196 wounded and 1,979,556 missing.[8]

Then came World War II, which started in Europe in 1939 when Germany invaded Poland. World War II ravaged cities and towns across Europe, Asia, Africa and the islands of the Pacific. There were two belligerents: The Allies including the Soviet Union, USA, UK, China, France, Poland, Canada, Australia, New Zealand, South Africa, Yugoslavia, Belgium, Netherlands, Greece and Norway; and the Axis-aligned nations of Germany, Japan, Italy, Hungary, Romania, Finland, Bulgaria, Independent States of Croatia, Slovakia, Vichy France, Thailand, Manchukuo and Iraq. With over 100 million military personnel mobilized, it was the most widespread war. World War II ended after the Allies (USA) dropped atomic bombs on the Japanese cities of Hiroshima and Nagasaki, leading to Japan's unconditional surrender in 1945.

It was significant for massive action carried out against civilians, such as the Holocaust, and the only use of nuclear weapons in warfare.

It is estimated that 52,199,262 people died during World War II, making it the deadliest conflict in human history.

The war strained the military, financial, scientific and civilian resources of the countries involved to such an extent that it left many on the verge of collapse and ushered in a new world order. The United States and the Soviet Union emerged from World War II as global superpowers and soon became locked in a tense ideological and military competition known as the "Cold War" – largely as a result of strong disagreements about the configuration of the postwar world. The Eastern Bloc was created by the Soviet Union and eastern European countries, later formalized under the Warsaw Pact (1955–1991). Meanwhile, USA and western European countries established alliances such as the North Atlantic Treaty Organization (NATO) – with containment of communism as an objective. Although neither of the main protagonists ever officially came into direct fighting, an indirect geopolitical conflict was waged through military coalitions and force deployments to "vulnerable" states, "proxy wars,"* espionage, propaganda wars, a nuclear arms race – and other technological competitions such as the "Space Race." Some of the most crucial stressful points in the Cold War were the Berlin Crisis in 1961 and the Cuban Missile Crisis in 1962 – which brought the world closer to a nuclear war than ever. The Cold War ended after the Soviet Union collapsed in 1991, leaving the United States as the dominant military power and Russia in possession of most of the Soviet Union's nuclear arsenal.[9]

One of the main proxy wars during the Cold War was that in Vietnam between 1959 and 1975. The Vietnam War turned into the longest military conflict in US history. It was a military struggle fought between North Vietnam and the National Liberation Front (NLF) on the one hand and the United States and South Vietnam on the other. The United States entered the war to prevent a communist takeover of South Vietnam as part of their wider strategy of containment.

Hostilities in Vietnam, Laos and Cambodia claimed the lives of more than 58,000 Americans and wounded a further 305,000. During the conflict,

---

* Proxy wars: When opposing powers use third parties as substitutes for direct confrontation.

approximately 3 to 4 million Vietnamese from both sides were killed, in addition to 1.5 to 2 million Laotians and Cambodians who were drawn into the war.[10]

Another Cold War proxy war was the Soviet–Afghan war between 1979 and 1989, in which the Soviet Union supported the Marxist government of the Democratic Republic of Afghanistan against the Islamic Mujahedeen Resistance – which was supported by several countries, including the USA, UK, Saudi Arabia, Pakistan, Egypt and other Muslim nations.

The Soviet–Afghan war left more than one million Afghans and 13,000 Russians dead. During the 1980s, half of all the refugees in the world were Afghan.[11]

It is estimated that during the war five million Afghans, one-third of the prewar population, fled to Pakistan and Iran. An additional two million were displaced within the country.

Apart from the various Soviet Union–NATO Cold War inspired conflicts that kept much of the violence at arms-length and somewhat out of sight for the main protagonist nations, there were several other regionally inspired wars. One example was the Iran–Iraq war, which began in 1980 when Iraq invaded Iran, following a long history of border disputes. In addition, Iraq wanted to dominate the Persian Gulf region, fearing an insurgency amongst its long-suppressed Shia majority, who were influenced by the Iranian Revolution. As well as using conventional warfare, Iraq made extensive use of chemical weapons such as mustard gas against Iranian troops and civilians – as well as against Iraqi Kurds. The war ended in 1988, when Iran accepted the terms of a UN Security Council resolution. Iran had around 500,000 casualties and Iraq around 150,000. As is the case in many wars, both countries received foreign support – but interestingly, some countries, such as the USA and Soviet Union, provided support at different times to both countries.[12]

Most of the above wars were, at least in principle, largely ideologically motivated. Yet, others were more motivated by acquisition of resources: for example, the Gulf War ("Operation Desert Storm") was triggered when Iraq – under Saddam Hussein – invaded Kuwait in 1990 with the apparent aims of acquiring that nation's large oil reserves, cancelling a large debt

Iraq owed Kuwait, and expanding Iraqi power in the region. This was met with international condemnation, and the UN Security Council imposed sanctions against Iraq. Under the leadership of the USA and UK, a coalition force of 34 nations launched an offensive against Iraq – with most troops coming from the USA, Saudi Arabia, UK and Egypt. Around \$40 billion of the \$60 billion war costs was paid by Saudi Arabia.[13] The war ended in 1991 after the coalition forces liberated Kuwait and advanced into Iraqi territory. It is estimated that the coalition suffered 240 deaths and 776 injured, whereas the Iraqis suffered in the range of 10,000 to 100,000 deaths.[14]

Of course, there were many, many other wars during the 20th century, with a whole host of underlying political, ideological and resource constraint motivations. A short list of post-1945 wars includes the following:

Greek Civil War (1946–1949), **French Indochina War** (1946–1954), **Pathet Lao War** (1950–1954), **Khmer Issarak War** (1950–1954), **First Kashmir War** (1947–1948), **Korean War** (1950–1953), **Algerian War of Independence** (1954–1962), **Suez War** (1956), **Laotian Civil War** (1959–1975), **Cambodian Civil War** (1967–1975), **Yemen Civil War** (1962–1970), **Sino–Indian War** (1962), **Second Kashmir War** (1965), **Six-Day War** (1967), **Warsaw Pact Invasion of Czechoslovakia** (1968), **Bengali War of Independence** (1971), **Lebanese Civil War** (1975–1991), **Ogaden War** (1977–1978), **Cambodia– Vietnam War** (1977–1991), **China–Vietnam War** (1979), **Falkland Islands War** (1982), **Israeli Invasion of Southern Lebanon** (1982–2000), **US Invasion of Grenada** (1983), **Third Balkan War** (1991–2001), **the Chechen War** (1994–Present), **The Congo War** (1998–2002)…

And certainly there were others.

So the 20th century was not exactly peaceful, even if the Cold War managed to keep much of the violence at arms-length and out of sight for citizens of protagonist countries.

And how has the 21st century started?

Frankly, badly:

On September 11, 2001, terrorists crashed two hijacked planes into One and Two World Trade Center. In the space of two hours, the towers collapsed and not long after that, 7 World Trade Center collapsed as well.

Nearly 2,800 people died, including 343 fire fighters, 23 police officers, 37 Port Authority police officers, and more than 2,200 civilians.[15]

September 11, 2001 set the tone for global violence at the beginning of the 21st century. The hijackers crashed a third plane into the Pentagon in Arlington, Virginia, just outside Washington, DC. A fourth plane crashed before reaching the hijackers' objective in Washington, DC – into a field near Shanksville in rural Pennsylvania. There were no survivors from any of the flights. The terrorist attacks killed 2,973 victims in New York, Washington and Pennsylvania and claimed the lives of citizens from 77 countries.[16]

The United States rapidly enacted the USA PATRIOT (Uniting and Strengthening America by Providing Appropriate Tools Required to Intercept and Obstruct Terrorism) Act of 2001. This facilitated law enforcement agencies' ability to search telephone, e-mail communications, medical, financial and other records; eased restrictions on foreign intelligence gathering within the USA; expanded scope for the Secretary of the Treasury to regulate financial transactions of foreign individuals and entities; and broadened the remit for law enforcement and immigration authorities to detain and deport immigrants suspected of terrorism. Other nations imposed similar counter-terrorism measures.

Al-Qaeda leader Osama bin Laden initially denied any link with the attacks, but in 2004 – shortly before the US presidential election – acknowledged al-Qaeda's involvement and his direct links to the attacks.

The "War on Terrorism" was launched and two countries re-emerged as "unfinished business" from the end of the 20th century: Afghanistan and Iraq.

Apparently, the very same people that had been supported during the 1980s and 90s were now being identified as "*terrorist*" enemies. [17,18,19]

The War in Afghanistan began on October 7, 2001, when the USA and British military launched "Operation Enduring Freedom." The stated aims of the invasion were to find Osama bin Laden and other high-ranking Al-Qaeda members to be put on trial; to destroy the Al-Qaeda organization; and to remove the Taliban regime that supported and gave safe harbor to it. Another ongoing operation is the International Security Assistance Force (ISAF), which was established by the UN Security Council at the end of December 2001 to secure Kabul and the surrounding areas.

However, it took until May 2011 for US forces to track down and kill Osama bin Laden. Afghanistan remains an insecure and unstable country, and insurgent bombings are regularly in the news. In fact, during the first seven months of 2010, an estimated 1,859 civilians were killed by improvised explosive devices.[20] So far there have been 1,749 coalition deaths, of which 1,060 are American. At least 5,831 Americans have been wounded in action.[21] There are no accurate estimates for the number of Afghan insurgents and civilians killed. On several occasions, there have been reports of Afghan civilians being killed by American bombs.[22]

A case for war against Iraq also gained momentum. In his presentation to the UN Security Council on the US case against Iraq, the US Secretary of State Colin Powell stated: "...the United States knows about Iraq's weapons of mass destruction as well as Iraq's involvement in terrorism."[23]

In January 2003, the US Secretary of Defense Donald Rumsfeld said:

Iraq poses a serious and mounting threat to our country. [Saddam Hussein's] regime has the design for a nuclear weapon, was working on several different methods of enriching uranium, and recently was discovered seeking significant quantities of uranium from Africa.[24]

A few months later on March 20, 2003, the military invasion of Iraq began. Eventually Saddam Hussein was captured, and was tried and executed by the Iraqi government. However, after the invasion no weapons of mass destruction were found.[25]

So far the war on Iraq has claimed the lives of 4,731 US and coalition forces.[26] There have been several attempts to estimate the number of Iraqi casualties. According to The Associated Press, in the period between March 2003 and April 2009, there were 110,600 violent deaths. Iraq remains one of the most dangerous places in the world. In 2010, the Iraqi army's chief of staff, stated that the Iraqi army would require American support for another decade before it would be ready to handle the country's security on its own.[27] According to the UN High Commissioner for Refugees (UNHCR), since the US-led invasion of Iraq in March 2003, an estimated 4.7 million people have been displaced both within and outside Iraq.[28]

Given such hostilities within the first decade of this century, in 2003 Nobel Laureate Richard E. Smalley identified terrorism and war as one of the top ten biggest problems facing mankind for the next 50 years.[29]

The 2005 Human Security Report documented a significant decline in the number and severity of armed conflicts since the end of the Cold War in the early 1990s. However, the evidence examined in the 2008 edition of the Centre for International Development and Conflict Management's study *Peace and Conflict* indicated that global conflicts were on the increase again.[30]

As for the term "terrorism," there is no universally agreed and binding definition in criminal law. Of course, the term is politically and emotionally charged, and this greatly compounds the difficulty of defining a single meaning: studies have found over 100 definitions.[31] Yet terrorism is assumed to indicate deliberately creating and exploiting fear in order to attain political objectives and change. An abiding characteristic of terrorism is the indiscriminate use of violence against noncombatants for the purpose of gaining publicity for a group, cause or individual.[32] The concept itself may be controversial as it is often used by state authorities to delegitimize political or other opponents, and potentially legitimize the state's own use of armed force against opponents (a force that may itself be described as "terror" by those opponents.) Terrorism has been practiced by a broad array of political organizations for furthering their objectives. It has been practiced by both right- and left-wing political parties, nationalistic groups, religious groups, revolutionaries and ruling governments.[33]

The newspaper headlines show that war and terrorism (however you define it) are clearly alive and kicking in the 21st century:

Financial Times, 21 December 2010: "NATO troops killed in Afghanistan crash"[34]
Financial Times, 19 September 2010: "Two car bombs in Iraq capital kill 10"[35]

So the 21st century continues with the same violent streak as the previous one. And at time of writing we are now at war again in Libya – with the UN Security Council passing resolutions against the government of Muammar Gaddafi and military action from NATO and other Arab states. "Where will it end?" is *The Economist* magazine's article on the subject.[36] Well, judging from history maybe this is just part of an endless process of humans waging war on others.

And what of other forms of social turmoil beyond war and terrorism? In November 2009, under the headline "Delayed explosion," *The Economist* asked the question as to whether 2010 would be a year of social unrest given the global fall in incomes and rising unemployment. The magazine quoted

Admiral Dennis Blair, the US Director of National Intelligence, as declaring that the risk of global political instability triggered by the economic crisis had become America's "primary near-term security concern." Also others, such as the heads of the IMF and the UN, had issued warnings about the danger of crisis driven social unrest – with associated potential violence from street protests and loss of general security to civil war. As such, and in the light of Economist Intelligence Unit (EIU) data, 2010 was predicted to be a year of upheaval, given a sharp rise in unemployment, increased poverty and inequality, weakened middle classes and higher food prices in many countries. Through analyzing country factors such as degree of income inequality, the state of governance, levels of social provision, ethnic tensions, public trust in institutions, the history of unrest and the type of political system, *The Economist* forecast that:

77 out of 166 countries assessed were at very high or high risk of social unrest in 2010 – with 22 in the very high risk category.

Unsurprisingly, sub-Saharan Africa was well represented in the EIU's predictions for high-risk categories: accounting for about one-third of the total high-risk group. Another quarter of the high-risk countries were deemed to be in Eastern Europe, the region hardest hit by the crisis, and with many underlying characteristics associated with unrest. Otherwise high-risk countries were dotted all around the globe: with several in Latin America and Asia—including China. But in Europe protests had toppled governments in Latvia and Iceland, and even historically stable countries such as France and UK were considered at some risk of social unrest. On a map, only the large geographic areas of the top left (USA, Canada) and the bottom right (Australia, New Zealand) appear safe zones.

Table 8.2 indicates the risk of social unrest for individual countries as predicted for 2010 by *The Economist*/ EIU for different countries.[37]

It is illuminating to review these predictions in hindsight. And it has to be said *The Economist* and EIU should be congratulated – in many instances the alerts for potential upheaval were indeed warranted. Economic-crisis-related street protests and general social unrest did hit many countries in 2010 – while others still seem to be waiting on tenterhooks for possible outbreaks in 2011. Police presence visibly increased in preparation for social unrest in many countries. For example, Greece experienced protracted violence attributed directly to austerity measures launched by the socialist government in return for emergency loans to tackle the country's debt crisis:

> Three Athens bank employees died on Wednesday in a blaze started by a petrol bomb thrown as the city erupted into violence during a march by tens of thousands of striking workers angry at deep spending cuts.[38]

Occasionally, high-risk countries have descended into full-blown civil war – such as Ivory Coast (Cote d'Ivoire).[39]

It is also interesting to note just how difficult it is to forecast such things. For example, in 2010 Tunisia was on the same medium risk of social unrest rating as several hitherto stable European countries. But by late 2010/early 2011 an intensive campaign of civil resistance and street protests had led to a full "*Jasmine Revolution*." Few had predicted the speed at which the turmoil would spread to Egypt – with the subsequent overthrow of President Mubarak – and on to violent revolutionary waves of demonstrations and protests across the Middle East and North Africa. While turmoil was expected in countries such as Algeria, Djibouti, Iraq, Sudan and Yemen, few expected the troubles that ensued in the likes of hitherto very stable Bahrain, Jordan, Oman, Kuwait, Lebanon and Saudi Arabia.[40]

Ultimately, such instability in the region spread to one of the countries judged as having lowest risk of social unrest in 2010: Libya.

For 2010, Libya was judged in the same low likelihood category of social unrest as the USA, Canada, Australia and New Zealand – and lower risk than many traditionally secure countries. Yet in 2011, the country descended into civil war.

Apparently therefore, social unrest – and its potential for subsequent violence and even war – has a high component of unpredictability.

Yet the outcomes of violence and turmoil are often more predictable. The ongoing Somali Civil War demonstrates that once an area becomes unstable it can be extremely difficult to regain social cohesion. The upsurge in attacks by Somali pirates reflects decades of political unrest, maritime lawlessness and severe economic decline in the region. Since 2005, international organizations such as the International Maritime Organization and the World Food Program, have highlighted the rise in acts of piracy off the Gulf of Aden,

Table 8.2: The risk of social unrest for individual countries in 2010

Continent	Risk of social unrest	Countries
Africa	Very high	Chad, Democratic Republic of the Congo, Cote d'Ivoire (Ivory Coast), Guinea-Bissau, Madagascar, Sudan, Zimbabwe
	High	Algeria, Burkina Faso, Cameroon, Central African Republic, Congo (Brazzaville), Djibouti, Eritrea, Ethiopia, Gabon, Guinea, Kenya, Mali, Mauritania, Niger, Nigeria, Zambia
	Medium	Angola, Benin, Egypt, Ghana, Lesotho, Morocco, Mozambique, Namibia, Senegal, South Africa, Swaziland, Tanzania, Togo, Tunisia, Uganda
	Low	Botswana, Libya
	Unrated	Western Sahara, Somalia
America	Very high	Bolivia, Ecuador, Haiti
	High	Argentina, Belize, Dominican Republic, El Salvador, Guatemala, Guyana, Honduras, Jamaica, Mexico, Nicaragua, Panama, Venezuela
	Medium	Chile, Colombia, Paraguay
	Low	Brazil, Canada, Costa Rica, Cuba, Greenland, United States, Uruguay
Asia	Very high	Afghanistan, Bangladesh, Myanmar, Pakistan, Tajikistan, Uzbekistan
	High	Armenia, Cambodia, China, Georgia, Indonesia, Korea (North), Kyrgyzstan, Nepal, Philippines, Sri Lanka, Thailand
	Medium	Azerbaijan, Bhutan, India, Korea (South), Malaysia, Mongolia, Turkmenistan, Vietnam
	Low	Japan, Taiwan, Lao

Europe	Very high	Moldova, Bosnia
	High	Albania, Bulgaria, Croatia, Greece, Hungary, Latvia, Montenegro, Romania, Russia, Serbia, Turkey, Ukraine
	Medium	Andorra, Belarus, Estonia, France, Iceland, Ireland, Lithuania, Portugal, Slovenia, Slovakia, Spain, United Kingdom
	Low	Austria, Belgium, Cyprus, Czech Republic, Denmark, Finland, Germany, Italy, Luxembourg, Netherlands, Poland, Sweden, Switzerland, Norway, Vatican City
Middle East	Very high	Iraq, Iran, Yemen
	High	
	Medium	Israel, Jordan, Lebanon, Saudi Arabia, Syria
	Low	Bahrain, Kuwait, Oman, Qatar, United Arab Emirates
Oceania	Very high	Papua New Guinea
	High	
	Medium	
	Low	Australia, New Zealand

Source: Economist Intelligence Unit/*The Economist*, 2009.

Arabian Sea and Indian Ocean coastlines of Somalia. Given that this area is one of the busiest shipping lanes in the world – southern access to the Suez Canal – piracy has contributed to a substantial increase in general shipping costs, impeded the delivery of shipments, and been a burden on the global economy.

Piracy-linked insurance rates for ships rose to $20,000 per voyage in 2009 from an estimated $500 in 2008: a 40-fold increase.[41]

Piracy in the Gulf of Aden cost Maersk Line, one of the biggest global shipping lines, $100 million in 2010. For 2011 the company expects these piracy-related costs to double to cover insurance premiums, hardship allowances and re-routing vessels.[42] Many ships now require a military escort in this area.[43] Such lawlessness is also adding to Somalia's problems in other ways. The UN and others have suggested that illegal fishing and dumping of toxic waste in Somali waters by foreign vessels has severely constrained the ability of locals to earn a living and forced many to turn to piracy instead. The UK Department for International Development stated that, between 2003 and 2004, Somalia lost about $100 million dollars in revenue due to illegal tuna and shrimp fishing by foreign trawlers.[44]

Another example of global lawlessness is the illegal drug trade, which is directly linked to violent crime in both developing and developed nations.[45] In the USA in the late 1990s, the Federal Bureau of Investigation estimated that 5 percent of murders were drug-related. And after a crackdown by US and Mexican authorities, as part of tightened border security in the wake of the September 11 attacks, violence inside Mexico surged – with the Mexican government estimating that 90 percent of the killings were drug-related. According to the BBC:

In Mexico alone, between 2006 and 2010, 28,000 people were killed in the drugs war.[46]

In terms of consumption, the world's largest illegal drug markets – and thus drug-related problems – are: cannabis in North America, Oceania and western Europe; cocaine in North America and some parts of western Europe; and opiates in Asia and Europe. Synthetic drugs such as amphetamines, meth-amphetamine and ecstasy are another part of the global drug mix. While there is evidence to suggest that illegal drug use has leveled-off in developed countries, there is considerable concern that production and consumption may be growing in emerging and developing nations.[47,48]

Threats and opportunities

While the 21st century clearly has not started well, according to the National Intelligence Council (NIC) of the USA, nor are we on course towards a more peaceful world any time soon. In its report *Global Trends 2025*, the NIC warns of several threats and the potential for a century that, in some respects, could be less stable than the last bloody one. In contrast to the relatively stable "bipolar" (USA–Soviet Union) or "unipolar" (USA-dominated) international systems in place since World War II, the NIC argues that the shifts in geopolitical power (see Global Trend 2) will lead to a new, more unstable "multipolar" international system in the coming decades, with various nations exerting considerable power.

In summing-up the 21st-century threats of war, violence and social unrest, I can do no better than quote directly from the NIC report:[49]

> Despite the recent financial volatility—which could end up accelerating many ongoing trends—we do not believe that we are headed toward a complete breakdown of the international system, as occurred in 1914–1918 when an earlier phase of globalization came to a halt. However, the next 20 years of transition to a new [multipolar] system are fraught with risks. Strategic rivalries are most likely to revolve around trade, investments, and technological innovation and acquisition, but we cannot rule out a 19th-century-like scenario of arms races, territorial expansion, and military rivalries…
>
> Terrorism, proliferation, and conflict will remain key concerns even as resource issues move up on the international agenda. Terrorism is unlikely to disappear by 2025… In the absence of employment opportunities and legal means for political expression, conditions will be ripe for disaffection, growing radicalism, and possible recruitment of youths into terrorist groups. Terrorist groups in 2025 will likely be a combination of descendants of long established groups—that inherit organizational structures, command and control processes, and training procedures necessary to conduct sophisticated attacks—and newly emergent collections of the angry

and disenfranchised that become self-radicalized. For those terrorist groups that are active in 2025, the diffusion of technologies and scientific knowledge will place some of the world's most dangerous capabilities within their reach. One of our greatest concerns continues to be that terrorist or other malevolent groups might acquire and employ biological agents, or less likely, a nuclear device, to create mass casualties...

We believe ideological conflicts akin to the Cold War are unlikely to take root in a world in which most states will be preoccupied with the pragmatic challenges of globalization and shifting global power alignments. The force of ideology is likely to be strongest in the Muslim world—particularly the Arab core. In those countries that are likely to struggle with youth bulges and weak economic underpinnings—such as Pakistan, Afghanistan, Nigeria, and Yemen—the radical Salafi trend of Islam is likely to gain traction.

Types of conflict we have not seen for a while—such as over resources—could reemerge. Perceptions of energy scarcity will drive countries to take actions to assure their future access to energy supplies. In the worst case, this could result in interstate conflicts if government leaders deem assured access to energy resources, for example, to be essential for maintaining domestic stability and the survival of their regimes. However, even actions short of war will have important geopolitical consequences. Maritime security concerns are providing a rationale for naval buildups and modernization efforts, such as China's and India's development of blue-water naval capabilities. The buildup of regional naval capabilities could lead to increased tensions, rivalries, and counterbalancing moves but it also will create opportunities for multinational cooperation in protecting critical sea lanes. With water becoming more scarce in Asia and the Middle East, cooperation to manage changing water resources is likely to become more difficult within and between states.

The risk of nuclear weapon use over the next 20 years, although remaining very low, is likely to be greater than it is today as a result of several converging trends. The spread of nuclear technologies and expertise is generating concerns about the potential emergence of new nuclear weapon states and the acquisition of nuclear materials by terrorist groups. Ongoing low-intensity clashes between India and Pakistan continue to raise the specter that such events could escalate to a broader conflict between those nuclear powers. The possibility of a future disruptive regime change or collapse occurring in a weak state with nuclear weapons also continues to raise questions regarding the ability of such a state to control and secure its nuclear arsenals.

Undeniably, this comes from an US perspective, but it is probably worth the rest of us taking note of these views of the world's only real "policeman." More specifically, and still from a US perspective, Admiral Dennis Blair, Director of National Intelligence, outlines "a complex and rapidly shifting international security landscape" in his foreword to the 2009 National Intelligence Strategy (NIS) report – which pinpoints threats to US interests emerging from particular nation-state players:

> Iran poses an array of challenges to US security objectives in the Middle East and beyond because of its nuclear and missile programs, support of terrorism and provision of lethal aid to US and coalition adversaries.
>
> North Korea continues to threaten peace and security in East Asia because of its sustained pursuit of nuclear and ballistic missile capabilities, its transfer of these capabilities to third parties, its erratic behavior and its large conventional military capability.
>
> China shares many interests with the US, but its increasing natural resource-focused diplomacy and military modernization are among the factors making it a complex global challenge.
>
> Russia is a US partner in important initiatives such as securing fissile material and combating nuclear terrorism, but it may continue to seek avenues for reasserting power and influence in ways that complicate US interests.[50]

The NIS report also identifies nonstate and sub-state factors as increasingly impacting international security. For example: violent extremist groups planning to use terrorism – including the possible use of nuclear devices if they can acquire them; insurgents attempting to destabilize vulnerable states; transnational criminal organizations, such as drug trafficking groups, that may penetrate and corrupt markets, destabilize nation-states, and provide weapons, hard currency and other support to insurgents and violent criminal factions. Furthermore, a continuation of various Global Trends is likely to present strategic security challenges. For example: the global economic crisis could accelerate and weaken security by fuelling political and social turbulence; failed states and ungoverned spaces offer safe haven to terrorists and criminal organizations; as states anticipate the effects of climate change or reducing finite resources, they may engage in conflict on issues such as contesting water supply, seeking to secure energy sources, opening transport routes and new territorial claims.

Clearly political and business leaders have a crucial role to play in working together to mitigate such general and specific destructive threats. If leaders do not act responsibly and ethically in the coming years, there are plenty of scenarios that lead to very unpleasant results.

On the other hand, *if* such challenges can be managed in a mature way by the world's leaders, then some positives are definitely possible.

From a business and personal career perspective, certain business sectors (such as defense, construction, insurance and energy) have, historically, done well financially from periods of conflict. Yet there are clear ethical issues relating to identifying profit making opportunities resulting from war, terror and social unrest in the 21st century. Nevertheless, it should be recognized that historically many social and technological advancements have happened during, and in the aftermath of, periods of turbulence. Throughout history, such periods of conflict have often been a spur to a greater sense of urgency to improve, more focused work in research and development, and less importance given to purely financial return on investment motives.

As a result, periods of uncertainty have historically given a boost to innovative advancements. In the area of medicine, many advances in the treatment of injuries and illnesses have occurred during wartime. Similarly, many advances in modern flight were initially developed for military use. And many other general technological advances are made through military spending – for example, US Department of Defense's Advanced Research Projects Agency was apparently instrumental in developing early versions of the Internet in the 1960s.

Similarly, positive changes in society have been attributed to periods of social unrest. For instance, increased civil liberties were attributed to the American Civil War, and greater gender equality – or women's liberation – resulted from social changes between World War I and II. In many respects, the aftermath of war and turmoil offer the opportunity to create and build more sustainable infrastructures, societies and political systems.

Nevertheless, the greatest opportunity of all has to be to achieve such human improvements *without* the need for the kind of bloodshed that has epitomized human history – and particularly the 20th century. To work towards socially stable environments that do not create the undertones upon which war, terror and social unrest need to propagate has to be the greatest human challenge. And perhaps everyone from global political and business leaders to citizens – of all colors, creeds and origins – has some obligation to work towards this goal. While not being naïve in expecting a totally harmonious world within the short – or even medium term – the alternative to working towards such a goal is to have a 21st century with more soldiers, police and war toys and less tolerance, compassion and freedoms. As previous negotiations to avoid conflict or to bring disenfranchised terrorist groups into the fold have shown, some concessions will most likely be needed in the quest for the greater prize of peace. Ultimately though, peace is the only state in which win-win is possible. With any form of war, terror or social unrest somebody loses – and history has shown that, beyond childish games, the humans on the losing side are often not the "baddies."

It is probably no coincidence that the global regions that have encountered most unrest and conflict in the late 20th and early 21st century are those with an abundance of oil. And as the NIC report clearly indicates, there is the grave potential of governments increasingly going to war to assure supplies of one of the bedrocks of modern society: *energy*. This is the topic of the next Global Trend.

Global Trend 9

Energy

"As Steven Chu, the US Energy Secretary, puts it, each modern American has the equivalent of 100 servants working for them, thanks to the use of oil, gas and electricity."

Ed Crooks, Energy Editor, *Financial Times*[1]

Yet it is not just the modern citizens of the USA that have become used to consuming vast amounts of energy. It would seem that the whole world is addicted to the stuff. From the discovery of fire and the harnessing of wind through to the industrial revolution and the dawn of the nuclear age, energy resources have been central to our well-being, to our economies and social improvement. Indeed, the *Financial Times* "Special Report on the Future of Energy" contends that every great change in living standards has had a revolution in energy use at its heart. Certainly before man discovered fire, life would have been pretty uncomfortable and precarious. Harnessing the forces of nature to make life easier, more productive or simply just possible has been at the core of human development throughout the ages.

Think about what distinguishes the modern world from our ancestors, and no doubt many things come to mind. New ways of living, new ways of eating, new ways of doing things, new products, new clothes, new gadgets… The world has changed utterly. Now try to think of any of these changes that haven't required energy to move things, transform raw materials into products, to process things and people or to power any of our modern gadgets. Without energy everything stops. Most of the trappings of modern life disappear. Stop and think for a moment about the amount of energy we take for granted in our daily lives: the energy required to keep over 400 tonnes of metal airborne for 12 hours – in the form of a modern aircraft;* the energy to power millions of miles of electricity grid and our 24/7 broadband

---

* A Boeing 747 has a maximum take-off weight of 442,000 kg (975,000 lb).

connections; the energy to extract the ore, transport it around the world, convert it into a 2-tonne* steel car and then drive it 100,000 miles; the energy to harvest, transform, package and transport everything from T-shirts from China to breakfast cereals from Argentina. The amount of energy we consume to sustain our 21st century lifestyles is truly astounding.

Quite simply energy – in all its forms – makes the modern world go round.

While our forefathers relied upon real horsepower to transport products around the world, we rely upon the mega-horsepower of internal combustion and jet engines. From the very moment our ancestors woke up in the morning they had to rely upon their own leg-work to get them around and obtain sufficient calorie intake to keep those legs working for the (often short) duration of their lifetime. Until relatively recently, there were no buttons to press, no light switches, no self-powered machines, elevators, kettles, vehicles... In the past, keeping warm required a lot more than a twiddle of a dial. Searching for food entailed a lot more than a car trip to the air-conditioned, super-illuminated supermarket.

I know this is largely stating the obvious, but it is worth dwelling on for just a few moments. If you didn't want to do something yourself in the past you really did need those servants working for you. Perhaps not the full 100, but it really was that simple – only if you were fabulously wealthy could you relax a little from the daily grind by paying less fortunate beings to do the chores. Otherwise, you had no choice but to live within your own energy constraints – of calories consumed versus exercise done – and take whatever nature threw at you. But humans seem to be endowed with an innate ability to search for easier or more productive ways to do things and greater levels of comfort. So gradually and with great ingenuity *Homo sapiens* started to harness the power of nature: burning wood and dung to keep warm, and harnessing the forces behind water and wind – to push boats around and to power ingenious cogged contraptions in flour mills etcetera.

For centuries, even millennia, that was pretty much that. We had pretty low energy consumption expectations. Until, one day, humans got to a particular point in innovative ability and stumbled upon the vast underground stores of

---

* The gross vehicle weight of a regular family saloon car is around 2 tonnes (over 4,000 lb).

millions of years of fossilized solar energy in the form of ex-photosynthesizing forests.

And with the discovery of fossil fuels there was an explosion in energy usage.

While charcoal from chopped wood had been used for ages to get the heat required to smelt metals and so on, it wasn't until big deposits of coal were technologically accessible that the industrial revolution really took off – starting near the coalfields of Britain and then spreading to Europe, North America and the rest of the world. Suddenly here was a very, very, very concentrated form of stored energy, and anywhere with accessible coal could hop onto the accelerating economic development bandwagon. From coal came steam. From steam came the power to drive all the factories, trains and steamships. Conversely, no coal (or coal beyond the technological reach at the time) – no economic progress.

With further ingenuity oil came gushing out of the ground in the late 1800s and early 1900s. This proved to be an even more concentrated and potent fossil fuel than coal – more convenient to transport, as it can flow through pipes, and readily combustible in all sorts of conditions. Of course from crude oil comes even more explosive refined gasoline, diesel and the multitude of other fuels that power the greater portion of the world we currently live in (in addition to all the oil based products from soap to fibers, from fertilizers to plastic toys, from tarmac to paint.)

Beyond the new-fangled combustion engines, the fossil fuels were used to generate another new-fangled energy form supply: *electricity*. Since the first electricity-generation plants in the 1880s and subsequent rapid global roll-out, this energy form has become another basic requirement for life today. But electricity doesn't just come from nowhere – it first needs to be generated by another form of energy. Thus the electricity that we have come to depend upon comes from electricity-generating power stations which, in turn, are based upon fossil fuels, nuclear reactors, or the "modern" (but actually very traditional) "alternative" electricity generating energies of water (hydro), wind and solar power.

Yet another energy form was added to the arsenal of ways to power electricity-generating stations with the development of atomic physics in the early 20th century, and subsequent application during World War II: *nuclear energy*.

Of all the energy forms, nuclear power perhaps best indicates the high stakes involved with human beings' thirst for ever increasing amounts of energy. With the March 2011 nuclear crisis in the Fukushima Daiichi plant in Japan it is clear that it is possible to get some calculations wrong with severe implications for the long term. Many will be thinking that if the well-organized and technically capable Japanese can make such mistakes, then heaven help some other nations that are, figuratively, playing with fire.

Granted, the issue of nuclear energy has been pushed up the global political agenda in the wake of the Japanese earthquake-induced nuclear failures, but even beforehand the insatiable demand for energy and its volatile supply issues have usually kept energy-related issues on the front pages of the press for most of the last decades. So much so, that *"extreme energy price volatility"* is one of the main issues that keeps the world's leaders awake at night. The World Economic Forum report *Global Risks 2011* projects such volatility as "highly likely" within 10 years and with an economic impact of over $500 billion.[2]

It was already becoming apparent that two forces would shape the world's energy system this century. On the one hand, the need to secure energy supplies in a world of rapidly growing demand will increasingly influence policy-making and geostrategic positioning. The ongoing presence of many developed countries such as the USA and Europe in the Gulf region and China's growing role in Africa are illustrations of this trend. On the other hand, the international scientific community has reached a near-consensus on climate change being man-made, leading to an increasing acknowledgement of the need to cut greenhouse gas emissions. This has led to rapid development of *"alternative"* and renewable energy sources, a trend which some see as the beginning of a paradigm shift away from oil, coal and gas.

These ongoing debates about energy are manifold and complex. Just to give a quick snapshot, as I am writing this on Thursday March 31 2011, I have by my side copies of the last few days' *Financial Times* – a quick scan of the front pages' headlines reveals the profound impact energy issues have upon the world at the beginning of the 21st century:

*"**Qatar boost for Libya's Rebellion**: First Arab recognition for Gaddafi opposition. Move eases way for oil sales to fund insurgency."*

*"**Merkel blames Japan crisis for defeat**: Angela Merkel, German chancellor, has blamed Japan's nuclear crisis, triggered by this month's earthquake, for*

the "very painful defeat" suffered by her ruling party in the state of Baden-Württemberg."

*"**Radioactive water leak:** Dangerously radioactive water has leaked from Japan's Fukushima Daiichi nuclear power station in the latest breakdown of containment systems at the plant."*

*"**China clean energy drive:** Private investors sank a record $243 billion (€172 billion) into renewable energy last year – 30 percent more than in 2009."*

*"**Opec set for export revenue of $1,000 billion:** Record if crude oil stays above $100 a barrel."*

*"**Obama urges more oil:** Barack Obama, US president, called on oil groups to raise energy output as a temporary solution to US's dependence on foreign oil."*

Perhaps equally indicative of the position energy plays in the modern world is the first advert to jump out from the pages of the FT – for an energy group Enel – announcing:

"Our energy will always be powered by your dreams..."

Energy appears to be one of those constant "hot topics" in the media and as such is not always covered in a rational way. The number of energy-related studies produced and quoted in the media is staggering and it becomes a daunting challenge to separate personal opinion, speculation, vested interest or indoctrination from rational "fact."

So, resisting the temptation to get emotional, let's take a step back and look at the underlying issues behind the energy debates in as objective a manner as possible...

The term "energy" has many different meanings in a great variety of fields. Scientists define it as the ability to do work – such as the ability to move an object. Energy comes in different forms such as thermal (heat), radiant (light), kinetic (motion), electrical, chemical, nuclear and gravitational and these forms can be designated as either *primary* or *secondary*. Primary energy sources include forms such as solar, wood/ biomass, gravitational/ hydropower, wind/ waves/ tidal, oil/ coal/ natural gas (fossil fuels), and chemical/ nuclear. Each of these forms can be used to produce secondary energy forms – the most common of which are steam power, electricity (grid, batteries, etc.), hydrogen and some versions of hydropower.

This is important: a primary energy source is needed to produce a secondary energy form – so just because you drive an electric car, it doesn't mean that a fossil fuel is not being burned in some electricity generation plant somewhere else.

Furthermore, the primary energy sources can be divided into two groups: *renewable* – an energy source that can be easily replenished; and *nonrenewable* – an energy source that we are using up and cannot re-create. The modern world's dependence upon abundant energy, combined with the realization that the fossil fuels upon which we largely depend are nonrenewable – and thus finite – has inevitably resulted in polarized debate. One particular bone of contention is the issue of "peak oil" or "Hubbert's Peak" – which refers to the point at which global oil production reaches a peak, and from then on starts a permanent decline. As the *Financial Times* recently stated:[3]

Global oil production last year suffered its biggest percentage fall since 1982, but it still does not sound like oil is reaching Hubbert's Peak, when reserves start to fall and prices rise inexorably. That inflection point will arrive some day, but it remains a moving target, continuously delayed by new data and discoveries. M. King Hubbert, the geologist after whom the theory is named, predicted US oil production would peak in 1970, and it did. But he did not anticipate the growth of global trade or the improvements in oil industry technology and geological knowledge.

Depending on editorial lines, we are anything between being already past peak oil or still far from it.[4] Yet with companies venturing into ever more challenging and expensive environments to extract oil (such as deep-water rigs and tar sands), no-one seems to question that much of the easy-to-get stuff has gone, that prices will rise as demand outstrips supply, and that one day the oil will run out. In fact, the UK Energy Research Centre states that:

A peak in conventional oil production before 2030 appears likely and there is a significant risk of a peak before 2020. Given the lead times required to both develop substitute fuels and improve energy efficiency, this risk needs to be given serious consideration.[5]

Another major energy-related sticking point is the issue of CO_2 emissions. In spite of the scientific consensus that climate change is largely man-made (see Global Trend 4), media reports questioning the relationship between fossil fuel CO_2 emissions and global warming still abound. Yet, against a backdrop of growing environmental concern, what doesn't seem to be in debate is that the energy sector today contributes 80 percent of CO_2 emissions and 60 percent of total man-made greenhouse gas emissions annually. As such, the need for all nations to reduce their carbon emissions has become a key political issue. Yet almost 70 percent of global annual metric tons of CO_2 emissions come from just 10 countries: China (6,701 million metric tonnes CO2); USA (5,769 million tonnes); Russia (1, 587 million tonnes); India (1,324 million tonnes); Japan (1,236 million tonnes); Germany (789 million tonnes); Canada (573 million tonnes); UK (523 million tonnes); South Korea (489 million tonnes); and Iran (466 million tonnes).[6] Can you imagine what a million metric tons of carbon dioxide gas looks like?

Worldwide, energy demand has grown astronomically in recent years – with primary energy demand increasing by more than 50 percent since 1980.

As a result of the financial crisis, primary energy consumption growth actually slowed by 1.4 percent in 2008, as did growth for each of the fossil fuels – but consumption will soon resume its upward trend if government policies do not change.[7] All the net growth in energy consumption came from the rapidly industrializing non-OECD economies. For the first time, non-OECD energy consumption surpassed OECD consumption. China alone accounts for nearly three-quarters of global growth.[8]

Manufacturing industry is the end-use sector that globally consumes the most energy, with a 33 percent share; followed by households (29 percent) and transport (26 percent). CO_2 emissions also follow a similar breakdown, with manufacturing contributing 38 percent; households 21 percent and transport 25 percent of all CO2 emissions.[9]

Five countries consume over half of the worlds' energy

These are: USA (20.35 percent of worldwide consumption), China (17.73 percent), Russia (6.06 percent), Japan (4.49 percent), and India (3.83 percent).

Adding another five countries accounts for two thirds of the world's energy consumption: Canada (2.91 percent), Germany (2.75 percent), France (2.28 percent), South Korea (2.12 percent) and Brazil (2.02 percent).[10] In terms of absolute consumption levels, among large countries the USA and Canada are by far the largest consumers of energy on a per capita basis. This level is around twice that seen in other parts of the OECD which in turn is far higher than in non-OECD countries. Between 1990 and 2005 energy use per capita in the OECD increased by 6 percent while the increase in non-OECD countries was only 1 percent. On average, energy use per capita in non-OECD countries is only 23 percent of the level seen in the OECD.

In terms of sources of energy, fossil fuels still represent 87.3 percent of all global energy consumption.

After all, fossil fuels have the added benefit that of all the primary energy forms they can be most easily transported to where they are needed in the world.

Oil remains the dominant fuel – generating 34.8 percent of all global energy consumption in 2008.

And despite this dropping from 38.7 percent over the last decade, more oil is used today than ever before.[11] Furthermore, demand for oil is expected to continue to grow, primarily driven by rising passenger travel and freight transport, and rapid expansion of emerging economies.

The usual suspects consume the lion's share of the oil: USA (23.9 percent of world total), China (9.3 percent), Japan (5.8 percent), India (3.3 percent), Russia (3.2 percent), Germany (2.8 percent), South Korea (2.7 percent), Canada (2.6 percent), Saudi Arabia (2.5 percent) and France (2.3 percent).[12]

Yet, on the supply side, the list of top ten producers brings a few surprises: Saudi Arabia (12.6 percent or world total), Russia (also 12.6 percent), USA (8.0 percent), Iran (5.4 percent), China (4.8 percent), Mexico (4.4 percent), Canada (4.1 percent), United Arab Emirates (3.5 percent), Venezuela (3.4 percent) and Kuwait (3.3 percent).

Figure 9.1 is a quick look at the major movements of oil around the world. It gives a good summary of who does what: the USA, Europe, Japan and China are net consumers whilst the Middle East, former Soviet Union, Africa and Latin American countries are net producers.

Figure 9.1: Largest inter-area oil movements by volume, thousand barrels per day

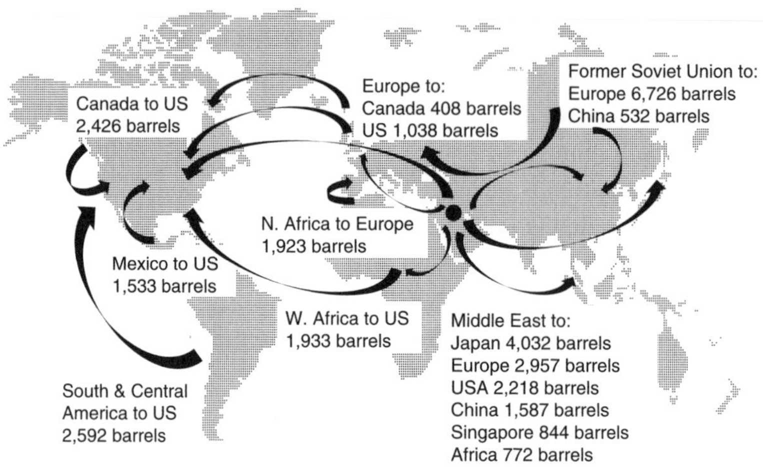

Canada to US
2,426 barrels

Europe to:
Canada 408 barrels
US 1,038 barrels

Former Soviet Union to:
Europe 6,726 barrels
China 532 barrels

N. Africa to Europe
1,923 barrels

Mexico to US
1,533 barrels

W. Africa to US
1,933 barrels

Middle East to:
Japan 4,032 barrels
Europe 2,957 barrels
USA 2,218 barrels
China 1,587 barrels
Singapore 844 barrels
Africa 772 barrels

South & Central
America to US
2,592 barrels

Source: Energy Security: Oil Key players and movements, *The Financial Times*

Looking through the above list of top producers it is perhaps no great revelation that, although seldom used as an official justification for war, oil is alleged to have been the source of several political and military conflicts – past, present and future.

This is even more the case when looking at the countries with biggest proven reserves for the future. Again Saudi Arabia tops the list with 21.3 percent of the world's total. But then come the interesting ones: Iran (11.2 percent), Iraq (9.3 percent), Kuwait (8.2 percent), UAE (7.9 percent), Venezuela (7.0 percent), Russia (6.4 percent), Libya (3.3 percent), Kazakhstan (3.2 percent), and Nigeria (2.9 percent).

Not exactly renowned as the most popular tourist destinations. In fact, perhaps there is a link between top proven oil reserves and bottom desirable places for a relaxing holiday in pleasant surroundings. Yet, most importantly, these countries have high reserves to current production ratios – indicating tremendous potential value in future years.

After oil, comes coal as the second most important global energy source – providing 29 percent of the world's needs in 2008.

It is still a major fuel used across the world for electricity power stations – for example in the USA coal accounts for approximately 50 percent of electricity generation. In fact, despite its dirty image, use of coal has increased in recent years. Furthermore, after centuries of mineral exploration, the location, size and characteristics of most countries' coal resources are well-established. The top ten countries in terms of proven recoverable coal reserves are: USA, Russia, China, Australia, India, South Africa, Ukraine, Kazakhstan, Serbia and Poland.[13]

After coal comes natural gas, which accounts for 23.5 percent of the world's energy consumption.

World natural gas production grew by a robust 3.8 percent in 2009, the strongest volumetric growth since 1984. The top three natural gas producers are: the Russian Federation with 19.5 percent of total worldwide production; the USA with 19.2 percent; and Canada with 5.7 percent. Yet the distribution of proven reserves follows a similar pattern to that of oil: with the energy-endowed Middle East topping the list with over 40 percent of worldwide proven reserves, and Europe and Eurasia with 34 percent. The rest of the world combined has less than 25 percent of world natural gas reserves. The top three countries with the most proven natural gas reserves are: Russia with 23.4 percent of the world's total reserves; Iran with 16 percent; and Qatar with 14 percent.

After the 87.3 percent of worldwide energy needs met with fossil fuels, come the rest.

The first of the rest is, perhaps surprisingly…

Hydropower energy – providing 6.3 percent of worldwide energy needs.

This primary energy source makes use of the potential energy of falling water – usually stored behind dams. It is regarded as the most widespread and flexible of the renewable energies and represents 87 percent of renewable energy. Global hydropower output increased by 2.8 percent in 2008, with China accounting for the entire world's net increase, and Chinese output rising by 20.3 percent on strong capacity growth and increased rainfall. However hydropower is somewhat restricted to those countries with adequate geography and climate. The top three producers and consumers of hydroelectric power are: China with 18.5 percent of the world total; Canada with 11.7 percent and Brazil with 11.5 percent of global hydropower production.

Then comes nuclear energy: the technology that emerged from war and in many people's eyes has never fully distanced itself from associations with the destruction it is able to cause.

Nuclear energy provided 5.5 percent of energy needs worldwide in 2008.

The top three producers of nuclear energy were: the USA with 23.4 percent of total worldwide production; France with 16.1 percent; and Japan with 9.2 percent. All of this nuclear power was created by nuclear *fission*. Nuclear fuels undergo fission (splitting) when struck by free neutrons and in turn generate neutrons when they break apart. This creates a self-sustaining chain reaction that releases huge quantities of energy – millions of times that released from a similar amount of chemical fuel such as gasoline.

Thus, while nuclear fission is a very tempting source of energy, there are two significant downsides – as we have found out from the likes of nuclear problems at Three Mile Island (USA), Chernobyl (Ukraine), and now Fukushima Daiichi (Japan). Firstly, chain reactions are great for bombs but *very* hard to control for safe energy supply. Secondly, the products of nuclear fission are usually far more radioactive than the heavy elements used as fuel – and remain so for *very* long periods of time... tens, hundreds, thousands and even millions of years. Just consider the half-lives* of this short list of nuclear fission waste products: Technetium-99 (220,000 years), Iodine-129 (15.7 million years), Neptunium-237 (two million years), Plutonium-239 (24,000 years). The technical challenges are clearly daunting, given the extremely long periods of time that radioactive wastes remain deadly to living organisms. Governments have had limited success in implementing long-term waste-management solutions to completely isolate such radioactive wastes from the biosphere.

Yet, off many people's radar screens is another nuclear option that doesn't seem to pose such dangers: nuclear *fusion*.[14]

This works by joining (colliding) two "heavy" hydrogen atoms together to form the relatively inert element helium, a neutron plus a *lot* of energy. This is the process powering the Sun and stars, and the UK Atomic Energy Authority

---

* Half-life: The time required for the radioactivity of material to be reduced to half its initial value by radioactive decay.

believes that nuclear fusion "is one of the most promising options for generating large amounts of carbon-free energy in the future." The main problem is that nuclear fusion is very difficult to make happen and, whilst some experiments have yielded promising results, we haven't yet worked out how to make it happen on a generating-plant level. But many scientists are somewhat optimistic. The Joint European Torus (JET) website for Europe's largest nuclear fusion device states that:

> A vigorous world-wide research programme is under way, aimed at harnessing fusion energy to produce electricity on Earth. If successful, this will offer a viable alternative energy supply within the next 30–40 years – with significant environmental, supply and safety advantages over present energy sources.[15]

Watch this space. Time will tell if this "other" nuclear power becomes viable or not.

Beyond nuclear power come all the "alternative energy" sources including wind, solar, biomass, geothermal and wave energy. While these energy forms are sometimes seen as new solutions to emerging energy dilemmas, in fact some of them are very old concepts that humans have been tapping into for millennia. With new technologies however, these renewables do potentially represent a way forward for some of the 21st century's energy needs. For example, it has been found that the integration of wind-generated electricity into regional or national supply systems can be readily achieved.

Wind energy to generate electricity is therefore growing fast, with technology of wind turbines improving dramatically over the last couple of decades.

In fact, since 1990 worldwide wind energy capacity has doubled every 3½ years. The size and energy-generation potential of both onshore and offshore wind turbines continues to grow – with blade diameters of up to 110 meters. That is big.

Solar power is catching up with wind as the fastest-growing source of renewable energy.

Between 2004 and 2008, new investment in the sector grew from just $600m to $33.5bn. Global sales of photovoltaic modules for terrestrial applications are growing at about 35 percent per annum. Furthermore, there is a growing trend towards the incorporation of passive solar into new building designs, which can reduce conventional energy consumption by as much as 75 percent.

The burning of renewable biomass currently provides around 1.3 percent of the world's electricity, but this could rise significantly over the next 50 years.

What is now known as biomass includes some of the most familiar and long-used energy sources in human history – wood, straw, grass, charcoal and animal excrement, usually dried and burned for heat. But this list is being extended to include municipal solid waste, sewage, industrial, crop and animal residues.

While geothermal energy is still a small contributor to energy production worldwide, advances in drilling techniques are opening up new areas for possible exploitation.

The World Geothermal Congress indicates that the total installed capacity of geothermal heat pumps in 2005 was nearly triple what it was in 2000. Also, tide and wave energy are currently minor contributors to worldwide energy production, but a number of new approaches are being tested including floating buoys, oscillating columns and bottom-of-sea systems that could prove viable in the coming years.

Threats and opportunities

There are obvious dangers at society, business and individual levels of exponentially increasing energy demand – with an over-reliance upon the chemically and politically volatile fossil fuels. How the world faces up to the twin challenges of securing energy supplies and reducing the climatic impact of CO_2 released from burning such quantities of oil, coal and gas will shape this century and beyond.

Of prime importance for any modern economy is the issue of energy security. At the beginning of the 21st century, nations face a stark choice.

Any society that has any aspirations of developing and sustaining a modern economy with the trappings of modern life simply *has* to have access to huge levels of reliable energy. Just to keep things ticking over – let alone any desire for growth – requires huge energy intake. The use of indigenous reserves or the ability to access a well-provided and affordable international market have enhanced region's energy security and provided affordable, reliable power to drive economies and development. Yet, with the threat of peak oil – whether past, present or future – supply disruptions are likely to increase and exacerbate pressures to provide secure and steady energy.

Despite an overall decline in oil's share of energy supply, the world remains, by and large, oil-dependent. The knowledge that oil is a finite resource, which will one day be used up, places further pressure on investors and the economic system as a whole. While the notion of peak oil itself is not controversial, its consequences on mankind are. Opinions range from avid proponents of free markets who claim that market mechanisms ensure a natural transition away from fossil fuels, to doomsday prophets who already see humanity on the brink of an energy-slump-induced collapse. The market argument suggests that according to the hypothesis of market efficiency and the law of supply and demand, oil prices will be driven up by increasing demand, which in turn will provide greater economic incentives for the development of alternative energy solutions. The main counter-argument is that markets are not always efficient, as recent financial turmoil has demonstrated. Also, the time-horizon of investors might not be in the same ballpark as the time-frame required to develop technologies allowing the shift away from oil. While the normal return-on-investment horizon is usually framed within the decision-taker's lifespan, the development of an alternative to oil may well be the work of generations.*

If an energy source does dry up – or if demand outstrips supply, sending prices soaring – many things will simply grind to a halt… unless of course new sources are found or more energy-efficient ways of doing things emerge.

---

* The ongoing ITER projects, for example, aim at providing mankind with "an environmentally benign and universally available resource" based upon nuclear fusion (as opposed to current fission-based nuclear power stations) by the last quarter of the 21st century. The true time-frame of the ITER project, which is sponsored by China, the EU, India, Japan, South Korea, Russia and the USA, becomes apparent when bearing in mind that its origins date back to 1985. See *The way to new energy*. ITER. http://www.iter.org/. Accessed July 2011.

And fast. Yet the urge to find big new sources of reliable, clean energy must be tempered with an objective and honest evaluation of both the positives and negatives involved. There is no sense in "jumping out of the frying pan into the fire."

At the time of writing, no country better indicates the underlying energy predicament than Japan. As an industrialized modern economy it is hooked on energy, but with no natural fossil fuels of its own it is reliant upon energy imports. In an attempt to safeguard against the potential volatility of the global fossil-fuel trade, the strategic decision was taken to invest in nuclear. For any country to feel it necessary to build nuclear reactors on a coastline that has historically been hit by earthquakes and tsunamis clearly indicates that the stakes are high in this energy bet. Apparently no open, objective and honest evaluation of the potential risks and impacts was fully carried out at political, business or citizen levels. And with the March 2011 nuclear crisis and leakage of radioactive material from the Fukushima Daiichi plant it is clear someone got their calculations wrong. Many people are likely to pay a high price for years to come.

Until the recent Japanese disaster, many countries had made the gamble on nuclear as the only clean energy form that can deliver the amounts required to get us out of the current energy and climate hole. While nuclear is not alone in its potential for horrifying catastrophes (just look at the harm caused by the BP Deepwater Horizon incident), it may deserve even more caution given the possible very long-term threats to life on this planet if anything should go wrong. And it should be remembered that nuclear fission has inherent drawbacks that are very, very, very hard (perhaps read "virtually impossible") to fully control for the full duration of the long-term radioactive threat posed by the chain reaction and deadly waste products involved. After all, what nation in the world would consider themselves as technically adept and self-disciplined as the Japanese? As a qualified mechanical engineer, trained in techniques such as "Failure Modes and Effects Analysis," I find it utterly astounding that well-informed human beings would dare put a nuclear fission plant anywhere near an area of seismic activity. How did we reach such a point of blind energy dependence regardless of the possible consequences?

Nevertheless, such disasters should not prevent human endeavor to find ways of solving the energy dilemmas we face. The threat now is that all investment in nuclear is cut. The worldwide nuclear industry is threatened with politicians and business leaders pulling the plug on planned investments. That could be a mistake. While the safety record and potential for future nuclear *fission*-related accidents needs to be openly and honestly considered amongst policy-makers, businesses and citizens, care should be taken not to "tar all nuclear power with the same brush." Nuclear *fission* may well be discredited but nuclear *fusion* still represents a potentially safe solution to our energy-supply problems in the not-too-distant future. However, nuclear fusion clearly needs continued investment for the coming decade or two for any chance of this to be realized. Ultimately it is a technology gamble – but one that just could pay off.

Most industrialized nations are moving towards a similarly insecure energy position to that of Japan – with some potentially hard realities to face-up to. Most emerging economies are also now well and truly following the same energy intensive path to growth and the prospect of a better life. As a result rapidly increasing energy consumption is sweeping through the emerging nations such as Brazil, Russia, India, and China (the BRICs – see Global Trend 2). The wisdom of maintaining such developed and emerging nation trajectories has to be questioned by all. Clearly there will be huge pressures to match supply with demand. Yet what are the limits in human demand for energy? History would indicate that humans have nothing in their DNA to self-impose such limits – in which case the quest for squeezing more and more energy out of existing nonrenewable fossil fuels sources will continue. At some point, though, that is likely to hit diminishing returns and then new forms of energy – plus some form of self-constraint – are likely to become more attractive.

In the meantime, what of the climate concerns? In this respect, the International Energy Agency proposes nothing less than an "energy revolution":

> Any effective strategy to mitigate climate change must depend on a rapid shift in patterns of production, transmission and use of energy, in short, an energy revolution. New technology development and deployment is essential in this regard, as is illustrated by IEA projections that describe the contributions that technology can make to steering us away from today's unsustainable energy trend, towards one that would still meet rising energy needs while preserving the world's climate.[16]

While the IEA recognizes the immense challenges that will be faced in launching such an energy revolution at a time when the world is suffering from an economic crisis (see Global Trend 1), this mitigation of threats points the way to significant potential opportunities – both in terms of finding new energy sources and developing more energy efficient ways of doing things.

Collaborative efforts between policy-makers, business leaders and citizens present tremendous opportunities on both the supply and demand side.

On the supply side, none of the currently available "alternatives" can match the fossil fuels or nuclear for their convenience and plain oomph. For example, it is unlikely that wind, solar, wave or hydropower are going to power a commercial plane anytime soon. Hence, the threats posed by classical fossil fuel energy generation will remain for the foreseeable future, but opportunities linked to alternative energy generation and energy efficiency increases will arise as new technologies gain momentum. As a result, such energy forms will probably have an important role to play in reducing the pressure on oil by helping in the generation of electricity. Furthermore, with increasing primary energy demand with the rise of emerging economies the price of conventional, finite fossil resources is likely to rise in the medium to longer term (despite short-term fluctuations). In turn, this is likely to provide economic incentives for the large-scale development of alternative and renewable primary energies.

Thus all energy forms – fossil fuels, nuclear, hydro, wind, solar, biomass, wave and geothermal – are likely to be called upon to create an appropriate "mix" of global energy outputs with reduced environmental impact. Therefore there are obvious supply side opportunities in developing and marketing appropriate methods, processes and technologies in the following areas: extracting more from proven fossil reserves and exploiting currently unfeasible ones through improved extraction methods; improving research and exploration methods to identify new reserves; and developing "clean" technologies to facilitate the shift to more abundant fossil fuels (coal, natural gas, oil shale and tar sands, etc.) *without* increasing CO_2 or pollution levels. And, of course, there are big opportunities in continuing to develop and promote non-fossil-fuel and renewable primary energy forms. Despite current and often publicized limitations, human history has shown just what can be achieved with continuing innovation. The alternative energy forms do have an important role to play in 21st century energy – so expect a dammed valley, wind farm or shiny-topped building near you soon.

On the demand side, there are many further opportunities in developing and marketing appropriate methods, processes and technologies to reduce energy consumption. There are a whole host of technologies that can already be applied to this problem – from automatic switch-off systems to better insulated homes, from more efficient transport systems to "smart" grids. New technologies will continue to emerge. Education to improve awareness is another big opportunity for policy-makers and business leaders – taking care to avoid the temptation of slick advertising campaigns promoting products as "green," when in energy terms they ultimately depend upon the same dirty coal-fired power stations. For example, electric cars recharged from an electric grid based upon fossil fuels might not address the underlying energy problems, but rather just move the primary energy consumption and pollution to someone else's back-yard. The important thing is to reduce *overall* energy consumption – and especially reduce reliance upon nonrenewable *primary* energy.

Global moves to kick the age-old human energy-addiction and "*Save it!*" would probably not go amiss.

Great opportunities for political and business leaders and individuals lie in increasing awareness of the issues at hand. While there are serious energy-related challenges facing humanity, excessive pessimism is perhaps unnecessary. Mitigating the threats will clearly take a great deal of effort, and would be much better undertaken with some foresight and preparation in order to avoid painful knock-on problems. Yet even if humanity's hand is forced by circumstances (which, unfortunately, currently looks likely), human history indicates that solutions will be found. Whether such solutions can be found and applied in time will depend upon the degree of human imagination and ingenuity applied to the associated problems. Serious solutions really are needed for the serious energy problems, and fast. But then "necessity is the mother of invention."

It is human beings' insatiable appetite for more and more energy that is one of the prime components of the immense human "global footprint" and the impact we are having upon ecosystems and the decline in biodiversity. These are the topics of the next Global Trend.

Global Trend 10

Ecosystems and Biodiversity*

"Our lives depend upon biological diversity. Species and ecosystems are disappearing at an unsustainable rate. We humans are the cause. The consequences for economies and people will be profound. Business as usual is not an option. I call on every country and each citizen of our planet to join together in a global alliance to protect life on earth. Biodiversity is Life. Biodiversity is our Life."

Ban Ki-Moon, United Nations Secretary-General[1]

As many schoolchildren know, the Dodo was a flightless bird unique to the Indian Ocean island of Mauritius. The impact of a combination of human hunting and habitat destruction, along with nest-plundering by imported voracious invaders such as cats, dogs, pigs and rats set the utterly defenseless creature upon a path towards inevitable oblivion. Within a century of the species' discovery by the first European colonizers of the paradise island – around the end of the 17th century – the unfortunate creature was no more. The last official sighting was in 1662, with a few stragglers perhaps hanging on in more remote areas for a couple of decades longer. The Dodo became an ex-Dodo. Extinct beyond any question of uncertainty. "As dead as a Dodo" in fact.

Yet, while we have focused this expression for extinction upon this one unfortunate creature, we could probably just as well make reference to a whole host of other creatures. Scientists understandably seem to hate to use the "extinct" word because it is very difficult to prove and takes many years

---

* An ecosystem is a dynamic complex of plant, animal, and microorganism communities and inert environmental components interacting as a functional unit. Biodiversity is the variance in living organisms from all sources, including terrestrial, marine and other aquatic ecosystems, and the ecological systems of which they are part. This includes diversity within species, between species, and diversity of ecosystems.

of fruitless searching: some experts liken the difficulties to "proving" that the mythical Loch Ness Monster does not exist. And given the finality of the term, its use can result in less funding for conservation work. Having said that, there are a whole host of animals that are classed as probably or possibly extinct and that have not been seen for many decades. So in the years to come we could just as easily be saying: "*As dead as a* [insert your favorite animal or plant here from the following]...*broad-faced potoroo; Eastern hare wallaby; desert rat kangaroo; thylacine; pig-footed bandicoot; red-bellied gracile opossum; bulldog rat; long-tailed hopping mouse; Indefatigable Galapagos mouse; Martinique muskrat; Ilin Island cloudrunner; Pallid beach mouse; Little Swan Island hutia; Marcano's solenodon; Christmas Island Shrew; Guam flying fox; Nendo tube-nosed fruit bat; New Zealand greater short-tailed bat; Sturdee's pipistrelle; Caucasian wisent; Bubal hartebeest; Schomburgk's deer; Queen of Sheba's gazelle; Saudi gazelle; Pyrenean ibex; Sea mink; Japanese sea lion; Caribbean monk seal; Bali tiger; Caspian tiger; Javan tiger; Japanese wolf; Mexican grizzly bear; Tarpan; Syrian wild ass; West Coast spotted kiwi; Korean crested shelduck; pink-headed duck; Auckland Islands merganser; Javanese lapwing; slender-billed curlew; Canarian black oystercatcher; Antillean cave-rail; New Caledonian rail; Wake Island rail; Marquesas Swamphen; Columbian grebe; Alaotra grebe; Guadalupe storm-petrel; passenger pigeon; Ryukyu woodpigeon; Sulu bleeding heart; thick-billed ground dove; Choiseul crested pigeon; red-mustached fruit dove; Negros fruit dove; New Caledonian lorikeet; Paradise parrot; Glaucous macaw; Carolina parakeet; Guadalupe caracara; laughing owl; Puerto Rican barn-owl; Cuban pauraque; Vaurie's nightjar; Siau scops-owl; turquoise-throated puffleg; imperial woodpecker; ivory billed woodpecker; bush wren; Tachira antpitta; Hawaiian honeyeaters; Chatham Island bellbird; Lord Howe gerygone; Nuku Hiva monarch; Guam flycatcher; short-toed nuthatch vanga; North Island piopio; South Island piopio; Huia; white-eyed river martin; red sea swallow; Moorea reed-warbler; Rueck's blue flycatcher; Chatham Islands fernbird; black browed babbler; Aldabra brush warbler; Rodrigues babbler; Kosrae Island starling; mysterious starling; Pohnpei starling; bourbon crested starling; Grand Cayman thrush; Bonin thrush; Cozumel thrasher; black-lored waxbill; slender-billed grackle; Bachman's warbler; Sempler's warbler; tawny-headed mountain finch; etcetera; etcetera; etcetera; etcetera...*"[2]

The list of extinct, probably extinct or possibly extinct is apparently *ad infinitum*. What is even more sobering is that the above is a very restricted list of certain mammals and some bird species. Not to speak of fish, insects, plants, reptiles and so on.

> **Many, many creatures have apparently disappeared from the face of the planet in the last 100 years.**

Nor does the above cohort include the countless living things that appear on all the other classification lists of *extinct in the wild,** *critically endangered, endangered, vulnerable and near threatened* of the comprehensive, objective, and reputable International Union for Conservation of Nature (IUCN). While it is difficult to prove beyond any doubt, it is reasonable to suspect that the vast majority of these extinct or close-to-extinct animals have disappeared – or are disappearing – as a result of human activity or negligence. One of the most recent and high profile cases – probably on account of it being one of the "smiley" creatures that we humans feel an affinity – has been the Yangtze River dolphin, *Baiji* – or "Goddess of the Yangtze" as it is nicknamed in China. Populations of this mammal declined rapidly towards the end of the 20th century – probably on account of the combination of rapid industrialization, pollution, overfishing, increasing river transportation and hydroelectricity installations. The animal was declared "*functionally extinct*"[†] in 2006 after failed conservation efforts and an unfruitful expedition to find any dolphins alive. So, notwithstanding the occasional blurry image of something looking like a *Baiji* (or a Loch Ness Monster) it would seem that yet another species has passed into the history books: "*As dead as a Baiji.*"

Perhaps mankind's rise is inextricably linked to other species' fall. The only species that do not appear to be in danger are those which have aligned themselves to our way of doing things – and then often annoy us in their plague proportions.

The "Global Risks Landscape" prepared for the 2011 World Economic Forum identifies "biodiversity loss" as one of the most likely risks facing the world (actually on par with such probable events as storms and cyclones, flooding and corruption). In other words, the world's political and business leaders see biodiversity loss as pretty much inevitable in the coming decade. The perceived economic impact was put at over $250 billion, to say nothing of the countless losses in so many other immeasurable areas.[3]

---

* Those species for which the only specimens that remain are in human captivity.

[†] Functionally extinct: Whilst there may be a few specimens still alive, the population is no longer viable. There are no individuals able to reproduce, or the small population of breeding individuals will not be able to sustain itself.

In tune with such inevitability, it would seem that most adults are pretty resigned to the fact that many cute, soft and cuddly – as well as the distinctly prickly, scary and disgusting – species simply will not be around for our children's lifetime. Well at least we have zoos for those that have no livelihood in the wild. And for the extinct ones, there are at least museums. For many people, that is apparently that. For any species that doesn't fit with the trajectory of human development there are clear signs towards the exit, and if they would be so kind as to shut the door on the way out that would inconvenience us even less.

Were you aware that the United Nations had declared 2010 the "International Year of Biodiversity"?

If so, you were better informed than me. The whole year had passed before I knew about this UN initiative. And it is a subject with which I had thought I was relatively aware – especially with two nature-mad young sons that have to put everything on hold to inspect a passing ant.

In his introductory message to launch the UN International Year of Biodiversity, Ban Ki-Moon spelled out that these issues go well beyond the disappearance of a few – or even a lot – of flora and fauna here and there. The loss of biodiversity has an inevitable impact upon the ecosystems upon which we, as human beings, depend. While we live our daily lives in our human designed techno-bubble, cushioned from the harshness of nature and buffered against environmental changes by the trappings of modern cultures, the human species is fundamentally dependent upon the underlying ecosystems of which we are an integral part. By plundering at ever-increasing scales all the things we have come to expect and enjoy from nature over countless thousands of years it would seem that we are biting the very hand that feeds us. It is clear that biodiversity plays an important role in ecosystem functions that provide numerous services that humans need to survive – let alone flourish. These services are essential for human well-being: in terms of basic material for life, health, good social relations, security and freedom of choice and action.

Nevertheless, at present there are few studies that link changes in biodiversity with changes in ecosystem functioning to changes in human well-being. Presumably, this is because such research is extremely hard to do. It is much easier to conduct research in a laboratory with test tubes and gadgets, or sit in front of a computer playing with spreadsheets and statistics, than it is to spend years in a rainforest being bitten by all manner of insects with the aim of determining causal links between the incredibly complex dynamics of nature.

So, as a result of high-level concerns about such ecosystem changes
and a lack of quality information on the issue, the Millennium Ecosystem
Assessment was initiated in 2001 on the request of the then UN Secretary-
General Kofi Annan. The objective was to:

> … assess the consequences of ecosystem change for human well-being and
> to establish the scientific basis for actions needed to enhance the conserva-
> tion and sustainable use of ecosystems and their contributions to human
> well-being.[4]

In a similar manner to the Intergovernmental Panel on Climate Change
(IPCC) (See Global Trend 4), the Millennium Ecosystem Assessment (MEA)
assembled 1,360 experts and scientists to synthesize information from the
scientific literature and relevant peer-reviewed datasets and models; incorporating knowledge held by the private sector, practitioners, local communities and indigenous peoples between 2001 and 2005. Also, as with the IPCC
reports for climate change, the MEA seems to represent the most complete
picture we have as to what has been happening over the last decades in terms
of ecosystem changes and biodiversity loss. The assessment investigated the
full range of ecosystems occurring on planet Earth: from the relatively undis-
turbed, such as natural forests, to mixed human-natural landscapes, to ecosystems intensively modified by humans, such as agricultural land and urban
areas.

A particular focus of the MEA was upon what it terms "ecosystem
services" – in other words, the benefits that people obtain from ecosystems:
provisioning services – such as food, water, timber and fiber: *regulating services*
that affect climate, floods, disease, wastes and water quality: *cultural services*
that provide recreational, aesthetic and spiritual benefits: and *supporting services* such as soil formation, photosynthesis and nutrient cycling.

The 155-page MEA synthesis report essentially comes up with four main
findings:

1. Over the past 50 years, humans have changed ecosystems more rapidly
   and extensively than in any comparable period of time in human
   history – largely to meet growing demands for food, fresh water,
   timber, fiber and fuel. This has resulted in a substantial and largely
   irreversible loss in the diversity of life on Earth.

2. The changes made to ecosystems have contributed to substantial gains in human well-being and economic development, but these gains have been achieved at growing costs: such as the degradation of many ecosystems; increased risk of further "nonlinear" accelerating, abrupt or irreversible changes; and the exacerbation of poverty for some groups of people. These problems unless addressed, will substantially diminish the benefits that future generations obtain from ecosystems.

3. The degradation of ecosystem services could grow significantly worse during the first half of this century. While some may benefit from over-exploiting ecosystems, the costs of potentially irreversible changes borne by society are often higher.

4. The drivers of biodiversity loss and ecosystem change are either steady, show no evidence of declining or are increasing in intensity. Therefore, the challenge of reversing the degradation of ecosystems while meeting increasing demands for their services would involve significant changes in policies, institutions, and practices that are not currently under way.

These findings are supported by a lot of evidence. For example, between 1960 and 2000, the demand for ecosystem services grew significantly as world population doubled to 6 billion people and the global economy increased more than sixfold.

To meet increased demand over 40 years, food production increased roughly two-and-a-half times, water use doubled, wood harvested for pulp and paper production tripled, installed hydropower capacity doubled, and timber production increased by more than half.[5]

It comes as no surprise that such rapid change in natural resources exploitation, and the way that we use land and water, has had devastating effects upon ecosystems in many regions in the last decades. More land was converted to cropland in the 30 years after 1950 than in the 150 years between 1700 and 1850. Cultivated systems (croplands, shifting cultivation, confined livestock production, or freshwater aquaculture) now cover one quarter of the Earth's terrestrial surface. Looking at a map, the only large untouched areas consist of the arid desert lands in North Africa, Australia and the Middle East, the frozen tundra of Alaska, Canada and Russia, and the continent of Antarctica. The opportunities for further expansion of cultivation are diminishing in many regions of the world as the proportion of land suitable for conversion to intensive agricultural use continues to decline. On the other hand, in some areas improved agricultural productivity has reduced the pressure for agricultural expansion. Since 1950, cropland area in North America, Europe and China has stabilized, and even decreased in the case of Europe and China. Cropland area in the former Soviet Union has decreased since 1960. As for water, the amount of water impounded behind dams has quadrupled since 1960: three to six times as much water is held in reservoirs as in natural rivers. Water withdrawals from rivers and lakes have doubled since 1960.

Though humans have been modifying land to obtain food and other essentials for thousands of years, we are living in a time of unprecedented rates of land use and land-cover change. Our actions are presently driving drastic changes in ecosystems and environmental processes at local, regional and global scales. The current rates of land-cover change are greatest for tropical moist forests and for temperate, tropical, and flooded grasslands, with a 14 percent loss for each between 1950 and 1990. Approximately 10–20 percent of the world's dry-lands are degraded. This is directly harming the population living in these areas, but also has indirect negative effects upon a greater population through biophysical impacts (such as dust storms and greenhouse emissions) and socioeconomic impacts (such as human migration and deepening poverty). Similarly, in the last decades of the 20th century, approximately 20 percent of the world's coral reefs were lost and an additional 20 percent degraded. Also, in countries for which sufficient data exist (which only accounts for half of the area) about 35 percent of mangrove area was lost during this time. Both reefs and mangroves provide invaluable services – not least in terms of moderating the effects of storms and flooding.[6,7]

As a result of all this human activity, it is clear that biodiversity is in decline. We know that the number of species on the planet is reducing – and fast. Global studies of a number of species (e.g. fish, amphibians, mammals, birds, insects.) show declines in the majority of populations. Of course, we know that extinctions of species are also a natural phenomenon as nature adapts and evolves to changing climates and conditions.

From the fossil record, we have been able to ascertain that less than one species in every one thousand became extinct every millennium of Earth's evolution.

> **A long-term average "natural" extinction rate is 1 species per thousand species per millennium.**

Yet there are approximately 100 well documented extinctions of birds, mammals and amphibians over the last 100 years – a rate 100 times higher than natural background rates of extinctions that were typical over Earth's history. Including less documented – but still highly probable – extinctions, the rate is up to 1,000 times higher than the fossil record extinction rates. Based upon current trends:

> **Millennium Ecosystem Assessment models estimate future species extinction rates to increase to over ten times the current rates: more than ten thousand extinctions per thousand species per millennium. Or 1,000 percent decline in species per millennium: 1 percent extinction per year.**

That is a simply stunning level of projected biodiversity loss, and one that cannot be remotely matched by the emergence of new natural species. While at first glance 1 percent extinction per year may not seem much, clearly it will not take long to get down to levels of biodiversity at which it is utterly impossible for any higher forms of mammals, birds, amphibians, fish, or plants to sustain a living in such a diminished web of life or food chain. In fact, some 10 to 50 percent of well-studied higher taxonomic groups (mammals, birds, amphibians, conifers, and cycads) are currently threatened with extinction, based on IUCN criteria.

And, while we are not there yet, humans are, ultimately, just another one of the several thousands of species that may be threatened with future extinction from ecosystems and biodiversity collapse.

The "Living Planet Index" (see Figure 10.1) is an aggregate indicator of the state of the world's biodiversity: measuring trends in natural populations of a variety of wild species. The index currently incorporates data on the abundance of 555 terrestrial species, 323 freshwater species, and 267 marine species around the world. As a whole, in 2000 the Living Planet Index was only

Figure 10.1: The Living Planet Index

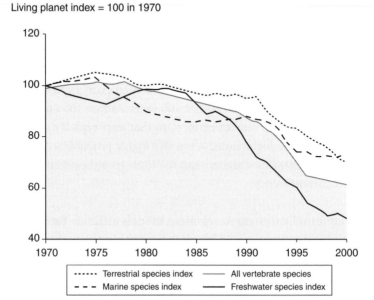

Living planet index = 100 in 1970

Legend:
- ······ Terrestrial species index
- — — Marine species index
- —— All vertebrate species
- —— Freshwater species index

Source: Millennium Ecosystem Assessment, 2005

60 percent of what it had been in 1970. In other words, based upon a sample of species that we know about:

There is 40 percent less abundance of life now than there was in 1970.

As for the different vertebrate species: the freshwater species index fell by about 50 percent, the terrestrial species index by about 30 percent, and the marine index by around 30 percent over the same period. Even more worrying is the accelerating trend for reductions in populations. From a more or less flat, stable line in the 1970s, vertebrate populations entered a precipitous decline from the 1980s onwards. A nosedive might be a better way of expressing it.

An extrapolation of these trends would suggest that we are heading towards a Living Planet index of ZERO by the year 2050.

Yet another cause for concern is just how little we *actually* know about the richness of biodiversity in the first place. The dimensions of biodiversity are hard to get to grips with and are thus relatively poorly quantified. Hence documenting ecosystem and biodiversity patterns is truly difficult. Even knowledge of taxonomic diversity, the best known dimension of biodiversity, is incomplete and strongly biased toward the species level, mega fauna, temperate systems, and components most used by humans. This results in significant knowledge gaps, especially regarding the status of tropical systems, marine and freshwater biota, plants, invertebrates, microorganisms and subterranean biota.

For these reasons, our best estimates of the total number of species on Earth range anywhere from 5 million to 30 million. We simply do not know with any greater certainty. Yet, irrespective of the actual global species richness, it is clear that the 1.7–2 million species that have been formally identified represent only a small portion of total species diversity.

While we consider ourselves fairly knowledgeable about – or at least have put a name to – over half of nearly 100,000 estimated species of vertebrates and around 300,000 estimated plant species, there are other important species groups about which really we know very little. We have names for less than a third of around 200,000 estimated crustacean species (barnacles, crabs, lobsters, shrimps, krill and so on). This is about the same for about 300,000 estimated mollusc species (snails, clams, squids, octopuses etc.). Our knowledge of the estimated 400,000 or so nematodes (roundworms) is, frankly, minimal. And the same goes for protoctista (algae, slime mold, ameboids etcetera) and chelicerata (arachnids). Of fungi, we have named around 200,000 species of an estimated 1.5 million species. And for insects and myriapods (centipedes and millipedes) we have managed to name a grand total of around 1 million of an estimated total of 8 million species.

So we really do not know much about the wildlife around us. We do not have much idea as to what is happening to the populations of these unknown species – nor, perhaps more importantly, do we really have much clue as to the potential impact upon our lives if they were to disappear. But we can be reasonably certain that the disappearance of many of the species that we have evolved with will not end well for our own species.

Let's just take one insect that we do know something about: the humble bee. This useful creature provides pollinating services with a commercial value estimated at around $300 million per year in the UK and $14 billion in the USA. Yet populations of bees have been collapsing worldwide, with corresponding high level concerns about food production. According to the Executive Director of the UN Environment program:

> **Of the 100 crop species that provide 90 per cent of the world's food, over 70 are pollinated by bees – and their populations have been collapsing worldwide.[8]**

Various studies have linked the worrying decline in bee numbers to reduced plant diversity – especially in areas of large commercial monoculture. The French government has even launched a project to sow a variety of nectar-bearing flowers along roadsides in an attempt to stem the decline in honeybees.[9] Put bluntly, given that such a high proportion of the food in our stomachs requires bee pollination, our survival depends upon the survival of the bee. And we are only beginning to understand the complex web of life that the bee depends upon to survive.

Yet the bee is just one insect superfamily – what of the impact of the other nearly 8 million insects and myriapods that could be on the verge of extinction without our knowing about it? There is simply no way that we can tell what could happen if there were large-scale extinction of such species. But we do know that it most likely wouldn't be good news.

Much of the problem comes down to habitat destruction, and one habitat that is being relentlessly destroyed is the rainforests. In the past six decades, 60 percent of rainforest has been destroyed and two-thirds of what remains is fragmented – making it more susceptible to being cleared in the near future. And such destruction is proceeding at a furious pace.

> **In the past decade around 13 million hectares of the world's forests, an area the size of England, have been lost each year.**

Most of this was tropical forest razed for agriculture. Much of the tree felling was illegal.[10]

Perhaps even more sobering than what is happening on land and in the air, is how we have been exploiting the oceans over the years. In every ocean in the world, one or more important targeted fish stock has been classified as collapsed, overfished, or fished to their maximum sustainable levels, and at least one-quarter of important commercial fisheries are designated with a high degree of certainty as "overharvested." In 2007, the UN FAO estimated that 52 percent of fish stocks are fully exploited, 19 percent are overexploited, 8 percent are depleted – with the remainder either moderately exploited or recovering from depletion.[11]

As the MEA biodiversity synthesis report states:

> Fishing pressure is so strong that over much of the world the biomass of fish targeted in fisheries (including that of both the target species and those caught incidentally) has been reduced by 90 percent relative to levels prior to the onset of industrial fishing.

As much as 90 percent of targeted fish have been removed by industrial fishing.

Commercial fishing largely targets the top predators, which are also the larger fish in the ocean. Such overfishing of these large species – sharks, tuna, marlin, swordfish and so on – has changed the composition of the oceans, modified interactions among species, and resulted in the targeting by fishing fleets of previously less desirable species that feed lower in the food chain.

Figures 10.2 and 10.3 show the estimated global marine fish catch from 1970 to 2000, and the trend in average depth of catches between 1950 and 2000. The tonnage of global fisheries landings peaked in the late 1980s and is now declining despite considerable excess fishing capacity and tremendous continuing human effort to catch and sell fish. An indication that it is getting harder to find fish to catch is that the average depth of catch has gone from around 170 meters in the 1950s to nearly 300 meters in 2000. It would appear that on a global level the easier-to-catch, shallower species have already been sucked-up or poisoned.

Rather than being a budget food for children to squirt ketchup on to, perhaps fish fingers are destined to become an expensive delicacy. After all, before pollution and overharvesting came close to wiping out the oyster from the waters of Britain, they were a subsistence food of the poor. In fact, it was only deliberate artificial breeding that saved the oyster from extinction in the UK.[12]

Another impact of human activity is that the distribution of (a reduced set of) species on Earth is becoming more homogeneous. All agricultural animals do well in this human-dominated world and the genetic diversity of these is also being whittled down to the most productive (see Global Trend 5: Water and Food). Domestic pets have also done well over the millennia – both in our homes and those that have escaped into the wild to fend for themselves,

Figure 10.2: Estimated global marine fish catch, 1970–2000

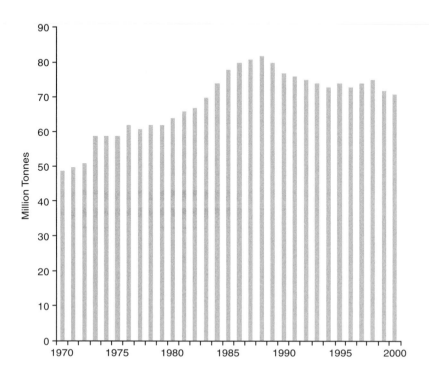

Source: Millennium Ecosystem Assessment, 2005

usually at the expense of natural, local species. The same applies to a host of pests that follow us around to scavenge off our wastes, plague our crops, or suck our blood (literally*).

> There are not many corners of the world today where the natural flora and fauna has not been adversely affected by species introductions, both intentionally and inadvertently, through increased human travel and trade.

---

* For example, the nasty little Asian tiger mosquito has been hitching rides around the planet with human transport systems and is extending its scope across North America and Europe. Its life-cycle seems ideally suited to that of the human world and there are increasing concerns about its ability to spread diseases such as dengue and yellow fever.

Figure 10.3: Trend in mean depth of catch 1950–2000

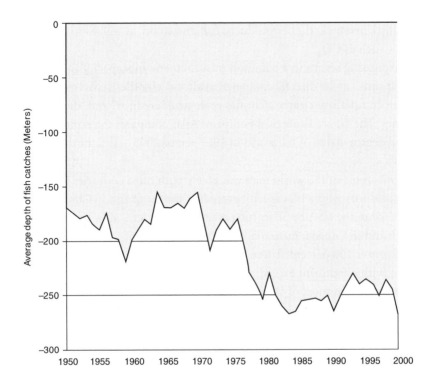

Source: Millennium Ecosystem Assessment, 2005

But all this goes further than purely ecosystem and biodiversity loss. A good deal of it comes down to whether human's insatiable demand for ecosystem services exceeds the finite capacity of the "biosphere" to supply that demand on a sustainable basis. In other words, whether the capacity of ecosystems – or "biocapacity" – can meet the demand and regenerate given the levels of exploitation to which they are subjected by humans: the "ecological footprint." The Global Footprint Network (GFN) was established in 2003 to improve the scientific rigor behind "ecological footprint accounting" and to assess whether humans are on a sustainable development path or not. The ecological footprint metric measures the amount of biologically productive land and water area required to produce all the resources an individual, population, or activity consumes, and to absorb the waste they generate, given prevailing technology and resource management practices. This area can then be compared with biocapacity: the ability of a given amount of area to produce crops, livestock, timber products, fish and so on, as well as to sequester wastes – such as CO_2.[13]

By expressing results in a common measurement, biocapacity and ecological footprints can be directly compared against each other across the world. And this comparison clearly identifies ecological "creditor" and "debtor" countries. The GFN's Ecological Footprint Atlas compares the ecological creditor and debtor status of the world in 1961 versus 2005 – and the differences are stark.

In 1961, most of the world map was green, with most countries being ecological creditors with a biocapacity exceeding the footprint: in China by up to 50 percent; the USA by 50 to 100 percent; the Soviet Union by 100 to 150 percent; and in Canada, Australia, New Zealand, most of Latin America and Africa by over 150 percent. There were only a limited number of ecological debtors, with a footprint exceeding the biocapacity: in India and Pakistan by 0 to 50 percent; in most of Western European by 0 to 100 percent; Egypt by 50 to 100 percent; and in Israel and Japan by 100 to 150 percent.

But by 2005, the global situation had dramatically changed. The global map had changed from green to largely brown. Now the majority of countries are ecological debtors, where their footprints exceed their biocapacity. Of course all the old ecological debtors are still debtors but now their footprints exceed biocapacity by even more: in many cases by over 150 percent. Now most nations in Eastern Europe, North and Central America, North Africa, the Middle East and Asia (including China) are also ecological debtors with a footprint exceeding biocapacity: mostly between 50 and 150 percent. Several sub-Saharan African nations have also joined the ecological debtor bandwagon.

The only ecological creditors left seem to be those *big* countries with a lot of space and relatively few people: Canada, South American nations, Russia, Australia, New Zealand and some African nations. Yet even for these ecological creditor nations a net surplus of biocapacity does not necessarily mean these countries are managing their ecological assets in a sustainable manner either as they may simply be exporting all their resources to debtor nations.

Overall the trend is clearly towards more ecological debtors with footprints exceeding biocapacity – often by over 150 percent.

With demand upon ecosystem services exceeding the capacity of the planet to meet that demand the projected trajectory is clearly unsustainable. In other words, turning resources into waste faster than waste can be turned back into resources puts us into "global ecological overshoot," depleting the very resources on which human life and biodiversity depend. As such, it now takes the Earth one year and five months to regenerate and absorb what humans use and dump in a year. And what of the future? Using UN data for moderate forecast scenarios for "business as usual" continuing current population and consumption trends the GFN computes that:

While today humanity uses the equivalent of 1.4 planets to provide the resources we use and to absorb our waste, by the middle of the century – if not earlier – we will need the equivalent of two Earths to support us.[14]

From where we are now, it will take rapid reduction of global ecosystem service consumption and dumping in order to get back to an ecologically sustainable path by 2050.

Threats and opportunities

Without a doubt, mankind has accomplished a lot in our short time on this planet. From humble beginnings we have invented gizmos and ways of doing things that cocoon our modern daily lives from the often harsh laws of nature. But this is an illusion: human beings are not separate from nature, we are part of it. What is more, despite our utter dependence upon the natural balances of things, there is clear evidence of a relentless increase in human pressure on the very ecosystems that support us. A whole host of organizations, such as the World Wildlife Fund (WWF), continue to work hard to bring the issues of human footprint, ecosystem decline and biodiversity loss onto the global agenda. Yet such issues are uncomfortable and hard for many to stomach. Perhaps as a result, efforts to raise awareness and to modify behaviors often seem unable to make any lasting impact beyond a large-scale change of Christmas card designs. This is a slur on our disregard of the consequences of our actions upon the environment around us: an environment which we, as one of several million other species, have been evolving with for a long time.

Failure to recognize and face-up to the Global Trends in ecosystem and biodiversity decline is perhaps the single biggest threat that they pose.

After all, in his book *Collapse: How Societies Choose to Fail or Succeed,* Professor Jared Diamond identified obviously destructive practices such as deforestation, habitat destruction, over-hunting and fishing, and the intro- duction of invasive species as sparking the rapid decline of past societies.[15] The challenge for humans of the 21st century is to avoid making the same mistakes.

With a failure to recognize such trends, it would seem that our actions will continue to cause losses in biodiversity and changes in ecosystem services at an increasing pace. While extinction has always been a natural component of evolution, human beings' actions are considerably increasing the rate at which other species' populations are declining. And, unchecked, such human driv- ers of ecosystem decline will inevitably have a significant detrimental impact upon societies, organizations and individuals – possibly starting with a dom- ino effect in the food chain.

Exploitation of ecosystems beyond their capacity for regeneration or absorbing wastes is not a good idea. Beyond a "get rich quick" mentality it makes no sense and will cause untold problems in the medium and longer term. While many individuals may benefit from activities leading to det- rimental ecosystem change, improved valuation techniques and growing knowledge about ecosystems reveal that the full costs borne by society often exceed the benefits. Even when the benefits and costs of ecosystem changes are not entirely known, a precautionary approach may be justified when costs could be high or changes irreversible. The pattern of "winners" and "losers" associated with ecosystem changes has not, perhaps, been adequately taken into account in traditional political, social, organizational or house- hold decisions. On the other hand, some of the world's poorest can only survive today by plundering nature, yet are the first of many to lose out from biodiversity collapse or decline in ecosystem services. Such practices are not sustainable and the world's political and business leaders would leave a tre- mendously positive legacy for future generations by implementing solutions to such problems.

In light of all such threats the recommendations made by the Global Footprint Network seem to make sense: there is a need for global coopera- tion and engagement at all levels of government, business and individuals to ensure more ecologically sustainable ways of doing things in the 21st cen- tury. Global agreements, tighter governance, greater scientific understanding, more responsible practices and changed consumer habits will all be needed to combat such profound ecological threats. Supporting environmental groups in their push for biodiversity and ecosystem conservation programs is probably in the interests of all. Establishing guidelines relating to new species* introduction seems the best way to contain this threat in the face of increased international travel and trade.

Beyond the clear negative implications of ecosystem damage upon societies and individual well-being, what of the impact on business? Pavan Sukhdev, formerly head of Deutsche Bank's global markets business in India, led a study called "The Economics of Ecosystems and Biodiversity" (TEEB), which found that preserving biodiversity in areas most at risk of species loss would yield between $4,000 billion and $5,000 billion a year in business benefits. The *Financial Times* Special Report on Sustainable Business article "Bad for biodiversity is often bad for business" quoted Pavan Sukhdev as saying:

> All economic activity and most of human well-being whether in urban or non-urban setting is based on a healthy, functioning environment. Nature's multiple and complex values have direct economic impacts.[16]

Dax Lovegrove, head of business and industry at the WWF, was also quoted:

> There is a dangerous assumption that companies can continue to rely on ecosystem services, especially when those ecosystems are in such rapid decline... Businesses need to think differently or fail.

Such views are not confined to "green" campaigners. Certainly the cost associated with a change in ecosystem can be huge. As just one example, the 1990s Newfoundland cod-fisheries collapse alone cost an estimated $2 billion and the loss of tens of thousands of jobs. As a result of such high-profile business failures, a survey of top executives conducted by the consultancy McKinsey found that over half believed biodiversity should be one of the top ten items on the corporate agenda. More encouragingly, about six in ten saw protecting biodiversity as more of an opportunity than a threat.

---

* Including genetically engineered.

So what about the opportunities in the ecosystem and biodiversity Global Trend? The WWF's Living Planet Report 2010* provides some scope for optimism:

> There are emerging solutions, at both national and local levels. Far-sighted governments will see the opportunity to gain national economic and societal competitiveness through approaches such as valuing nature and allocating resources in a manner that provides societal prosperity and resilience.[17]

The same goes for far-sighted companies and individuals. Opportunities will abound as markets become more aware of the human footprint, and demand is likely to increase for products that take into account the ecological impact at every step of the supply chain. Companies can also use their leverage to drive positive, ecologically sustainable consumer habits. More research will likely be needed to develop and implement waste management solutions that are geared towards reducing harmful waste and pollution. Where such technologies already exist, they often need improving to make them economical and applicable on a large scale. With increased regulations and resource prices pushing up costs for businesses, there is likely to be a need for technologies that help improve resource efficiency – reducing usage and wastage of natural resources.[18]

We have seen that a narrow focus on short-term drive for profits is an irresponsible business approach that often leads to negative implications in the broader society. In any case, the development of more ecologically sustainable models of responsible business stewardship is likely to lead to more stable businesses, and improved society and environmental conditions for business growth.

There is still plenty of uncertainty with how this Global Trend will play-out, and this should weigh heavily on current decisions at all levels. Paying more attention to the early-warning signals in ecosystem change will help prepare for potential, and quite possibly sudden, negative future impacts. In the past, natural climate and ecological changes have, for the most part, been slow enough for many species – including human beings – to adapt. But with the frenetic changes of the last decades, such gradual change cannot be assumed.

---

* Coproduced with the Global Footprint Network and the Zoological Society of London.

Ecological "tipping points" are capable of sparking ecosystem collapse of proportions that could be extremely detrimental to human well-being. In addition, loss of ecosystem and biodiversity resilience increases human vulnerability to other Global Trends – notably climate change. And, conversely, anthropogenic climate change (see Global Trend 4) is highly likely to exert yet more pressure on natural ecosystems.[19]

Clearly, major decisions need to be made relating to ecosystem decline and biodiversity loss and how we should react to it. Uncertainty is no excuse for inaction. After all, even with uncertainties related to developing lung cancer, most smokers have changed their ways.

Mother Nature has certainly extended a helping hand to mankind over thousands of years. Perhaps now is time to repay the favor.

Firm empirical evidence to identify specific causal links between ecosystem decline and human well-being may not be forthcoming for another few decades. However, it does not take a rocket scientist to predict that, unless humanity responds in an appropriate manner, the way this Global Trend is going is likely to cause considerable discomfort across various "quality of life" dimensions – including economic, social, cultural, and health dimensions.

Health – and its changing nature – is the topic of the next Global Trend.

Global Trend 11

Health

"Smallpox was the worst disease in history. It killed more people than all the wars in history. In the last century it killed 500 million people. In 1967 the World Health Organization embarked on what was an outrageous program to eradicate the disease... and in 1980 we declared the globe free of smallpox... Soon we may see the eradication of polio."[1]

Dr. Larry Brilliant, Physician, Epidemiologist, Former Director of Google.org.* Participated in the World Health Organization (WHO) Smallpox Eradication Program

"85 percent of the global disease burden for cardiovascular disease is in developing countries... yet 90 percent of the resources are in the 'West.' Who is at risk? Anyone who visits Africa... if you get chest pains, shortness of breath, sweating; you are having a heart attack. Will you fly back to the US, Europe? No. You will die."[2]

Dr. Ernest Madu, Cardiologist and Clinical Investigator, Founder of the Heart Institute of the Caribbean

These quotes of Doctors Brilliant and Madu reflect the dual-nature of changing health panoramas entering the 21st century. On the one hand there are the infectious diseases – resulting from the transmission of pathogens such as viruses and bacteria. And on the other are the slow-progressing, long-lasting or recurrent chronic diseases such as heart disease, stroke, cancer, chronic respiratory diseases and diabetes.

---

* Google.org is the charitable arm of Google – the Internet search engine company.

On the infectious disease side, smallpox was truly awful. A picture of an afflicted child covered from head to toe by the hideous blisters and hard, deep pustules has to be one of the most moving images you could ever see. With an overall mortality rate of 30–35 percent – and up to 80 percent in children – the airborne *Variola major* virus, once inhaled, showed no mercy. Malignant and hemorrhagic forms of smallpox were usually fatal. Throughout the world everyone from kings to paupers was terrified of the disease which attained deity of death status in some cultures. The mummified body of Ramses V of Egypt indicates death from smallpox. Those lucky enough to survive the onslaught of the invasive virus could be blinded or suffer limb deformities for life. The terrifically lucky were "just" covered with lifelong scarring. As recently as 1967, the WHO estimated that 15 million people contracted the disease.

To eradicate such a cruel killer and maimer really does indicate that human beings are, indeed, capable of amazing things. It was no mean feat, taking concerted and sustained effort, dedication and organization at a global level to outsmart such a sinister virus. Yet, we are also capable of complicating health issues. The disparity between the rich and poor worlds is an ever present factor in ensuring that some live in deplorable conditions in which they inevitably become sick, and others live sedentary or opulent lifestyles that are simply not healthy. With both rich and poor worlds providing the conditions for incubating new diseases and generating new health problems, our actions in this globally connected world also enable the rapid transmission of new diseases with transport and travel habits and the transfer of unhealthy lifestyle habits.

Thus, having accomplished incredible goals in health during the 20th century, new challenges are emerging that will present distinct threats and novel opportunities for improving health and extending well-being in the 21st century. In the World Economic Forum's Global Risks Landscape 2011, the world's leaders recognize the dual infectious and chronic disease battle fronts. Infectious diseases are perceived as likely to cause global problems within the next ten years and have an economic impact of over $250 billion. Chronic diseases are deemed to be even more likely to present problems in the next decade, and with an even greater economic impact of nearly $500 billion. In fact, chronic diseases are rated on a similar risk-impact level to that of global water security. Of course, such a cold assessment says nothing of the human suffering caused by either infectious or chronic health conditions.[3]

Before delving into the specific evolution patterns of infectious and chronic diseases, let's take a step back and ask the question: *What is health, and to whom should health-care be directed?* According to the constitution of the World Health Organization:

> Health is a state of complete physical, mental and social well-being and not merely the absence of disease or infirmity. The enjoyment of the highest attainable standard of health is one of the fundamental rights of every human being without distinction of race, religion, political belief, economic or social condition. The health of all people is fundamental to the attainment of peace and security and is dependent upon the fullest co-operation of individuals and states.[4]

Article 25, Paragraph 1 of the United Nations Declaration of Human Rights states that:

> Everyone has the right to a standard of living adequate for the health and well-being of himself and of his family, including food, clothing, housing and medical care and necessary social services.[5]

Yet, it is plain to see that we live in a world that still does not meet such high ideals. If health really is a human right, then why are so many people not covered by basic health-care systems? Is it the responsibility of the state? And in any case, how attainable is this ideal and how relevant is it?

The priority status given to – and the ensuing political and social controversy surrounding – President Barack Obama's healthcare reforms in the USA demonstrate the complex and emotional issues behind this topic. Issues of health and healthcare provision in the 21st century are fiercely debated across many countries. While the debates are very different in character depending upon the nation, or group of nations in question, certain things are the same. For example:

According to WHO, health is a top concern for citizens in all countries.[6]

When people are asked to name the most important problems that they and their families are currently facing, financial worries often come out on top, with health a close second. Of most countries, between 30 percent and

50 percent of populations cite health as the most important concern before other issues. In certain nations this proportion goes over 60 percent – perhaps corresponding to where good health cannot be taken for granted, such as Bangladesh and Uganda.

Despite the worldwide importance given by citizens to the issue of health, the divergence in quality and scope of healthcare access between nations is shocking. We are living in a bipolar world regarding healthcare, divided by a line called "wealth." Citizens of those countries with a GDP per person in excess of $20,000 – such as the western European and Scandinavian nations, Czech Republic, Slovenia, the USA, Canada, Japan, Taiwan, Hong Kong, South Korea, Singapore, Australia, New Zealand, Brunei, Israel, Kuwait, UAE, Qatar, Oman – can all expect to live beyond 75 years old.[7]

Yet, poor sub-Saharan countries with GDP per person of under $2,000 – such as Zimbabwe, Congo, Central African Republic, Somalia, Burundi, Mali, Sierra Leone, Mozambique, Chad, Zambia, Lesotho, and Guinea-Bissau, have life expectancies of under 50. Violence and war will take their toll in some of these places, but poor health is probably the bigger underlying cause of death. For example:

Even in war-torn Iraq in 2009, the average life expectancy was still just under 70, while the poor health conditions in Afghanistan lead to life expectancy of under 45 years.

Perhaps even crueler in these poor countries are the statistics for children dying.

In the poor sub-Saharan states and Afghanistan over 200 children die before the age of 5 for every thousand live births. This compares with much less than 10 child deaths per thousand births for most rich countries.

With child mortality rates in developing nations of over ten times higher than in developed nations, there are many knock-on negative social and economic impacts. Such problems are exacerbated by the lack of availability of healthcare for the poor – often because it is beyond their financial reach or simply because there is inadequate infrastructure in place in poorer nations to institute improvement programs.[8]

It has been shown repeatedly that poverty is strongly correlated to low levels of general health. With poverty come many problems including lack of hygiene – and other social ills such as drug use and violence. Furthermore, poor countries often lack adequate healthcare systems and many lives are lost due to lack of treatment. Yet more lives are lost due to lack of proper mechanisms to contain the spread of infectious diseases. Nevertheless, even though things may look bad now, they were a lot worse before. In fact, there has been considerable global improvement. For example:

If children were still dying at the 1978 rates, there would have been 16.2 million deaths globally in 2006. In fact, there were *only* 9.5 million deaths as a result of better education, better drugs, improved access to water, better sanitation and improved antenatal care.

A good part of the improvements in worldwide health are due to greater allocation of funds towards healthcare related issues. According to the WHO *World Health Report*, the global health economy grew faster than gross domestic product (GDP) from 2000 to 2005. In absolute terms, adjusted for inflation, this represented a 35 percent growth in the world's expenditure on health. With such public and private healthcare investment there has been a tendency of convergence towards improved health in a large part of the world.

Yet, in both developed and developing nations, spending on health services most often benefits the rich more than the poor. In other words, the people with the most financial means, and whose needs for healthcare are often less, consume the most care. Those with the least financial means and, generally, with the greatest health-related problems, have access to the least care. Thus the substantial progress in health over recent decades has been deeply unequal between rich and poor in both developed and developing nations. Even more illuminating is that many are actually pushed into poverty *because* of healthcare costs:

Over 100 million people annually fall into poverty through paying for high healthcare expenses.

In addition, while several countries have, undoubtedly, made great improvements in health, others, particularly in the African region, have stagnated or even lost ground. On the one hand, many countries such as Oman, Mongolia and Morocco made significant improvements in reducing child deaths of the under-5s, from over 150 deaths per 1000 children in 1975 to considerably less than 50 in 2006. On the other hand, poorer countries such as Zambia are increasingly lagging behind, and are still recording similar levels to 1975 at around 160 deaths per 1000 children under five.

The online resource Worldmapper claims to show "the world as you've never seen it before," and certainly in terms of public and private health spending it lives up to the promise. Using WHO data, Worldmapper creates some perspective-challenging images that can only be likened to those "wibbly-wobbly" mirrors in fairgrounds... you know, the ones that make you look short and fat or tall and thin. By re-sizing the area of each country according to its total public or private healthcare expenditure the world as we know it changes form into something really rather grotesque. The Northern American countries, Europe and Japan take on a form of utter obesity for both public and private spending. The Latin American, African and Asian continents, on the other hand, become emaciated for private spending – and completely skeletal for public health spending.[9]

In most developed countries, especially the USA, western Europe and Japan, a combination of public and private systems of health insurance covers a substantial portion of the population. However, sustainability of these systems is always a matter of debate. For example, in the USA more than 46 million people are not covered by any form of health insurance. The rest of the population is covered under schemes which are placed under more and more stress.[10]

In the USA alone, government spending on healthcare is expected to double from $1.6 trillion to $3.1 trillion between 2002 and 2012.[11]

Higher spending on health is generally associated with better outcomes in terms of lower infant mortality and increased life expectancy. Nonetheless, living for more years is not necessarily desirable if many of those extra years are spent suffering from poor health. What is more important is the concept that people live longer lives and in better states of health. A common measure used to summarize this healthy life expectancy is the "health adjusted life expectancy" (HALE). This is an estimate of the number of healthy years, free from disability or disease, that a person can expect to live based on current trends.*

---

* The average number of years spent in unhealthy states is subtracted from the overall life expectancy, taking into account the relative severity of such states.

Figure 11.1, the WHO *World Health Report* graph of HALE against total
health expenditure highlights some insightful issues. Firstly, it confirms
the general trend that increased spending leads to a longer, healthier life.
Residents of those countries that spend the most on health – such as Sweden,
Germany and the USA – also tend to have longer, healthy lives. For example:

**Sierra Leone spends less than $100 per person on healthcare and
the result is an average healthy life expectancy of less than 30 years.
Conversely, Sweden has a per capita health expenditure of over $2,500
and the average health-adjusted life expectancy is over 70 years.**

However, a second observation is that some countries appear to achieve
longer, healthy lives with less expense. The best performing country, with
average HALE exceeding 75 years, is Japan, which spends less than Sweden,
Germany or USA. Even more pronounced is Finland, which manages to
achieve an average HALE of 70 years – which is higher than that in the USA
for at least $1,500 less expense. Some other surprises can be seen, for example:

**The average person in Tajikistan can expect to have an equally long and
healthy life as the average American: about 69 years. But the level of
healthcare spending is over 25 times higher in the USA.**

Clearly, other factors are also at play such as diet and lifestyles.
Nevertheless, as the WHO report states: "Such differences suggest that how,
for what and for whom money is spent matters considerably."

The WHO outlines several counter-productive issues and practices in the
industrialized world that complicate the allocation of health spending. For example, there has been disproportionate focus of health expenditure on hospital
treatment and curative services rather than primary prevention and health promotion measures that could prevent up to 70 percent of the burden in the first
place. Also, the excessive sub-specialization of healthcare providers and the narrow focus of many health programs has become a major source of inefficiency
that prevents more effective holistic approaches for continuing care. In OECD
countries, the 35 percent growth in the number of doctors in the last 15 years
was driven by rising numbers of specialists (up by nearly 50 percent between
1990 and 2005)– compared with only a 20 percent increase in general practitioners. Furthermore, as many as 25 percent of 65–69-year-olds and 50 percent

Figure 11.1: Health-adjusted life expectancy (HALE) and health expenditure

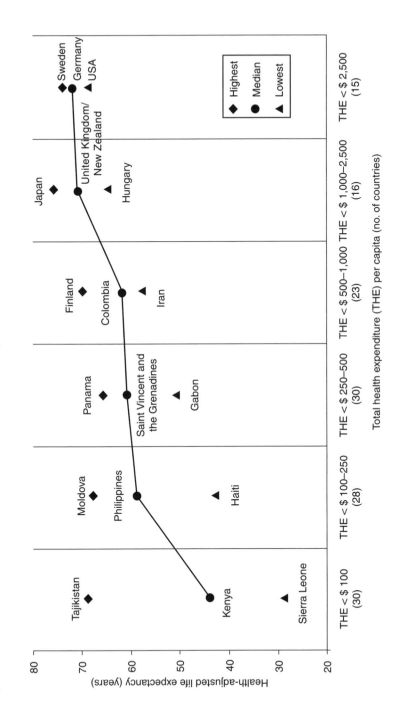

Source: *The World Health Report 2008*, WHO

of 80–84-year-olds in developed countries are affected by two or more chronic health conditions simultaneously. This creates higher levels of complexity for service delivery, which increases costs beyond the drugs or treatments themselves.

As a result of their differing healthcare contexts, profiles of major causes of death differ considerably between developing and developed countries. In high-income countries the top ten leading causes of death (with the number of people killed) in 2002 were: coronary heart disease (1.34 million); stroke and other cerebrovascular diseases (0.77 million); trachea, bronchus, lung cancers (0.46 million); lower respiratory infections (0.34 million); chronic obstructive pulmonary disease (0.30 million); colon and rectal cancers (0.26 million); Alzheimer's and other dementias (0.22 million); diabetes mellitus (0.22 million); breast cancer (0.15 million); stomach cancer (0.14 million).

In low-income countries the top ten killers are: coronary heart disease (3.10 million); lower respiratory infections (2.86 million); HIV/ AIDS (2.14 million); perinatal conditions* (1.83 million); stroke and other cerebrovascular diseases (1.72 million); diarrheal diseases (1.54 million); malaria (1.24 million); tuberculosis (1.10 million); chronic obstructive pulmonary disease (0.88 million); road traffic accidents (0.53million).

Therefore, both high- and low-income countries have something in common: the largely chronic conditions of coronary heart disease, respiratory infections, strokes and pulmonary disease are big killers of both rich and poor. Beyond these nonselective illnesses the main causes of death for the rich are other chronic conditions such as cancers, dementias, and diabetes (killing a total of 1.45 million). For the poor, nearly 2 million die around the period of childbirth (perinatal conditions); over 2 million of HIV/ AIDS and a total of nearly 4 million died in 2002 because of the other infectious diseases of diarrhea, malaria and tuberculosis.

Therefore, chronic diseases account for almost all deaths in developed countries, but these same conditions often kill more people in developing countries. In addition, poorer nations suffer high death tolls from potentially preventable infectious diseases.

Diarrhea, malaria and tuberculosis alone kill nearly as many poor as all the top ten rich country causes of death put together.[12]

---

* Relating to the period around childbirth, especially the five months before and one month after birth.

The fact that road traffic accidents are also a major killer in poor countries is alarming for other non-health related reasons.

Another important difference between the rich and poor is the age when people die.

In high-income countries 70 percent of deaths are among people over 70; 29 percent for those between 15 and 69; and 1 percent for children from 0 to 14. In low-income countries only 22 percent reach the age of 70; 44 percent die between 15 and 69; and an incredible 34 percent die before age 14.

As you would expect, the worst black-spots are in sub-Saharan Africa, but South Asia and the Middle East and North Africa also have high death rates in pre-14-year-olds.

To put these statistics into perspective in terms of percentage of global population: less than 14 percent of people live in high-income countries; whereas over 50 percent live in low-income nations. The remainder of around 36 percent live in emerging market, middle-income countries.

Clearly, infectious diseases remain a prolific problem – mainly in poorer countries where various poverty-related conditions conspire to undermine improvement efforts. Yet, as the history of smallpox shows, infectious diseases may be more common amongst the poor, but the rich are certainly not immune. Another example of the vulnerability of everyone to the spread of such diseases was the influenza pandemic between 1918 and 1920.

Within only 11 months of the outbreak of "Spanish flu" there were 20 million deaths. The total death toll rose to anywhere between 50 and 100 million – representing 3 to 6 percent of the world population. Young, *healthy* adults were the most susceptible. About 500 million people – or one-third of the world's population – were infected as a result of increased travel as more rapid modes of transport made it easier for soldiers, sailors, and civilians to spread the disease.[13]

Transport systems and travel habits have become part of 21st-century lifestyles, and as such, risks of global infectious disease pandemics are heightened. A significant portion of healthcare coverage by the media in the past decade has been related with spread of infectious diseases. In the last ten years, there were several outbreaks of viral infectious diseases including SARS in 2003, H5N1 "avian" flu in 2008, and H1N1 "swine" flu in 2009. All of these diseases originated in poorer nations, but many people were surprised by the global reach and speed of transmission, as carriers of the virus travelled in airplanes to other parts of the world. The WHO confirmed that few countries escaped without any H1N1-related deaths.[14]

In the USA alone, the Centers for Disease Control and Prevention (CDC) estimate that between 43 million and 89 million cases of H1N1 occurred between April 2009 and April 2010. During this time there were between about 195,000 and 403,000 H1N1-related hospitalizations and between about 8,870 and 18,300 H1N1-related deaths. [15]

In August 2010, the WHO declared the H1N1 pandemic over and these diseases to be largely under control. In retrospect, some questioned the seriousness of the H1N1 outbreak when compared with seasonal flu, which claims between 250,000 and 500,000 lives worldwide each year.[16] Yet the issue of pandemics remains high on many experts list of concerns. In the Centers for Disease Control and Prevention paper relating recent infectious disease outbreaks to the Spanish flu pandemic, the authors (Taubenberger and Morens) state that:

> Even with modern antiviral and antibacterial drugs, vaccines, and prevention knowledge, the return of a pandemic virus equivalent in pathogenicity to the virus of 1918 would likely kill >100 million people worldwide. A pandemic virus with the (alleged) pathogenic potential of some recent H5N1 outbreaks could cause substantially more deaths.

Therefore, infectious disease pandemics originating in poor countries and rapidly spreading to the rest of the world remain a significant global threat.

Nevertheless, at present chronic diseases still constitute the lion's share of mortality, representing 60 percent of worldwide deaths. In 2005, 35 million people died from chronic disease.[17]

According to the WHO *World Health Report*, increasing levels of urbanization, aging populations and globalized lifestyle changes will combine to make chronic and noncommunicable diseases – including depression, diabetes,

Figure 11.2: Past and predicted impact of chronic and infectious disease 2004–2030

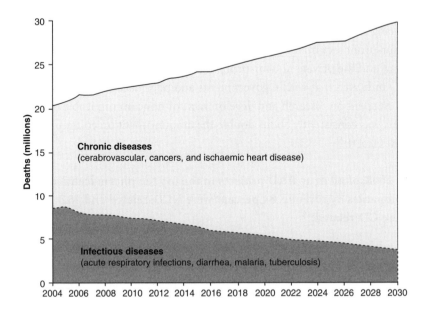

Source: *The World Health Report* 2008, WHO

cardiovascular diseases, cerebrovascular diseases and cancers – increasingly important causes of morbidity and mortality worldwide. Figure 11.2 shows the forecast future Global Trend towards increasing impact of such chronic and noncommunicable health conditions. Over the last few decades there has been an increase in deaths from chronic and noncommunicable conditions of cancers, heart failure and stroke, and the forecast is for this trend to continue. After all, by 2050, the world will count 2 billion people over the age of 60, around 85 percent of whom will be living in today's developing countries, mostly in urban areas.

In contrast to an increasing number of deaths from chronic disease, the forecast is for a Global Trend of decreasing impact of infectious diseases such as acute respiratory infections, tuberculosis, malaria and diarrheal diseases as general living conditions and access to adequate healthcare systems are expected to improve across the globe. However, this could be a dangerous assumption if continued efforts are not made to fight such tenacious diseases in poor countries.

Such past and forecast trends towards a greater burden of chronic diseases have affected levels of drug research and development (R&D). Total global financing for health R&D exceeded US$ 160 billion in 2005: with the private for-profit sector accounting for 51 percent of this, the public sector 41 percent and the private not-for-profit sector 8 percent. A 2009 study for the WHO indicated that within governments and pharmaceutical companies, the amount spent on research and development of noncommunicable diseases (NCD) was consistently about double the amount spent on communicable diseases (CD).*

In 2008, of all drug R&D projects in the top ten pharmaceutical companies by revenue, 84 percent were NCD-related and 15.3 percent were CD-related.[18]

The public sector has a similarly high level of R&D effort towards NCDs: cancer drugs constitute 31.5 percent of drugs in development; mental health drugs 22.4 percent and cardiovascular disease drugs 11 percent of relevant projects. Publicly funded cancer research alone absorbs the equivalent of – or more than – what flows into research for all CDs. Within the private not-for-profit sector, NCDs are also widely covered by charity funding, while CD funding remains almost exclusively in the realm of private foundations. Of the 2,900 medicines in development in 2008, only 13 were for tropical infectious diseases.

As a result of such skewed R&D funding towards chronic diseases and NCDs, there are concerns that the current system of drug development is neglecting diseases of the poor, and can be blamed for inequalities of healthcare between developed and developing countries. Worse still, such distortions in drug development could result in losing the battle against certain infectious

---

* The terms NCD and CD approximately correlate to the respective terms 'chronic disease' and 'infectious disease' and are often used interchangeably. NCDs include chronic, long duration and generally slow progression conditions such as heart disease, stroke, cancer, asthma, diabetes, osteoporosis, Alzheimer's disease and others. Yet NCDs are distinguished by their non-infectious cause. Not all chronic diseases are NCDs: for example, HIV/AIDS is a lasting medical condition requiring chronic care management, but is caused by transmissible infections.

diseases in poorer nations – especially in the light of increasing resistance of some diseases to existing drugs. For example, the primary drugs for tuberculosis are over forty years old and are quickly losing their effectiveness. Multidrug-resistant tuberculosis is already running rampant in endemic areas, and without badly needed novel compounds, it will continue to spread.[19] Even when effective compounds are found, inadequate funding for appropriate roll-out can severely restrict effectiveness – as was the case with artemisinin and malaria.[20]

Drug development costs have increased considerably over the last decades as there has been a greater use of high-cost services and procedures. For example:

The average cost to bring one drug to the market in 2010 was $1 billion, although other studies have results ranging from $500 million to $2 billion.

With such high development costs, pharmaceutical companies are keen to recoup investments as fast as possible once a drug is launched. This is especially true since the clock is ticking with patent lives of around 20 years – 10 to 13 of which are spent in drug development. In order to recoup investment and return a profit within the available time-frame, large affluent markets are ideal targets. In addition, it is less risky for companies to develop drugs for which there is already a known and increasing demand. It would seem that there is often little financial incentive for pharmaceutical companies to develop drugs for relatively poor markets, and "non-profitable" diseases that are predicted to decline. Such a model of drug development leads to a reduced realm of innovation and serving the same wealthier customers, leaving many important areas of healthcare without improved treatments.[21, 22]

The issue of patents is a particularly sensitive one. Extending patent lives gives more protection to drug developers and therefore a greater incentive to develop novel treatments. However, a delayed patent expiry also means a more expensive drug for a longer period of time before generic drug producers can legally produce a lower cost version. Higher patented-drug costs are borne by those who need the drugs. As a result, in developing countries, there has been strong pressure from interest groups and even the government to abolish patents and allow earlier low-cost generic production of certain drugs.

One example of this has been with antiretroviral drugs for the treatment of AIDS. According to the charity AVERT:

The availability of cheaper generic antiretroviral drugs has been instrumental in treating around 5.25 million HIV/ AIDS sufferers in low- and middle-income countries.

Such actions create strong disincentives for pharmaceutical companies to develop or market drugs in poorer countries. As such, many of the newer, more effective drugs are only available in richer nations where AIDS has passed from being a death sentence to a chronic illness. The same cannot be said of developing countries, where AIDS remains a big killer: sub-Saharan Africa alone still has two-thirds of AIDS patients, and prevalence rates in the area are six times that of the rest of the world.[23,24]

As a result of such complex relationships between governments and phar-maceutical companies, development of drugs for many infectious diseases seems to remain largely the domain of foundations and charities. Some of the world's richest individuals have dedicated their fortunes towards charitable health initiatives, such as the Bill and Melinda Gates Foundation, Medicines for Malaria Ventures, and the Global Fund to Fight AIDS, Tuberculosis and Malaria. The resulting treatments sometimes have the benefit of an acceler-ated approval process with regulatory authorities. However, barriers to effective development and roll-out of such drugs still include bureaucracy, inefficient distribution of funding, and improper incentives. Where certain pharma-ceutical companies have been working towards developing drugs for diseases that afflict developing countries, this seems to be more a gesture of corporate citizenship – either self-inspired or the result of government pressure – rather than an integral part of financially motivated corporate strategy.

In the corporate chase for profits in established, low-risk and wealthy markets, a heavily disproportionate amount of money is spent developing and marketing drugs that essentially serve the same function. Much of the advertising for drugs is for treatments for diseases of the affluent or for non-life-threatening diseases. One particular trend is the increased exposure of drugs in the public. Some of the best-known drug brands in the world are for non-life-threatening diseases many would not consider entirely necessary. They are known because they are heavily adver-tised, whether explicitly in media, or as references. One example is the increase of direct-to-consumer drug advertising in the United States. It has opened debates over the effectiveness of advertising, as well as ethical and economic implications. Viewers of drug adverts may request that doctors prescribe them more expensive drugs when cheaper or more effective alternatives are available.

Several questions arise from such practices: Is it wise to shift the decision making from the expert to the patient? Does superficial advertising confuse the patient rather than create understanding of the implications behind taking these drugs? Do such actions encourage the dependence or abuse of certain drugs? Such issues have potentially profound social implications.[25]

Threats and opportunities

What appears to emerge from the current picture of market-based healthcare activity is an increasing focus upon R&D and marketing directed at treatments for the established, wealthy markets of developed nations. This potentially leaves diseases of the developing world behind, further increasing the already considerable divergence between rich and poor worlds. With such current health scenarios, there would appear to be huge challenges to be faced before the WHO and UN human rights objectives of "health and well-being for everyone" can possibly become a reality of the 21st century.

Furthermore, the nature of health problems is changing in ways that were only partially anticipated, and at a rate that was wholly unexpected, as a combined result of global aging, the effects of urbanization, globalized lifestyle changes, accelerated worldwide transmission of communicable diseases, and the increased burden of chronic and noncommunicable disorders. The WHO World Health Report *Primary Health Care: Now More Than Ever* indicates that several other Global Trends in climate change, food security, social tensions will all have definite, but largely unpredictable, implications for health in the years ahead. Economic and political changes will challenge state and institutional roles to ensure access, delivery and financing of healthcare. Technological developments are creating new market opportunities, but are also driving increasing expectations for higher quality and longer-lasting health services.

According to the WHO, health systems seem to be drifting from one short-term priority to another, increasingly fragmented and without a clear sense of direction. As the WHO report states:

Today, it is clear that left to their own devices, health systems do not gravitate naturally towards the goals of health for all through primary health care… Health systems are developing in directions that contribute little to equity and social justice and fail to get the best health outcomes for their money. Three particularly worrisome trends can be characterized as follows: health systems that focus disproportionately on a narrow offer of specialized curative care; health systems where a command-and-control approach to disease control, focused on short-term results, is fragmenting service delivery; health systems where a hands-off or laissez faire approach to governance has allowed unregulated commercialization of health to flourish.

These trends fly in the face of a comprehensive and balanced response to health needs. In a number of countries, the resulting inequitable access, impoverishing costs, and erosion of trust in healthcare constitute a threat to social stability.

Clearly, public policy has a huge role to play in addressing such issues. Yet, as the *World Health Report* points out:

Despite the benefits and low relative cost of better public policies, their potential remains largely underutilized across the world. One high-profile example is that only 5 percent of the world's population lives in countries with comprehensive tobacco advertising, promotion and sponsorship bans, despite their proven efficacy in reducing health threats, which are projected to claim one billion lives this century.

The health sector's approach to improving public policies has been singularly unsystematic and guided by patchy evidence and muddled decision making – not least because the health community has put so little effort into collating and communicating these facts. For all the progress that has been made in recent years, information on the effectiveness of interventions to redress, for example, health inequities is still hard to come by and, when it is available, it is confined to a privileged circle of concerned experts. A lack of information and evidence is, thus, one of the explanations for under-investment."

To come close to accomplishing the WHO and UN human rights goals in the 21st century, several threats need to be addressed. Given the challenges we face on both infectious and chronic disease fronts, concerted efforts are needed to ensure medical innovation does not decline and is undertaken for the benefit of all. A recent trend has been for mergers and acquisitions of small biotech companies by large pharmaceutical companies to restock dwindling R&D pipelines, potentially reducing innovation in the industry overall. In the wake of drug recalls in the past decade, regulatory authorities are considering drug application submissions with more scrutiny, potentially leading to fewer drugs being released in the market.[26]

Without continued drug innovation, increased drug resistance could become a big 21st-century threat. Pathogens that cause diseases mutate and develop resistance to drugs over time, but such drug resistance is often hastened greatly by improper administration, improper adherence, or overuse of treatment regimens. As well as drugs for treating infectious diseases such as malaria and tuberculosis, several classes of important antibiotics – 70 percent of which are widely misused as growth promoters in animal feeds – are at risk of becoming ineffective in dealing with resistant "*superbugs.*"[27]

Demographic changes will increase the burden on public and private insurance and health delivery systems since the globally aging population is more likely to suffer from multiple chronic conditions. Further strain will be imposed by increasing numbers of children being treated with emerging conditions such as obesity, attention deficit hyperactivity disorder (ADHD), allergies and diabetes. In fact, in the USA in recent years drug spending for child illnesses has increased four times faster than general medication spending.[28] Without adequate measures, increasing levels of urbanization, sedentary lifestyles and new eating habits are likely to lead to further increases in existing chronic illnesses, the emergence of new medical conditions and increasing burdens on healthcare services. Ultimately, with a smaller working-age population to pay for them, the sustainability of the increasingly stretched existing insurance and delivery systems will be brought into question.

If existing systems do not evolve to deal with such challenges, costs will spiral, medical care will suffer and the health of society will be jeopardized. Without changes in the way that the current biased healthcare systems work, inequalities are likely to become more pronounced, leaving a greater proportion of the world's poor – both in developed and developing world – with health problems. As with a lack of economic opportunities for the underprivileged, if healthcare delivery systems continue to neglect those that need most care, there is clear potential for social unrest, especially if increasing numbers of people are forced into poverty through paying for ever-more-expensive treatments.

Several trends stand in the way of improving the efficiency and efficacy of healthcare systems in the face of new challenges. Increasing levels of sub-specialization, hospital treatment and curative services – at the expense of more cost effective holistic primary prevention and health promotion approaches – seems to be going in the wrong direction. With increased globalization and travel come increased risks of disease transmission and pandemics – especially if half of the world's population lives in conditions that are ideal for incubating and creating new infectious diseases. With recent outbreaks such as the H1N1 virus, many health infrastructures were found wanting. In the face of more severe outbreaks, there is the risk of failing international health systems unless steps are taken: firstly to reduce the possibilities of such outbreaks; and secondly to have adequate measures in place should they occur.

Thus there are many challenges to overcome in improving global health. Nevertheless, these challenges point the way to a number of opportunities: actions to mitigate the above threats in themselves represent opportunities to work towards a healthier world. In addition, there are several specific opportunities for governments, businesses and individuals to improve the outlook for future health.

Governments and businesses have a social responsibility to work together to ensure the continued innovation of appropriate drugs. Of course profits for private companies are crucial. However, without doubt, more efforts could be made to funnel greater investment into projects benefitting the poor, aimed at eradicating further grotesque illnesses and, in the process, ensuring less potential spread of such diseases to wealthier regions. Generous donations from the wealthy will always be welcome in doing battle with infectious diseases, however, for-profit businesses could probably shoulder a greater proportion of the burden than they currently do. Ultimately, it is not to anyone's benefit to have a world in which access to curing drugs is limited for the poor majority. With courageous and intelligent leadership, there will be ways of accomplishing the noble WHO and UN human rights goals without compromising healthy corporate profitability. A good place to start has to be working to rid the world of the scourge of various potentially eradicable infectious diseases, such as polio.

Other significant opportunities lie in improving infrastructure in developing countries to remove various causes of poor health to start with. Access to fresh water eliminates water-borne diseases such as cholera. Reducing the incidence of malnutrition and hunger improves general health of the population thereby reducing incidences of opportunistic infections. Other proactive steps such as the distribution of insecticide-treated mosquito nets – along with appropriate education on their use – can be cheaper than drug administration and ensure less of a disease burden on the society and economy of the nation.

Clearly, there are huge opportunities in terms of driving more cost-effective and efficient health delivery systems. A greater focus upon more effective holistic approaches of primary care, prevention and health promotion that can eliminate up to 70 percent of health problems in the first place has to be sensible. Improving general education towards avoiding health pitfalls can achieve a lot. After all, widespread educational campaigns relating to awareness of AIDS have been successful for many countries in containing the spread of the illness.

Working to reduce child mortality and to extend "healthy life expectancy" represents big opportunities beyond ethical considerations. Such issues are extremely important to the long-term prosperity of a country. Those nations – both developed and developing – that spend wisely on improving healthcare systems have the opportunity to reap the social and economic benefits from a more productive working population. Longer healthy lifespans have positive impacts on society as adults can care for future generations. Breaking the cycle of parents dying young in developing countries could have huge impact in many areas. Making sound investments and decisions in healthcare to look after the growing youthful populations in developing nations, could lead to a closing of the gap between rich and poor nations. Of course, with increased lifespans and expectations for quality of life come a multitude of increased business opportunities. For pharmaceutical companies, there will always be opportunities to develop new drugs and treatments that further extend and improve the quality of life. For individuals, a long, happy and healthy life is what we all seek.

The inequality of healthcare access has led to two different worlds, which need to be tackled in different ways. The current system of healthcare development, which strongly favors the rich, contributes to the divergence of these two worlds. In developed countries, citizens have access to expensive, cutting-edge medical treatments for diseases which many would question as strictly necessary. In contrast, millions of people in developing countries die each year due to lack of access to the most basic treatments for diseases that developed countries have largely forgotten.

We need to rise to the challenge of eradicating nasty existing infectious diseases, such as polio, as well as reducing the potential for worldwide transmission of new ones. If this can be achieved, there is tremendous potential for convergence of global healthcare as developing countries follow the same health trends towards more chronic conditions. With the combined efforts of the world focused upon dealing with a reduced set of illnesses, overall health can only improve. The example of smallpox eradication offers considerable cause for future optimism. Policy-makers, business leaders and motivated individuals have already shown that, with effort, they can work together to banish cruel diseases to the history books, as well as find new ways of treating emerging illnesses. If such efforts can be sustained into the 21st century, this can only improve overall social and economic development, and lead to more sustainable business models and rewarding lives.

Beyond diseases and lifestyles, there is another group of factors that can have a sudden and massive negative impact upon the health and well-being of individuals, businesses and societies: natural disasters. These are the topic of the final Global Trend.

Natural Disasters

"Disasters effect on average 200 million people every year... Earthquakes and droughts remain the main killers, but floods, hurricanes, cyclones and storms are the hazards that affect most people worldwide. Crowded cities. Unsafe constructions. Lack of urban planning. Destruction of natural buffers. Climate change. These all combine to expose more people to disasters... We are all at risk."

2010–2011 World Disaster Reduction Campaign,
United Nations International Strategy for
Disaster Reduction (UNISDR)[1]

The UN launched the World Disaster Reduction Campaign before the magnitude 9.0* earthquake and induced tsunami hit the northeast coast of Japan on March 11th 2011, killing 28,050, directly affecting 492,000 and with an estimated damage to the economy of $309 billion.[2] The earthquake itself was the biggest in Japanese history, one of the five most powerful earthquakes since modern records began in 1900, and triggered massive tsunami waves of up to 38 meters high that reached 10 kilometers (6 miles) inland. For sure, when nature decides to invoke its wrath, the human cost can be staggering:†

Every hour the toll keeps climbing. White coffin after white coffin is brought into a bowling alley in the town of Natori, lost life after lost life. Tatsuya Suzuki was searching among the names for his wife, Izumi... She

---

* Richter scale: a single number to quantify the energy contained in an earthquake. The magnitude is a base-10 logarithmic scale. An increase in magnitude of 1.0 indicates a shaking amplitude 10 times larger and an increase in energy released (which correlates to its destructive power) of about 31 times. An increase in magnitude of 2.0 is equivalent to a factor of 1000 times the energy released.
† This is even before taking into account further knock-on incidents resulting from the earthquake-damaged Fukushima nuclear reactor.

[had] handed [her] two children to her mother-in-law who pulled them inside just as the tsunami reached them. Izumi was swept away by the waves. "The kids keep smiling every day," says Tatsuya, with his little son perched on his lap. "They keep saying, 'Let's go and find mummy today.'"[3]

There were shortages of essential supplies, but people in the city would queue calmly for up to two hours at a time rather than taking from the empty shops. "Psychologically we had a common sense of not wanting any more confusion or panic, or any further peril, so we all helped keep public order," Machiko Konno says. "The queues at stores show that people are uneasy," she says..."In Japan people smile with their face and cry Inside..."[4]

With some regularity we watch on our television screens as societies of tearful mothers, fathers and children from often distant and unfortunate parts of the globe, struggle to come to terms with lost loved ones and shattered lives. While the media swoops on the hot stories of the moment, there is invariably still a wake of previous disasters where people are still coming to terms with the consequences of disaster years later. From August 23 to 29, 2005, Hurricane Katrina swept past Florida and through the Gulf of Mexico before clattering into New Orleans and Louisiana, killing 1,833 people, affecting 500,000 more, and causing damage in the region of $125 billion. Much of this was caused by storm surge floods overcoming man-made levees* that proved insufficient to protect low-lying areas. Again the human toll was striking:

America Williams, 34, evacuated on Sunday, piling into a sport utility vehicle with her boyfriend and 13 of his relatives – seven of them children. "They just told us to drive, to drive east or west to get as far from the storm as possible."... After two nights in three $50 rooms at a motel, the family ran out of money.[5]

I [Darryl Barthe] returned to New Orleans the first week of October to find my apartment in the Farber St John area totally destroyed... Whatever had not been destroyed by the six or seven feet of water had been looted... I asked a police officer what I should do to protect myself and he told me to arm myself and not be afraid to shoot someone... There was just a wave of despair across the whole place.[6]

---

* Dykes or embankments.

While the stoic Japanese coped in an incredibly orderly manner in the face of adversity, certain sectors of New Orleans' society did not react with such restraint and this added to the overall suffering. But Japan and the USA are both rich nations. Of course, natural disasters also affect poorer countries, and when they do it seems that even more people suffer. The floods in Pakistan from July 28 to August 7, 2010, that resulted from unprecedented heavy monsoon rains, killed 1,985 people and affected 20,359,496. One-fifth of Pakistan's total land area was under water: a flooded area similar in size to Italy destroyed more than 1.6 million acres of crops and made millions homeless. The UN Secretary General Ban Ki-moon noted that it was the worst disaster he had ever seen. An indication that most of these 20 million-plus affected were poor is that the estimated economic damage was put at a comparatively low $ 9.5 billion. Beyond the dollar values though, the human sorrow was considerable:

> We never thought the waters would rise so high. I was away at my aunt's house... My relatives said to wait until the tide ebbs, but it kept rising, and soon it was clear that my part of the city had drowned. My mother died... She was washed away. We haven't found her body. My brother is traumatized.[7]

> People are suffering with diarrhoea and nausea. I'm a doctor and I'm trying to help but have no transport or medicine. I'm sitting in front of a pregnant lady who needs medical assistance and there are no roads to take her to hospital... We don't have medicine. People are sick and I can't test to see whether it's a cholera outbreak. There is no electricity, no drinking water.[8]

The EM-DAT International Disaster Database classifies natural disasters into five categories. *Geophysical* disasters include events originating from solid earth such as earthquakes and volcanoes. *Meteorological* disasters are caused by short-lived (from minutes to days), small- to medium-scale atmospheric processes such as storms. *Hydrological* disasters, such as flooding or wet-earth movements (for example mudslides), result from deviations in the normal water cycle or overflows of bodies of water. *Climatological* disasters such as drought, extreme temperatures, and wildfire are caused by long-lived (from intra-seasonal to multi-decadal climate variability), medium- to large-scale atmospheric processes. The last EM-DAT category is *Biological* disasters such as epidemics and insect infestations.[9]

Beyond disasters associated with climate change, water scarcity and diseases (already discussed in Global Trends 4, 5 and 11), the World Economic Forum's Global Risks Landscape 2011, indicates that there are essentially three natural disaster fronts that worry the world's leaders: "storms and cyclones," with the highest perceived likelihood occurrence in the next decade of all the global risks and an estimated impact of over $250 billion; just behind in probability of occurrence comes "flooding," with an equal forecasted economic impact; and then "earthquakes and volcanoes," also with very likely perceived chance of occurring in the next ten years and with a potential impact of nearly $250 billion.[10]

Table 12.1 summarizes information on the world's costliest natural disasters since 1965 from data sources such as the IMF and World Bank.[11]

The Japanese earthquake and tsunami of 2011 could be the costliest disaster since comparable records began in 1965.

Not including any knock-on effects resulting from the failure of the nuclear power plant, provisional estimates released by the World Bank put the economic damage resulting from the disaster at anything between $122 to $235 billion, around 2.5 to 4 percent of GDP. The World Bank summarizes the impact upon the Japanese economy:

> If history is any guide, real GDP growth will be negatively affected through mid-2011. Growth should though pick up in subsequent quarters as reconstruction efforts, which could last five years, accelerate. The intensity of these efforts is likely to impact on the final cost of the disaster... Private insurers are likely to bear a relatively small portion of the cost, leaving a substantial part to be borne by households and the government.[12]

However, the impact of such a disaster has gone well beyond Japan: with considerable disruptions to financial markets and to international supply chains that pass through Japan, especially in automotive and electronic industries. The World Bank predicts further trade and finance implications from the earthquake and tsunami. Over the last five years, trade with Japan accounted for 9 percent of East Asia's total external trade. Thus the slow growth of Japanese GDP will also slow down other developing East Asian countries and influence the regional economics given resulting currency

Table 12.1: The world's costliest natural disasters since 1965

Natural Disaster	Year	Approximate economic loss ($ billion)	Approximate insured loss ($ billion)	% GDP loss in disaster year
Earthquake/Tsunami, Japan (provisional)	2011	230	30	4.1
Kobe earthquake, Japan	1995	200	10	1.9
Hurricane Katrina, USA	2005	170	80	1.0
Northridge earthquake, USA	1994	90	30	0.6
Sichuan/Wenchuan earthquake, China	2008	90	0	1.9
Irpinia earthquake, Italy	1980	70	0	2.6
Hurricane Andrew, USA	1992	70	40	0.4
Yangtze River floods, China	1998	50	5	3.0
Great Floods, USA	1993	50	5	0.3
Tangshan earthquake, China	1976	50	Unavailable	3.7
Spitak earthquake, Armenia	1988	50	Unavailable	1.9[a]
River floods, China	1996	50	0	2.8
Drought, USA	1988	40	5	0.3
Kalimantan forest fires, Indonesia	1982–3	40	Unavailable	9.3
Hurricane Ike, USA & Caribbean	2008	40	20	0.3
Niigata earthquake, Japan	2004	40	5	0.6
Eastern floods, China	1991	40	5	3.6
River Arno floods, Italy	1966	40	0	2.7
Loma Prieta earthquake, USA	1989	30	5	0.2
Friuli earthquake, Italy	1976	30	0	1.7

Source: "Natural disasters: counting the cost." *The Economist*. ([a]Estimate).

Figure 12.1: Estimated damage (US$ billion) caused by reported natural disasters 1975–2009

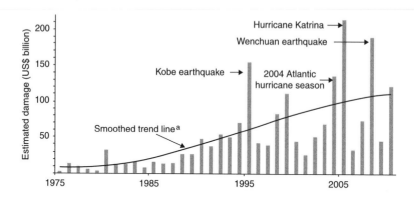

Source: EM-DAT: OFDA/CRED International Disaster Database. ([a]Polynomial function)

fluctuations. Moreover, Japan is a significant source of foreign direct investment which may decrease as capital is needed for reconstruction within Japan.

Clearly, such disasters are a global phenomenon, yet certain countries seem to crop up repeatedly as a result of their geographic position. It is interesting to note from Table 12.1 the relatively small proportion of economic losses that are actually insured. The wider impact upon the economic GDP is often considerable: 9.3 percent loss in GDP must have been an incredible shock to the Indonesians in 1982–3. Also noteworthy are the disasters that do not make it on to this list. For example the Indian Ocean tsunami in 2004, which caused around 250,000 deaths, does not feature in Table 12.1. As a result of low property and land values in the affected areas, economic losses amounted to *only* $14 billion. Thus poor countries are likely to be somewhat under-represented in such economic loss data.

So, what about Global Trends in natural disasters?

According to the EM-DAT International Disaster Database, natural disasters are happening more frequently over recent decades and with larger average yearly damage impact. Figure 12.1 shows the tremendously "spikey" nature of natural disasters from year to year. For example 1995, 2005 and 2008 were the years corresponding to the "big three" disasters, prior to Japan 2011, of Kobe, Katrina and Wenchuan. Smoothing out these spikes, EM-DAT

Figure 12.2: Natural disasters 1975–2009: numbers of people affected (line) and killed (bars)

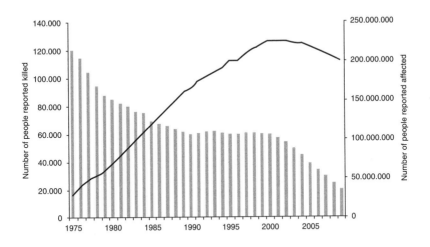

Source: EM-DAT: OFDA/CRED International Disaster Database

indicates that, overall, the average estimated yearly damage has been increasing since the 1970s.[13]

The number of country-level natural disasters reported has actually been on the increase for the last 4 decades. Since 1975, when around 60 disasters were reported, there has been a steady increase of the "linear interpolated" trends up to about 440 disasters reported in 2000. From 2000 to 2010 this increasing trend of reported disasters has flattened-off. The non-smoothed time trend of country reported natural disasters also indicates increasing peaks of 205 in 1983; 278 in 1990; 413 in 2000; 421 in 2002; 432 in 2005; before dropping back somewhat to 373 in 2010.

In line with this overall increasing trend in number of disasters reported, the number of people affected worldwide has increased each decade from under 50 million affected per year in the 1970s to over 200 million per year for the last decade.[14]

This trend in increasing numbers of people affected can be seen in Figure 12.2. Also shown in the graph is the trend of number of people reported killed by natural disasters. Despite increasing numbers of reported disasters and more people affected by disasters over the last decades, the good news is that fewer people have been killed. Since 1975, when about 120,000 people were killed per year by natural disasters, the number of fatalities has dropped to around 20,000 deaths per year. In fact, this decreasing trend in yearly deaths goes back to the early 1900s when approximately 500,000 were killed on average per year through natural disasters. In the early 20th century there were several particularly bleak "*anni horribiles*" – such as 1931 when close to 4 million people were killed in the single year, mostly in the Central China floods; probably the deadliest natural disaster of the century.

It would appear that, despite increasing levels of disasters, emergency planning and rescue teams are getting better at saving people.

The question is whether the apparent leveling-off of reported disasters and numbers of people affected between 2000 and 2010 is a reverse in the increasing trend or a momentary respite in a longer-term upward trend. Beyond increased transparency and reporting of disasters in the first place, unfortunately two drivers behind these trends would indicate the latter. Firstly, throughout the 20th century there were big demographic shifts, still continuing today, of mass migration to ever-larger cities – many of which are near to areas of seismic activity and/or rivers and coastlines susceptible to storms, tsunamis, flooding and other water-borne natural disasters. Secondly, there have been considerable, largely man-made, alterations to the environment such as climate change and deforestation which are likely to have a continuing effect both upon increasing severity of storms and a reduced ability of natural systems to absorb flash-floods, storm surges and the like.

A breakdown of disasters over the last 100 years, appear to support the hypotheses behind these two drivers of continuing upward trends in reported disasters and number of people affected. Of all the categories of natural disaster monitored by the EM-DAT International Disaster Database, flooding and storm disasters demonstrate a considerable "bulging" in increased number of reports from the middle of the 20th century onwards. There is considerably less, but still significant increase in reporting of associated "wet mass earth movements" and of droughts. Each of these is likely due to the combination of urbanization, climate change and general environmental degradation. Epidemics have also increased considerably as a result of increased travel, urbanization and water-borne illnesses – such as cholera – following floods and storms.

The number of reported earthquakes has also increased to a significant degree over the last fifty years. The United States Geological Survey (USGS) states that this is at least partially because of the tremendous increase in the number of seismograph stations in the world and the many improvements in global communications. The USGS also points to increasing exposure of humans to earthquakes:

> The population at risk is increasing. While the number of large earth-quakes is fairly constant, population density in earthquake-prone areas is constantly increasing... So we are now seeing increasing casualties from the same-sized earthquakes.[15]

So what of the last full year of natural disaster reporting: 2010?

Bluntly, according to the EM-DAT data, it was not a good year: and this despite the fact that 2010 did not have any of the above "biggest" economic impact natural events. According to Debarati Guha-Sapir, Director of the Centre for Research on the Epidemiology of Disasters (CRED):

> In 2010, 373 natural disasters were recorded in the EM-DAT database. They killed over 296,800 people, affected over 207 million others and caused more than US$109 billion of economic damages. The two most lethal disasters – the January 12 earthquake in Haiti, which killed over 222,500 people, as well as the Russian summer heat wave, which caused about 56,000 fatalities – made 2010 the deadliest year in at least two decades.[16]

After the earthquake in Haiti and heatwave in Russia, there were several other high-profile lethal natural disasters in 2010 including (with number of deaths): earthquakes in China (2,968), Chile (562), and Indonesia (530); floods in Pakistan (1,985) and China (1,691); landslides in China (1,765) and Uganda (388); and a cold wave in Peru (409).

The 296,818 total people killed through natural disasters was much higher in 2010 than the decade 2000 to 2009 yearly average of *only* 78,087. As the quote above suggests, the bulk of these deaths were due to the earthquakes and extreme temperature disasters during the year. Nevertheless, flooding also killed 8,119 people in 2010 compared to the decade yearly average of 5,401; landslides and general wet-earth movements caused 3,258 deaths compared to only 763 from 2000 to 2009. Conversely, there were many fewer storm-related deaths worldwide in 2010 compared to the previous decade: 1,367 versus 17, 222 respectively.

Deaths are the most immediately negative impact of such disasters, but the number of people killed is not the whole human impact story: there are also the longer-term repercussions upon all those affected by the disaster and the rebuilding of shattered communities. The numbers of people who lose their homes, livelihoods and possessions to drought, earthquake, extreme temperatures, floods, mass earth movements, storms, volcanoes and wild fires is staggering.

Between 2000 and 2009, the average number of people affected by natural disasters was 227,378,014 people per year.* That is over 3 percent of the world's population affected by natural disaster *per year.*

In 2010, a total of 207,677,316 people were affected by natural disasters worldwide. This total is somewhat below, but still on par with the previous decade's average. The vast majority of this 2010 total was affected by flooding: 178,866,521. From 2000 to 2009, flooding affected on average 94,850,811 people per year. Droughts and storms also had considerable impact over the decade, affecting an average of 75,489,671 and 39,720,117 people per year respectively.

The estimated economic damage of destroyed homes, infrastructure and livelihoods of $109 billion in 2010, was $10 billion more than the yearly average from year 2000 to 2009. Table 12.2 shows the ten most damaging natural disasters in 2010.

To give some perspective on the impact of disasters in 2010 over 40 percent of the population of Haiti were killed or affected; nearly 16 percent in Chile; and about 11 percent of the population of China and Pakistan.

A glance down the list of countries involved indicates that natural disasters are truly global phenomena with apparently few places offering true refuge from nature's not-so-occasional and somewhat random outbursts. Whilst nearly 85 percent of the people killed during the period 2000 to 2009 were in Asia, in 2010 this suddenly changed to 76 percent of deaths being in the Americas.

---

* Not including epidemics or insect infestations.

Table 12.2: The ten most damaging natural disasters in 2010

Country	Type	Estimated damage (US$ billion)	Number of people	
			Killed	Affected
Chile	Earthquake	30	562	2,671,556
China	Flood	18	1,691	134,000,000
Pakistan	Flood	9.5	1,985	20,359,496
Haiti	Earthquake	8	222,570	3,700,000
New Zealand	Earthquake	6.5	–	300,002
Australia	Flood	5.13	16	200,000
France	Storm	4.23	53	500,079
Mexico	Storm	3.9	12	230,000
China	Drought	3.6	–	60,000,000
Poland	Flood	3.2	16	100,000

Debarati Guha-Sapir, Director of CRED has some commonsense advice:

> … it is important to clearly understand the direct causes of deaths and destruction of livelihoods from natural disasters, and to act on them with effective relief response and preparedness measures.

This is where there is apparently huge discrepancy between different nations and parts of the world. Two of 2010's earthquakes demonstrate this. On January 12th a magnitude 7.0 earthquake struck Haiti. Just over a month later, on February 27, a magnitude 8.8 earthquake struck Chile, releasing about 500 times the energy and destructive power of the earthquake in Haiti.

In the Haiti earthquake, around 70 percent of homes and buildings collapsed killing over 200,000 people – or 2 percent of the inhabitants. The economic impact was 123.5 percent of GDP.

In Chile the human and economic impact of the 8.8 earthquake was still considerable, but nowhere near as devastating in human terms. Why? Because after a devastating magnitude 9.5 earthquake in 1960, strict building codes were implemented in Chile that ensured subsequent buildings were more resilient. Also people were educated about earthquake safety and better prepared to act appropriately when the earthquake struck. In Haiti, no such lessons had apparently been learned from the past, although the city of Port-au-Prince had been completely destroyed by earthquakes in 1751 and 1757. In September 2008, geologists had picked up minor quakes in Haiti and alerted the likelihood of an earthquake of greater intensity, yet the population remained largely unprepared. Had similar initiatives been taken in Haiti as in Chile, it is inconceivable that there would have been as much mayhem.

According to the US Geological Survey (USGS), geophysical activity is far from rare. In fact the USGS states:

> There's a 100 percent chance of an earthquake today. Though millions of persons may never experience an earthquake, they are very common occurrences on this planet. So today – somewhere – an earthquake will occur.[17]

Thankfully, however, the overwhelming majority of these are small seismic tremors. Based upon observations since 1900, scientists estimate that there are approximately 1.3 million earthquakes of magnitude 2 to 2.9 per year; 130,000 of magnitude 3 to 3.9; 13,000 of magnitude 4 to 4.9; 134 from 6 to 6.9; 15 big earthquakes per year of magnitude 7 to 7.9; and an average of 1 truly massive destructive earthquake per year with a magnitude over 8.0. But much of the problem with earthquakes and associated mayhem (such as triggered landslides, surface deformation and tsunamis) is the sheer unpredictability of the event. Lacking any way of forewarning populations to imminent danger can contribute hugely to the scale of devastation. Precise prediction of earthquakes remains a future possibility, only feasible after much more is learned about earthquake mechanisms. Nevertheless, we know that certain regions are higher-risk areas, associated with particular geological fault-lines. Albeit with notable exceptions, the majority of magnitude 8 and greater earthquakes since 1900 have occurred along the western and eastern pacific coastlines of the Americas, Asia and Oceania. While not being able to predict *when* it will happen, or the specific location of impact, scientists can calculate probabilities of potential future earthquakes. For example:

Within the next 30 years, the probability of a major earthquake occurring in the San Francisco Bay area is 67 percent and 60 percent in Southern California.[18]

While volcanoes have not had such large impact as earthquakes in recent decades, they do remain a significant, albeit often difficult to quantify, risk. After all, as many school children will know Pompeii was destroyed and completely buried under nearly 6 meters of ash and pumice during a long catastrophic eruption of the volcano Mount Vesuvius in 79 AD. From a long list of historical eruptions, some of the more recent costly ones have included: Nevado del Ruiz, Colombia in 1985, killing 21,800, affecting 12,700 with damage of $1,000 million; Mount St. Helen, USA in 1980 killing 90, affecting 2,500 and costing $860,000; Mount Pinatubo in Philippines in 1991, killing 640, affecting 1,036,065 and costing $211 million; and Bulusan in Philippines in 2010, affecting 14,161 people.

The USGS reports that there are about 1,500 potentially active volcanoes dotted around the globe. About 500 of these have erupted in historical time. Many are located along the Pacific "Ring of Fire." The most active volcano on earth, Stromboli, in Italy has been erupting nearly continuously for over 2,000 years. Even though scientists can anticipate volcanic eruptions by observing ground movement and changes in volcanic gases, volcanoes can still cause huge damage once they erupt. Even relatively small volcanoes can cause considerable disruption and economic impact. For example, the relatively minor volcanic eruption of Iceland's Eyjafjallajökull volcano in 2010 created ash that grounded flights and paralyzed intercontinental travel in and out of Europe for almost a week.[19]

While direct damage was limited, many businesses lost considerable revenue and incurred many complications, showing the vulnerability of the networked global economy to such Earthly "hiccups." Volcanoes are rare but potentially highly disruptive events that can expose tremendous human frailty in the face of unmanaged risk. The President of the European Volcanological Society, Henri Gaudru is quoted by the WHO Collaborating Center for Research on the Epidemiology of Disasters (CRED) as saying:

> While the Eyjafjallajökull eruption was not a relatively big one compared with others in the past, it has caused chaos on a massive scale. Other volcanoes in Europe, such as Italy's Vesuvius and Iceland's much bigger Katla, would create far more disruption if they were to erupt today.

While earthquakes and volcanoes are likely to be beyond human being's direct control, other natural disasters are more within human beings' sphere of influence. Increasing numbers of meteorological, hydrological and climatological disasters including floods, storms, extreme temperatures and droughts are an apparent result of changing climate, increasing pressure on water resources and environmental destruction (see Global Trends 4, 5 and 10).

> **Many of the 2010 disasters have been linked by experts to these largely human-driven environmental changes.**

For example, following the heatwave in Russia, unmatched in 130 years, that fueled the disastrous and deadly wildfires that destroyed one-third of the country's wheat crop, the Russian Federation President Dmitry Medvedev said:

> Unfortunately, what is happening now in [Russian] central regions is evidence of this global climate change, because we have never in our history faced such weather conditions in the past.[20]

According to the UNISDR, such events

> … underline the needs for all countries – both developed and developing – to plan ahead or face increasing economic losses in the face of a "new normal" marked by unpredictable and extreme weather patterns.[21]

Beyond the direct impact upon human life, all the different forms of floods, storms, extreme temperatures and drought can generate further complications for sustained livelihoods through changes invoked by the natural disaster – such as coastal erosion, inundation, island breaching and so on. A whole host of economic impacts can follow, from decreased tourism revenue, to damaged property, to loss of cultivatable land area, and more vulnerability to future disasters.

Nevertheless, the impact of each of these meteorological, hydrological and climatological hazards can be drastically reduced by proactive implementation of appropriate defenses, adequate infrastructure, and monitoring and early warning systems. Throughout history, human innovation has provided many solutions to problems posed by such natural forces. For example, the low-lying Netherlands has always faced-up to the hazards of nature through various ingenious flood and storm defenses. Now, faced with rising sea levels in the 21st century, the country has further prioritized flood protection.

At a cost of 450 million Euros, the *Maeslant Storm Surge Barrier* was built in 1997, with 22-metre high gates, the same length and twice the weight of the Eiffel Tower, creating a barrier straddling a 300-meter-wide river.

This in addition to a whole series of flood-protection systems, sea barriers, real-time data collection and monitoring designed to protect the Netherlands from any storm that nature has been capable of throwing at the country over the last 10,000 years. What is more, the Netherlands still plans to spend about 1 billion Euros per year on flood and storm protection for the next century.[22]

However, such solutions require money – which is in short supply in a country such as Mozambique, which faces largely the same natural hazards as the Netherlands. Mozambique faces increasing flood risk along a 2,700 km coastline, with more than 13 million people living in coastal and river delta areas, yet struggles to implement rudimentary flood defenses. The country has started to build embankments, elevate schools and move people to safer areas; however, as one of the poorest countries in the world, it lacks the resources to construct large-scale embankments costing $1,000 per meter. Furthermore, most people living in vulnerable areas rely on fishing or farming for survival today, so encouraging them to move away from their livelihoods in preparation for a possible disaster in coming years is a challenge.

Similarly, to improve the ability to cope with drought, dams, reservoirs, canals, desalination plants and other infrastructure can be built, and monitoring systems implemented. Again, such large-scale solutions are beyond the reach of many poorer countries. Also, technologies exist to prevent buildings from collapsing during earthquakes. Yet, while efforts are being made to make earthquake-resistant technology less expensive, it currently results in increased new-building costs of 5 to 10 percent. The cost of renovating old buildings to conform to earthquake standards is even higher – making it prohibitive for poor nations such as Haiti.[23] With volcanoes, the onus is upon evacuation of the local population. Hence volcano monitoring, hazard assessments and eruption warning systems provide a solution. Again, such constant hazard assessment is not without considerable cost and is generally only fully implemented in richer nations.[24]

Threats and opportunities

In 1756, the French philosopher Voltaire wrote of the Lisbon earthquake and tsunami disaster, where an estimated 10,000 people were killed:

> *Ce n'est pas le tremblement de terre qui fit mourir les gens à Lisbonne, c'est le fait qu'ils habitaient à Lisbonne.*[25]

Roughly translated: "It wasn't the earthquake that killed the people of Lisbon, but the fact that they were living in Lisbon." As the CRED Annual Disaster Statistical Review points out, even now, more than 250 years after Voltaire's letters, when earthquake strikes, unsafe buildings in urban sprawl remain a primary killer. Yet, now this problem is even graver, given that for the first time in history, the majority of the world's population now live in urban areas. Each day, almost 180,000 people move to cities around the world. As a result of such rapid growth, urban newcomers often encounter a lack of infrastructure, services, housing and property rights and are often obliged to live in unsafe places. Thus, expanding cities are placing an increasing number of people in the path of natural disasters of all forms. To add insult to injury, this is at a time when certain types of natural disasters are on the increase – largely as a result of human impact upon the climate, pressure upon water resources and destruction of habitat that would normally act as buffers against disasters.

Thus, Mother Nature's wrath continues to present considerable threats to mankind in the 21st century, compounded by several actions of our own doing. It should be remembered that human beings do have an impact upon meteorological, hydrological and climatological natural disasters. Working to reduce the human-driven disaster-magnifying effects in the areas of climate change, water resource pressure and ecosystem degradation (see Global Trends 4, 5 and 10) would be a good place to start attempting to reverse the trend of increasing exposure to flooding, storms, mudslides, drought, extreme temperatures and wildfires.

Beyond such broad efforts to reduce those natural hazards upon which we have some leverage, there are a number of more focused actions that should aim to remove as many people as possible from the path of *all* types of natural disasters. While demographic movements of people into at-risk urban areas is a trend likely to continue into the 21st century (see Global Trend 7), there are many things that can be done to manage and alleviate the hazards.

The distinct outcomes from the earthquakes in Haiti and Chile indicate that, given the chance, we are capable of reducing the numbers of deaths from such incidents. The overall trend in reducing mortality levels from natural disasters is a very optimistic one.

What is clear is that effective planning and reaction to catastrophes can make our societies more resilient to natural hazards. As such, all stakeholders; governments, businesses and citizens have important roles to play. While there are few ethical opportunities to be gained directly from the occurrence of natural disasters, there are many opportunities for decreasing levels of human exposure to risk and thus reducing death and suffering when nature inevitably does show its ferocious side.

Margareta Wahlström, the United Nations Special Representative of the Secretary General for Disaster Risk Reduction points to some areas of opportunity in managing the risks of natural hazards:

> Three factors affect our degree of risk: changes to our natural environment, the quality of the built environment around us, and whether awareness and knowledge is widespread enough for us to modify our behavior in response to these factors.[26]

Thus, three cornerstones to risk reduction against the day when disaster strikes: education and preparation, quality urban planning and building, and constantly updating awareness of the world around us.

Given the fairly high unpredictability of most potential natural disasters, being educated about the dangers and being prepared is vital. For example in the USA, the Federal Emergency Management Agency provides very practical advice and action plans for people in vulnerable zones:

> Earthquakes strike suddenly, violently and without warning. Identifying potential hazards ahead of time and advance planning can reduce the dangers of serious injury or loss of life."[27]

This refers specifically to earthquakes, but the points are equally valid for other natural hazards. Simple steps such as identifying safe places indoors and outside, education of families and communities, having disaster supplies on hand, and developing emergency communication plans are important elements of reducing risks when confronting the forces of nature. Apparently, just having a pair of sturdy shoes within reach increases your chances of survival.

Part of being prepared also means appropriate urban planning, for example to ensure people are away from areas susceptible to flooding. Linked to this are adequate building regulations to reduce the impact of natural disaster when it happens. In earthquake-prone areas this clearly means construction focused upon seismically safe buildings to avoid unnecessary death from building collapse.

In the end though, poverty is what puts a lot of people in the path of disaster. Outlining the circumstantial differences between the earthquakes in Haiti and Chile, *The Economist* article "Earthly powers" noted that "death by disaster is in many ways a symptom of economic underdevelopment." Similarly, wealthier societies are more likely to recover more quickly from such misfortune. The problem is that cases such as Haiti do not really stand a chance when faced with nature's power. After all, it is one of the poorest nations in the world, with illiteracy at around 45 percent and some 60 percent of people without access to basic healthcare services.

Efforts to reduce poverty in general are likely to pay dividends in reducing the impact of natural disasters. It is poverty that leads to those overcrowded cities and unsafe constructions on flood plains, unstable slopes and fault lines. Therefore, working to get the one billion people who live in slums across the world into better-quality accommodation will take many people out of nature's firing line. Further actions to educate the poor would also reap rewards: increasing understanding of natural hazard implications, leading to more informed choices, and enabling reading of safety instructions for what to do in case of emergency. Of course, access to basic healthcare services can be both part of the education process and the life-saving actions when disaster does strike.

Undoubtedly, richer nations are better able to face-up to whatever nature throws at them because they have the resources to implement costly solutions. With the increasing threats of exposure of more of humanity to natural disasters of all forms, it makes sense for these rich nations to put more efforts into further innovation of natural disaster solutions. Particular priority though should be given to cost-effective solutions that would benefit everyone, but also give a much-needed boost to poorer nations such as Haiti and Mozambique.

While it is true that many rich countries will continue to implement costly technology to protect themselves better against natural hazards, effective risk management does not have to be expensive and can be done equally well by poorer nations. Simple measures can be very effective at reducing mortality and the numbers of people affected. Regarding potential hazards, neither education nor basic preparations are necessarily expensive. The United Nations International Strategy for Disaster Reduction (UNISDR) is campaigning for such basic initiatives and promotes ten actions to help in "Making cities resilient"[28]:

1. Organization and coordination to understand and reduce disaster risk.

2. Assign a budget for disaster risk reduction, providing incentives for homeowners, low-income families, communities, businesses to invest in reducing risks.

3. Maintain up-to-date data on hazards. Prepare risk assessments and use these as the basis for urban development plans.

4. Invest and maintain infrastructure, such as flood drainage, and adjust to cope with climate change.

5. Assess the safety of schools and health facilities, and upgrade if necessary.

6. Apply and enforce realistic, risk-compliant building regulations and land-use planning principles. Identify safe land for low-income citizens and upgrade informal settlements.

7. Put in place disaster risk-reduction education and training programs in schools and communities.

8. Protect ecosystems and natural buffers to mitigate floods and storm surges.

9. Install early-warning systems and emergency-management capacity.

10. After any disaster, ensure the needs of the survivors are placed at the center of reconstruction.

Some funding is clearly necessary in achieving such resilience-generating actions, yet perhaps more important is the collaboration and cooperation between stakeholders. In the wake of Iceland's relatively small Eyjafjallajökull volcano that wreaked havoc upon international air travel in 2010, *The Economist* article "Earthly powers" argued that the issue of disasters is more about people and planning than the power of nature. While there is no existing technology to prevent earthquakes or volcanoes, or even for accurately predicting such events, "humans are not completely powerless in the face of nature: rather the reverse." After all, "the story of human development is one of becoming better at coping with them."

It is good that we have managed to reduce the death toll from natural disasters over the last century and this should continue. Now, though, we should be attempting to reduce the hazards in the first place, and at the same time reducing the more-than 200 million people exposed to natural disasters every year. In this respect the UNISDR's "Hyogo Framework for Action" – a ten year plan to make the world safer from natural hazards by building the resilience of nations and communities to disasters – is a big step in the right direction. The framework was adopted by 168 nations in 2005 following the Indian Ocean tsunami and is the first international plan to explain, describe and detail the work that is required from all different sectors and actors to reduce disaster losses. Much could be achieved without the need to resort to expensive rocket science. But to achieve adequate levels of resilience will need collaboration between governments, businesses and individuals to mitigate the natural hazards and exploit opportunities to defy death and reduce suffering.[29]

In May 2010, Port-au-Prince in Haiti was one of the cities that signed up to the UNISDR "Making cities resilient" campaign. We should sincerely wish them the very best of luck in becoming more prepared for next time. Yet, with twelve of the world's sixteen largest cities located near coasts, many in low- and middle-income countries and at risk from a whole gamut of potential hazards, big-impact natural disasters are not going to go away anytime soon. The United Nations Global Assessment Report on Disaster and Risk Reduction identifies other cities such as Dhaka in Bangladesh (the 9th-largest and one of the most densely populated cities in the world) as "disasters waiting to happen."[30] Concerted efforts are still needed to put natural disasters in their place. We should not all be at risk.

As we have seen, natural disasters have consequences that go beyond the immediate death of the unlucky and unprepared: they can have a lasting human and economic impact on the survivors. As the Japanese earthquake in March 2011 clearly demonstrates, they are especially damaging to those countries with economic difficulties, and can go on to negatively impact a world still struggling to emerge from an extended economic crisis: leading us back to the topic of Global Trend 1.

Facing Up to a Changing World

So, there you go. A dozen Global Trends that will change your personal and professional life, the way societies and businesses do things and the character of the world we all live in. The 21st century will be different to the 20th. From the economic crisis, through geopolitical power shifts, technological challenges, climate change, water and food, education, demographic changes, war, terrorism and social unrest, energy, ecosystems and biodiversity, health, to natural disasters, there are plenty of reasons to expect change.

At the beginning of the book I asked the question:

"How much time do you dedicate to thinking about the big issues that are likely to affect your personal and professional life in the next 20 years?"

Having reached this chapter, you have certainly dedicated more hours to such big issues than you would otherwise have done. As such you should feel some increased awareness of the "big picture." But is there a bigger picture still? Could other catalysts for change come from beyond these twelve areas?

Well yes, there is always the chance of our planet being blasted by meteorites, solar storms or "*super volcano*" eruptions that could threaten life on earth as we know it. We know these events have happened in the past and might happen again sometime again in the future. There is also an outside chance that aliens could land and change things forever. This is not meant to be sarcastic (well, not overly so), as it is probably important that someone, somewhere does consider such things and obtains more evidence to inform appropriate decision making processes. But, as far as I am aware, these are largely beyond our current knowledge or ability to do much about them.

When facing up to a changing world we have to draw the line somewhere. In my opinion, there are sufficient issues to contend with on this planet, without setting off on space odysseys for the time being. In any case, this is not a book about cataclysmic events, but a book about Global *Trends*. Trends that we do have a good deal of information about from the past and that can, with reasonable certainty, be projected into the coming decades. As you have seen, we have built up a considerable amount of knowledge regarding each of the twelve Global Trends and can, most definitely, modify actions based upon how we see them panning-out.

There are few things in life that we can be absolutely sure about, but one thing I am certain of: many of the details described in the previous chapters will change. Some of the details will be out of date before I have even finished penning the text. Nevertheless, I am fairly confident that most of the underlying trends outlined will continue well into the 21st century. Unless nature and/ or human beings drastically change behavior in the coming years to knock these trends off course it is highly likely that:

1. **The repercussions of the economic crisis are not going to disappear in the short term.** High levels of debt will be an issue for many years to come. In particular, the possibility that countries previously considered as sound investments will default on their debt will result in profound changes to the way things are done at international, national and local levels across political, business and personal domains. Twitchy investors, austerity measures and labor market reforms will herald a new postcrisis economic era.

2. **Geopolitical power will continue shifting away from the incumbent powers of Europe and the USA and towards emerging economic powerhouses such as China, India, Russia, Brazil and others.** Unless some other big events conspire to derail the increasing economic clout of these countries, they will only become more powerful at an international level. The 20th-century status quo will certainly change. Whether the transition to a new world order is a smooth one depends upon the behavior of all the actors involved.

3. **Technology will continue to develop, bringing new sources of "creative destruction."** Old ways of doing things will be challenged by disruptive technologies that bring potential improvements. Individuals, companies and even societies that aren't proactive will get left behind. Our grandchildren will be doing things we could only dream about, just as we are doing things our grandparents dreamed of. However, there are likely to be mistakes made along the way that present significant risks to us and the environment.

4. **The world will continue warming up and climate will change.**
Human greenhouse gas emissions seem set to continue rising. Extreme weather events are likely to become more common, with far-reaching global impacts. There are likely to be many losers, but some winners – which will complicate the achievement of international agreement. In general, human beings will have no option but to rise to the challenges posed and adapt as best they can, while attempting to counter the underlying drivers behind the rising mercury.

5. **The worsening problem of water scarcity will continue to impact food production for the foreseeable decades, especially as nonrenewable groundwater is used up or polluted.** Given that human life is impossible without water this will put huge pressure upon existing resources. Local and national conflicts are possible; new ways of treating and living with less water will need to be found. Agriculture will suffer and food prices are likely to rise. With increasing production pressures, more mouths to feed, increasing vulnerability of fewer crop varieties, and emerging health problems the world food chain is likely to change substantially.

6. **The importance of sound education will continue to increase.** The teaching of values, lifelong skills, literacy and numeracy will remain essential to equip future generations with the necessary tools to face-up to the challenges presented by other Global Trends. Individuals, communities and countries with poor education levels will lag further behind in many ways and be a drag on global development. Without significant effort the link between poor education and poverty will not be broken – either in developed or developing nations.

7. **The population of the world will continue to increase and then stabilize around 2050.** This will put pressure upon existing resources. Average ages will rise across the globe as people live longer. With low birth rates, developed nations are likely to suffer too few young workers to sustain ever increasing *"support ratios"* of the elderly and current pension schemes. Conversely, developing countries are likely to have an excess of young people without sufficient economic opportunities. Thus migration pressures are likely to increase.

8. **War, terror and social unrest will continue and potentially increase.**
The shift from the "*unipolar*" and "*bipolar*" international systems of the
second half of the 20th century towards a "multipolar" one is likely to
have some destabilizing effect, with the emergence of strategic rivalries.
Social unrest will remain a high risk in many countries. Pressures on
key resources, lack of employment and economic disparities are likely
to provide the conditions for social ills such as disaffection, radicalism,
piracy and organized crime.

9. **The world will remain, by and large, oil-dependent in the coming
decades, despite a decline in its share of energy supply.** An energy
"revolution" would be needed to change this trend but does not appear
to be forthcoming in the short term. With rising pressures both on the
demand and supply side, oil prices are likely to increase – albeit with
volatile fluctuations. This will lead to greater efforts to develop and
implement higher capacity alternative energy sources. Nuclear will
remain a tempting, but politically charged, option.

10. **Humans will continue to destroy ecosystems and biodiversity will
continue to decline**. With sustained human pressure on the environment, extinction rates will continue and possibly accelerate, putting
many terrestrial and marine ecosystems in danger of collapse. Possibly
after key high-impact food-chain collapses, more sustainable behaviors
will become necessary as other critical thresholds are approached. In
the meantime, more nations will become ecological debtors, consuming and dumping more than the Earth can sustain.

11. **Health and well-being for everyone will remain an unfulfilled goal.**
Chronic, noncommunicable diseases will kill more people in the 21st
century. Continuing economic disparity will maintain conditions for
infectious diseases to thrive in poor countries. With increasing global
travel, increasing drug resistance and limited drug innovation for such
illnesses, the risk of epidemics of new infectious diseases will remain high.
Without profound reorientation, current health systems will increasingly
struggle to deliver quality, affordable service.

12. **Natural disasters will affect greater numbers of people, but potentially kill fewer.** Hazard planning and rescue of victims will continue

to improve ability to cope with disasters. Nevertheless, more people will be exposed to increasing floods, storms, extreme temperatures and droughts. Earthquakes and volcanoes will remain ever present, intermittent, but high-impact hazards. Increasingly populous cities with inadequate planning and unsafe buildings will put many at risk – especially the poor. Several cities will remain disasters waiting to happen.

Each of the twelve Global Trends, in itself, has the power to impact us on a personal, family, organizational, society, national and international level. As such, each Global Trend represents an important area of serious analysis. Yet, as this book has hinted throughout, each trend is to an extent inseparable from the others, so any meaningful analysis cannot be done in isolation. Hence the need to see the big picture. Repercussions from the crisis will lead to geopolitical power shifts; which in turn will depend upon which nations have access to cutting-edge technologies; which will drive humans' response to climate change; which will dictate what happens to water scarcity and food production; which depends to a large degree upon the education levels of the global population; which will have a cause–effect relationship with demographic changes; which is a driver of war, terror and social unrest; also driven by humans' unquenchable thirst for energy; which has profound negative impacts upon ecosystems around the globe; degradation of which leads to poor general health; which is magnified by low resilience in the face of natural disasters. And to close the circle, the earthquake of Japan in 2011 has clearly shown that natural disasters can play a big role in further exacerbating economic crises.

All of the twelve Global Trends are inter-related. Each links to the next as the "Global Trends Clock" ticks all the way around the twelve trends. (Figure 13.1)

With every tick of the clock, each Global Trend presents clear new threats. With more consideration though, definite opportunities also emerge – even if many are simply a chance to mitigate, or possibly eliminate, the threats. The challenge for any rational human being is to put aside natural emotions of pessimism in the face of the genuinely disconcerting directions that many Global Trends are taking. Nor are such trends to be brushed aside with the irrational optimism that "things will all work out in the end." Outside Hollywood, in real life there is the chance of both happy and sad endings

Figure 13.1: The Global Trends clock

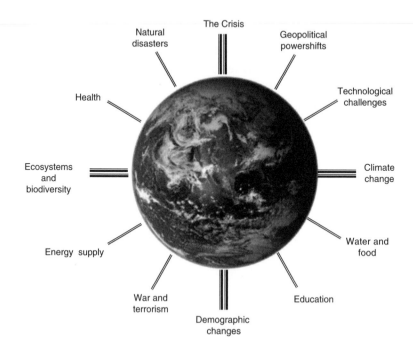

and it is up to us to do our utmost to ensure the former. The economic crisis has taught us that it is naïve to entrust such abstract and ethereal things as "market forces" to always act as some sort of benevolent, divine controller to protect the interests of the greater good.

No, we need to face-up to our changing world and confront these real issues with corresponding realism. Policy-makers, business leaders and citizens all have a role to play across local, national and international levels.

Throughout the book, I have referred several times to the World Economic Forum's *"Global Risks Landscape 2011."* The perception data from the corresponding Global Risks survey is graphed in Figure 13.2.* What is reflected by the 580

---

* Threats from new technologies (unintended consequences for human, animal or plant life from the release of agents into the biosphere by genetic engineering, synthetic biology or nanotechnology) appears as an outlier in this graph. However experts agreed subsequently that it was being underestimated. Other unlinked outliers such as 'Space Security' and 'Ocean Governance' in the original have been omitted from this graphic.

Figure 13.2: Perceived risks and related impacts over the next ten years

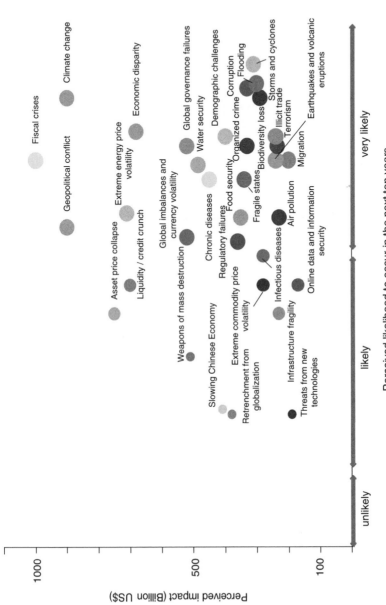

Source: Global Risks 2011 6th Edition. World Economic Forum

expert respondents to the survey is that most of the issues associated with each of the dozen Global Trends of this book fall within the *likely* or *very likely* categories of occurring within the next decade. In addition, they all have high economic impact well in excess of $100 billion, not to mention other forms of suffering.[1]

In the wake of the recent economic crisis, disease outbreaks, natural disasters, online security breaches and so on, I have often witnessed political and business leaders come up with phrases such as: "You can't plan for the unplannable." Such comments may give those who say them some comfort and allow them off the hook when something bad happens, but the truth is that we *can* plan for such things since we actually *know* a lot about them. What is more, faced with the possibility of a high-impact event, any sane human being carries out some form of scenario and action planning.

> **After all, faced with the fairly low likelihood, but high-impact potential repercussions of a car crash, conscious adults wear a seatbelt.**

In other words, any sensible person proceeds with caution knowing that the consequences could be grave. Thus, the most concerning things about these Global Trends are not the threats themselves, but the combination of a significantly negative impact along with the high likelihood of them actually happening within the next decade.

> **As the WEF Global Risk Landscape indicates, the individual threats posed by the twelve Global Trends are all in the high-probability and high-impact quadrant of the two-by-two matrix of Figure 13.3.**

When confronted with an even higher likelihood of a serious car accident, any sensible human being will either stop, or make darned sure that they were well prepared for the likely crash. Beyond wearing a seatbelt, they would also take out high risk insurance, modify driving habits accordingly and proceed with considerable caution. My contention is that similarly pragmatic scenario and action planning is necessary for the Global Trends at all levels of international, national and local society, from policy-makers and business leaders to individual citizens.

With some prior knowledge, most thinking people moderate habits *before* having an accident. Yet in the political and business world there has been a concerning move towards requiring conclusive "*scientific evidence*" before accepting that certain ways of doing things are not acceptable. At high political and business decision levels, the onus has often gone from the

Figure 13.3: Probability and impact: a guide to appropriate procedures

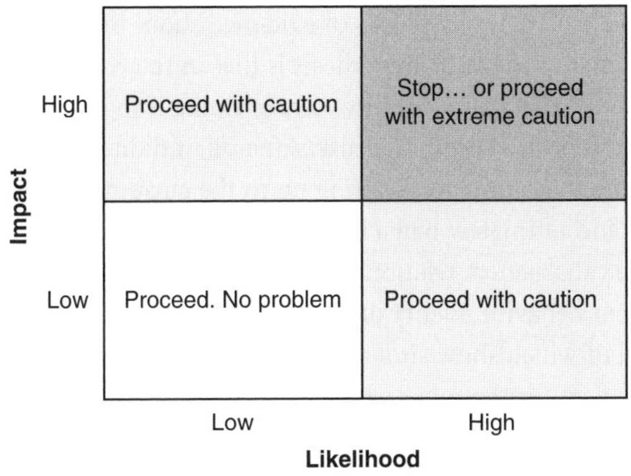

commonsense approach of applying caution when faced with high-impact risk, towards requiring up-front conclusive evidence that harm will definitely result before any moves are made to moderate clearly dangerous behaviors. This is waiting for the definitive proof that you will have a car crash before accepting it is a good idea to put on the seatbelt. All too often, I see otherwise smart people applying such pseudo-scientific logic in place of common sense, when in fact real scientific logic usually supports common sense.

The process of true science does involve empirical factual evidence (past car crashes.) Such evidence informs scientific theories from which hypotheses and predictions for the future can be made (regarding the likelihood of future car crashes). Another issue of real science is that evidence of an effect always happens *after* the cause. You simply cannot get proof of a cause before its effect. There is a time delay between cause and effect. Yet, armed with previous evidence-based theories, human beings can make rational and accurate predictions as to what is likely to happen if we continue with current ways of doing things. Thus a logical, scientific, intelligent approach allows us to formulate appropriate plans of action to mitigate or eliminate the threats (avoid the car accident), and exploit the opportunities (enjoy the journey.)

We already have a substantial amount of quality economic, historic and scientific evidence for each of the Global Trends. From this we can make

solid scientific hypotheses as to what is likely to happen in the coming years under various scenarios.

For example, backed-up by plenty of evidence about the way several Global Trends are going, my scientific hypothesis is that in the coming decades we will see plenty of proof that some current ways of doing things are not good. This is scientific, but it is also common sense. After all, it didn't require a rocket scientist to judge that the practices leading up to the current economic crisis were unsustainable and ultimately had a high chance of leading to financial collapse. It was a simple cause–effect relationship. Yet there were no seat belts, insurance plans or prudent behavior. Plenty of evidence is already in for the other Global Trends, several of which show similarly unsustainable behavioral patterns. We do not need to wait for the car crash before doing something about them: if we don't like where things are going, then we can take corrective action.

Conversely, if we think we are on the right path, then we can do things to ensure that we continue to benefit from such current trends. It is not all bad news by any means. After all, there are many "*good*" trends in process that should be continued, such as decreasing child deaths, increasing life expectancy, disease eradication, improving education and so on.

In his book *Collapse: How societies choose to fail or succeed,* Jared Diamond[2] identifies a number of factors that have contributed to the decline of some societies while others flourish. The Greenland Norse, the Easter Islanders, the Polynesians of Pitcairn Island, the Anasazi of North America, the Maya of Central America, and more modern examples, such as Rwanda and Haiti, are all societies that chose to fail. A wise man, drawing knowledge from various academic and practical spheres of knowledge, Professor Diamond makes the link between many of the historical issues that led to the failure of previous societies to problems facing the modern world: collapse of trade, climate change, water and food problems, overpopulation, hostile neighbors, energy shortages, and failure to adapt to environmental problems. While he didn't cover the full twelve, such problems are at the heart of the dozen Global Trends of the book you are holding. The impact of these issues goes beyond the society level, and is felt by organizations, of all shapes and sizes, and countless individual people.

Looking backwards, it is easy to see that societies have come and gone with some regularity throughout history: from the Egyptians, the Romans, the Incas, to the fall of Hitler's fascist Germany and Stalin's Soviet Union, and the opening-up of Franco's Spain and Mao's China. But also many presumed "normal" ways of doing things have changed: widespread slavery, sacrifices and corporal punishment have largely past into the history books as class and gender equality, social support systems and urbanization have emerged. The Stone Age, the Iron Age, the industrial revolution, the information age, the knowledge economy… Societies, businesses and individuals have had to adapt to such changing ways throughout history. The day-to-day of our grandparents' lives bears little resemblance to our daily reality. And, looking towards the future, change will continue its forward march. With so many pressures so early in the 21st century, it should be no surprise that many frameworks that we take for granted are likely to change. Paradigms will change whether we like it or not: either by force or by design.

In other words: "*Shift happens.*" Get used to it.

Nevertheless, we have a big advantage over previous societies and generations, in that we have a considerable amount of data, information and knowledge that we can now draw upon so as not to fall into the same pitfalls, whilst proactively charting a course to a brighter future. We can see where the Global Trends are going and the likelihood of paradigm change in many aspects of the world as we currently know it. As such the "*black swans*" introduced in the first chapter are plainly visible. The ignorance of the dinosaurs is no longer an excuse. With awareness, these black swans cease to be totally uncontrollable systemic shocks and become actionable issues. Furthermore, the *Last Samurai* showed that, after attaining awareness, failure to act in an appropriate manner is not an appealing option.

So, now that you are aware, what are you going to *do*: for yourself, your family, your organization and your society?

We are now in the second part of the problem relating to what to do about those black swans now that we can see them. With a view of the big picture, it is time to consider formulating action plans to reduce the negatives and maximize the positives from these Global Trends. This is where human beings have the ability to excel, yet often seem to get stuck. The moment of action is often the most challenging, but is what usually distinguishes the successful from the rest. It is at the moment of action where the aptitudes of *vision, awareness, insight* and *wisdom*, which I argued so strongly for in the first chapter, really come into their own. The problem is that faced with such a complicated array of issues where does one start?

Well actually it doesn't have to be so complicated. There are a number of business tools and frameworks that take such strategic issues down to the operational level of implementing appropriate actions to reduce risks and costs and increase the benefits and profits. The objective is the same when managing businesses or societies to minimize threats and maximize opportunities. In my particular area of real-world experience and business school expertise there has always been a clear mantra:

"Do more with less."

In other words, take actions to minimize the downsides whilst accentuating the upsides. In the world of business this usually takes the form of managing operations to provide better quality of product and service outputs with reduced inputs. The same can be applied to the management of threats and opportunities, and most of the successful approaches are simple ones that can be easily understood and communicated. Just one such commonsense approach that I have found works in the implementation of strategic goals in complex environments is that of the "*Pareto Analysis*." Many know of this as the "*80:20 rule*." The underlying principle is that for many management situations:

Roughly 80 percent of the effects come from 20 percent of the causes.

Or to put it another way, working diligently on 20 percent of the drivers will control for 80 percent of the outcomes. This is not trivial. Because of the way things are, about 80 percent of the threats can be mitigated by intelligently and rigorously working on 20 percent of the underlying problems. Similarly around 80 percent of the opportunities can be exploited by intelligently focusing upon the 20 percent priority actions that will reap most dividends.

In other words focus upon "*the low hanging fruit*" first.

In the same way that 80 percent of the fruit can be picked-off a tree in 20 percent of the time needed to pick all the fruit; in 20 percent of the time you can vacuum 80 percent of a room; with 20 percent well focused effort you can achieve 80 percent of the exam results; 80 percent of defects in a car plant come down to 20 percent of the causes; 80 percent of lateness will come down to 20 percent of excuses; 80 percent of customer satisfaction is achieved by focusing upon 20 percent of the service offering. Etcetera. (See Figure 13.4.)

Figure 13.4: Causes and effects: the 80:20 rule

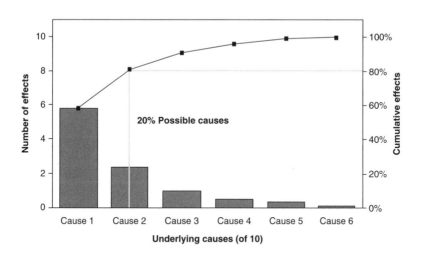

In any management situation, it makes sense to concentrate on those actions that will lead to most benefit with the least possible use of time, energy and resources. Only once the 80 percent easy-to-get fruit has been picked is it opportune to move on to the more difficult-to-reach stuff. To begin by expending effort on the 20 percent that is out of reach is not sensible, wastes a lot of effort and is usually demotivating. If, after picking the first 80 percent, there are resources and motivation to continue towards higher goals then it is time to move to the next phase: apply another 20 percent effort to the next 80 percent of easy-to-pick remaining fruit.

And so on until the goals have been reached. We do not live in a perfect world, so achieving 100 percent of the targets in the real world is a statistical impossibility: even more so in a single step. Thus trying to work on everything at the same time simply wastes valuable effort and resources and progress is inevitably limited. Nevertheless, this should not dampen enthusiasm for making "*continuous improvements*" towards the desired goals. But the only chance we have of getting there – as individuals, businesses or societies – is by taking small steps at a time: acting on that most important 20 percent of underlying causes at a time.

While being no "*magic wand*," this commonsense approach works, and is successfully implemented across all manner of organizational and business scenarios. So, why not apply it to provide some framework for maximizing opportunities whilst minimizing risks associated with the twelve Global Trends?

Now, it is time to do some more thinking as to how to go about managing and acting upon the dozen Global Trends to help reach our own goals. To do this, we need to identify those threats and opportunities that will have greatest impact upon what is most important to us. As you have read through this book, several personal, business and society threats and opportunities will have occurred to you. The next step is to "*brainstorm*," ideally in a focused team, a more complete list of threats and opportunities at whatever unit of analysis is most appropriate: nation, community, business, family, or just for you.

From this list of potential threats and opportunities, select those that are most likely to have the most impact in the coming years. Reduce the list down to the top 20 percent of most severe threats and most promising opportunities, and enter these into a table similar to Table 13.1 (under "Threats/Opportunities: 1, 2, 3, 4..."). Next, again ideally with a team, identify actions to address each of the priority threats and opportunities. Again reduce the list of actions down to the top 20 percent and enter into the table (against "Actions: A, B, C, D..."). In all of this process, stay ethical. Remember, if others lose out, ultimately there is a likelihood you will too.

Then work through the table indicating (with a dot) the threats and opportunities that are addressed by each action. Here the inter-relatedness of the Global Trends actually helps since you will invariably find that any particular action will work towards addressing several threats and opportunities. If there is further need to prioritize actions, those approximately 20 percent that address around 80 percent of threats and opportunities should be given highest priority.

By way of a few simple examples:

On a personal level, buying cheaper, fresher more nutritious, in-season foodstuffs from a local grocer – rather than more costly transported food of questionable nutritional value – is likely to impact upon an individual's dimensions of surviving the crisis, decreasing greenhouse gases, lowering energy requirements, reducing pressure on ecosystems, and reducing chronic illnesses. Not bad for one action.

On an organizational and business level, implementing cost-saving energy efficiency efforts will have similar impacts across several Global Trends, but on a bigger scale. Further actions such as investing in new technologies, creating new markets in emerging nations, collaborating with educational initiatives and health improvement programs will all have positive and profound impacts across many of the Global Trends. Similarly, implementing "*lean*" approaches to do more with less resources and reduced waste has to be a good idea in general.

Table 13.1: Translating awareness into action

Global trend	Threats/Opportunities	A	B	C	D	E	F	G	H	I	J	K	L	M	N	O	P	Q	R	S	T	U	V	W	X	Who?
The Crisis	1	•	•	•	•	•	•	•	•	•						•										
	2	•	•	•	•	•	•	•	•							•										
Geopolitics	3		•	•	•	•	•	•			•	•		•	•	•	•	•	•	•	•	•	•	•		
	4		•	•	•	•									•	•	•	•	•	•	•	•		•	•	
Technology	5			•	•	•	•	•				•		•	•	•	•	•	•	•	•	•	•	•	•	
	6		•	•	•	•	•					•	•	•	•	•	•	•	•	•	•	•		•		
Climate Change	7		•	•	•	•		•				•	•	•	•	•	•	•	•	•	•	•	•	•	•	
	8		•	•	•	•	•					•	•		•	•	•	•	•	•	•	•				
Water & Food	9		•	•	•	•	•					•	•	•	•	•	•	•	•	•	•	•				
	10				•	•	•					•	•	•	•	•	•									
Education	11	•			•	•	•				•	•	•	•	•	•	•				•	•	•	•		
	12	•		•	•	•	•				•	•	•	•	•	•	•			•	•	•	•	•		
Demographics	13			•	•	•	•	•						•	•	•	•	•	•	•	•	•	•	•		
	14			•	•	•	•	•					•	•	•	•	•	•	•	•	•	•				
War & Terror	15			•	•	•	•	•	•				•	•	•	•					•	•	•	•		
	16			•	•	•	•	•						•	•	•					•	•	•	•		
Energy	17				•	•	•	•					•	•	•	•						•	•	•		
	18				•	•	•	•						•	•									•		
Ecosystems	19				•	•	•								•									•		
	20				•	•	•																	•		
Health	21				•	•															•	•	•	•	•	
	22					•															•	•	•	•		
Natural Disaster	23				•	•															•	•	•	•	•	
	24					•																	•			
When?																										

On a society and national level, investing in good, solid education, particularly at lower levels will, undoubtedly, have positive impact across the board. Also, investments in primary healthcare and poverty alleviation efforts are likely to reap rewards across a number of the Global Trend threats and opportunities.

As the Global Trend clock indicates in Figure 13.5, there are not only strong cause–effect relationships going around the clock, but also between the opposite points: the crisis will be interconnected with demographic changes; geopolitical shifts inextricably linked with war, terrorism and social unrest; technological challenges links with energy supply; climate change is connected to ecosystems and biodiversity; water and food is related to health; education determines response to natural disaster. But as analysis of the threats, opportunities and actions chart will reveal, there are likely to be actions that work across several Global Trends, and the interconnections between Global Trends will become more complex, but still relatively manageable.

Now it is a question of joining the dots in the table. And what do you see? Well, firstly you will have a new, albeit possibly rather "*grainy,*" perspective on the global big picture. And secondly, you now have a simple way of "killing various birds with one stone" (a rather unfortunate, but effective metaphor) as each action is likely to be linked to several Global Trends. My suggestion is that this framework is a simple, effective and efficient way of getting the process of mitigating threats and maximizing opportunities underway. Later on, more complex tools and methods can be brought into play if needed.

In the end, any of the Global Trends can take center stage depending upon the perspective adopted. Ultimately, the point of departure is up to you and your intended goals. Depending upon what you want to gain from conducting such an exercise, the unit of analysis is also your decision: the planet Earth; the international system; your country; your region; your community; your business or organization; your family... or just you. When all is said and done, whatever perspective you take, YOU will always be in the middle.

With all this I can already hear the cynics saying: "*Isn't it ridiculous to expect to solve the world's problems with such a simple framework?*" Well, no I don't think so. Audacious maybe, but not ridiculous. The simplicity of such an approach is an advantage. After all, it was complex, overly sophisticated methods, that only a very few financial wizards truly understood, that got us into the current global economic doldrums. Of course, there are other more refined management approaches and tools that would go beyond such a simple analysis, but the 80:20 rule will go a long way towards achieving goals and is definitely a good start to help move the process along. I have been actively involved in many different business and organizational contexts since the mid-1980s and simple approaches such as these are the ones that genuinely solve problems rather than adding to them.

Perhaps one of the opportunities of the current times of economic crisis is a genuine return to sound values and common sense basics. Pragmatic, simple and holistic approaches are the ones that are most likely to get us out of the predicaments we are facing, as well as continue working towards a more prosperous, healthier and just world.

Now that we have identified many of the challenges, it is up to all of us to face-up to this changing world. To do this, it will be necessary to question the status quo and preconceived ideas. There will be a need to leave comfort zones, safety in numbers and avoid emotional "*noise*." Making good decisions requires continual digging beneath the hype and hysteria in order to obtain the best, most impartial, factual evidence available at the

Figure 13.5: The twelve Global Trends and YOU

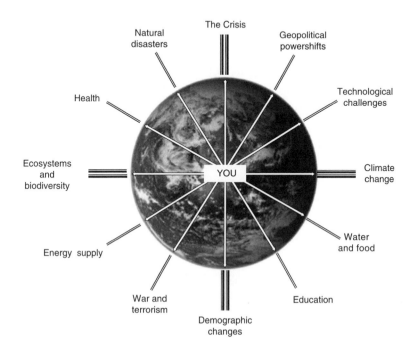

time. Given the number of vested interest groups, it is often quite a challenge to get to unadulterated facts, but it is important to stay focused and rational. As it has always been, it will be crucial to think for yourself and work towards your own conclusions. Above all, as time moves on, the ability to stay aware, to keep abreast of changes and to be prepared to act will be invaluable.

The aim of this book has been to present a coherent overview of the Global Trends and propose a simple framework to provide a basis against which policy-makers, business professionals and thoughtful citizens can inform decisions and guide appropriate action. Is the analysis and model complete? No, but it is a start. When looking into the future a complete analytical model is, frankly, impossible. The model presented here, on the other hand, is simple, flexible and intuitive enough to be clearly communicated and continually developed as time passes and as the Global Trends inevitably carry on evolving. Any such model, however rudimentary, that can help manage the potentially turbulent years ahead is better than no model at all.

In the face of a changing world, we all have three choices: to *act*, to *do nothing*, or to *react* when change inevitably happens. The dinosaurs did nothing because they weren't aware of any change: and look what happened to them. The Last Samurai were aware of potential change, but were too proud to adapt their old ways of doing things, arrogantly believing they would be able to react when the time came. They got it wrong. Of course, the ignorant and arrogant can be lucky. But there is also such a thing as improving your chances of success, and for that you *have* to act. No-one knows the future for certain, but with modern science, economics and a significant body of historical evidence at our disposal, we can have a pretty good idea as to where things are going. As such, we now have the benefits that previous generations did not have: we *can* look into the crystal ball, even if it is somewhat foggy. As Peter Schwartz outlines in his book *Inevitable surprises: thinking ahead in times of turbulence,* the keys in the scenario-planning process are to use your own judgment, plan a course, keep your eyes open, avoid denial and also consider some contingency plans.[3]

It is not simply a case of extrapolating past trends into the future, but reasoning why things have happened the way they did, predicting what could happen next and adopting an appropriate course of action. After scenario planning and implementing actions, given the uncertainties of the real-world, there is another thing that is highly recommendable: *stay flexible*. Charles Darwin is often misquoted as saying something along the lines of:

> It is not the strongest of the species that survives, nor the most intelligent. It is the one that is most adaptable to change.[4]

While Darwin's Victorian rambling style does not lend itself to simple interpretation, this popular paraphrasing from *The Origin of Species* does indicate that, throughout the history of our planet, if you weren't adaptable, then you had to be lucky enough to have the specific physical attributes to survive whatever change was coming. Modern humans do not have many physical attributes that really gives us a competitive advantage over anything else with more teeth, claws, fur or whatever than us. But we do have a decent brain, and we have always known how to use it to look forwards, plan for the future and act accordingly to improve our chances of success. Frankly, that is how we have made it so far as a species despite our other weaknesses. Looking forward, armed with knowledge and the courage to act, it is also possible to have some control over how we manage these 21st century Global Trends to our benefit. From international political and business leaders to the person on the street, with conviction it is possible to have considerable positive impact upon where your world is going; where your country, your organization, your community, your family, and ultimately, where your personal and professional life is going.

This is what facing up to a changing world is all about. It is not about pessimism or optimism, but about realism. Not worrying about the future, but instead getting ready for it. It is about using an increased awareness of the big picture to take better decisions and improved actions in the years to come. The end is not nigh, but we are entering a new era.

I wish you all the best with managing the twelve Global Trends to mitigate those threats and maximize opportunities… and, of course, with facing up to a changing world.

So, what will you do now?

References

Introduction

1. Goldin, Ian, 2009. Navigating our global future. *TED Global.* July, Oxford, UK. http://www.ted.com/talks/ian_goldin_navigating_our_global_future.html. Accessed March 2011.

2. The National Intelligence Council, 2008. *Global Trends 2025: A Transformed World.* Washington DC:US Government Printing Office. http://www.dni.gov/nic/PDF_2025/2025_Global_Trends_Final_Report.pdf. Accessed March 2011.

3. World Economic Forum, 2011. *Global Risks 2011 6th Edition: An Initiative of the Risk Response Network.* http://riskreport.weforum.org/. Accessed July 2011.

Global Trend 1   Repercussions of "The Crisis"

1. Wolf, Martin, 2011. How the crisis catapulted us into the future. *Financial Times,* February 1. http://www.ft.com/cms/s/0/5fc7e840-2e45-11e0-8733-00144feabdc0.html#axzz1CnOgSnXK. Accessed February 2011.

2. Ferguson, Niall, 2009. *The Ascent of Money: A Financial History of the World.* Penguin Books.

3. Kindleberger, Charles P., and Aliber, Robert, 2005. *Manias, Panics, Crashes: A History of Financial Crises.* 5th ed. Wiley.

4. Laeven, Luc, and Valencia, Fabian, 2008. Systemic banking crises: A new database. *International Monetary Fund Working Paper,* wp/08/224. http://www.imf.org/external/pubs/ft/wp/2008/wp08224.pdf. Accessed April 2011.

5. Barber, Lionel, 2008. How gamblers broke the banks. *Financial Times,* 16 December. http://www.ft.com/cms/s/0/4fc84eca-cb10-11dd-87d7-000077b07658.html. Accessed April 2011.

6. Ben S. Bernanke talks about four questions about the financial crisis. Speeches. The Morehouse College, Atlanta, Georgia. 14 April 2009. *Board of Governors of the Federal Reserve System.* Web. 14 April 2009. http://www.federalreserve.gov/newsevents/speech/bernanke20090414a.htm. Accessed May 2010.

7. President Obama announces financial regulatory reform. Speeches & Remarks. The White House, Washington DC, 18 June 2009. Whitehouse.gov. Web. 17 June 2009. http://www.whitehouse.gov/the_press_office/Remarks-of-the-President-on-Regulatory-Reform/. Accessed May 2010.

8. Roubini, Nouriel, 2009. Ten risks to global growth: An analysis of medium-term economic prospects. *Forbes.com* 28 May. http://www.forbes.com/2009/05/27/recession-depression-global-economy-growth-opinions-columnists-nouriel-roubini.html. Accessed May 2010.

9. International Monetary Fund (IMF), 2009. *World Economic Outlook: Crisis and Recovery April 2009.* Washington DC: International Monetary Fund. http://www.imf.org/external/pubs/ft/weo/2009/01/pdf/text.pdf. Accessed May 2010.

10. The White House, 2008. Declaration of G20. http://georgewbush-whitehouse.archives.gov/news/releases/2008/11/20081115-1.html. Accessed February 2009.

11. The Reserve Bank of India and the Bank of England, 2009. *Causes of the crisis: Key lessons*, G20 Workshop on the Global Economy. http://www.g20.org/Documents/g20_workshop_causes_of_the_crisis.pdf. Accessed April 2011.

12. The Committee for a Responsible Federal Budget, 2010. Washington, DC. http://stimulus.org/?filter0=80%filter1=%filter2=%filter3. Accessed June 20 2011.

13. The Israel Export & International Cooperation Institute, International Projects.http://www.export.gov.il/eng/SubIndex.asp?CategoryID=340. Accessed April 2011.

14. The global debt clock. *The Economist.* http://buttonwood.economist.com/content/gdc. Accessed February 2011.

15. Office for National Statistics, 2009 Annual Survey of Hours and Earnings (ASHE) Analysis by All Employees. http://www.statistics.gov.uk/downloads/theme_labour/ASHE-2009/2009_all_employees.pdf. Accessed February 2011.

16. Still scary. *The Economist*, 13 January 2011. http://www.economist.com/node/17902815?story_id=17902815. Accessed January 2011.

17. Time for Plan B. *The Economist*, 13 January 2011. http://www.economist.com/node/17902709?story_id=17902709 . Accessed January 2011.

18. Organization for Economic Co-operation and Development (OECD), 2010. Economic Outlook 88. http://www.oecd.org/home/0,2987,en_2649_201185_1_1_1_1_1,00.html. Accessed March 2011.

19. International Monetary Fund, 2009. Global financial stability report. http://www.imf.org/external/pubs/ft/survey/so/2009/RES093009A.htm. Accessed March 2011.

20. A special report on the world economy: The long climb. *The Economist,* 1 October 2009. http://www.economist.com/specialreports/displayStory.cfm?story_id=14530093. Accessed March 2011.

21. World Economic Forum, 2011. *Global Risks 2011 6th Edition: An Initiative of the Risk Response Network.* http://riskreport.weforum.org/. Accessed July 2011.

Global Trend 2   Geo-political Power Shifts

1. A special report on China and America: A wary respect. *The Economist,* 22 October 2009. http://www.economist.com/opinion/displaystory.cfm?story_id=14678579. Accessed April 2011.

2. Pesek, William, 2005. South Korea, Another "BRIC" in Global Wall. http://www.bloomberg.com/apps/news?pid=newsarchive%sid=aoJ4WG5LSf1s%refer=market_insight. Accessed June 20 2011.

3. World Economic Forum, 2011. *Global Risks 2011 6th Edition: An Initiative of the Risk Response Network.* http://riskreport.weforum.org/. Accessed July 2011.

4. Wolf, Martin, 2010. What the world must do to sustain its convalescence. *Financial Times,* 3 February.

5. Schott, Jeffrey J., 2009. America, Europe, and the new trade order. http://www.bepress.com/bap/vol11/iss3/art1/. Accessed April 2011.

6. Beattie, Alan, 2010. BRICS: The changing faces of global power. *Financial Times,* 17 January. http://www.ft.com/cms/s/0/95cea8b6-0399-11df-a601-00144feabdc0.html#axzz1LNttaagD. Accessed April 2011.

7. Warrell, Helen, and Bernard, Steve, 2010. Building BRICs. *Financial Times,* 15 January. http://librarydb.iese.edu:3176/cms/s/0/f246692e-01cf-11df-b8cb-00144feabdc0.html. Accessed April 2011.

8. Goldman Sachs, 2007. The N-11: More than an acronym. http://www2.goldmansachs.com/ideas/global-economic-outlook/n-11-acronym-doc.pdf. Accessed April 2011.

9. China and America: The odd couple. *The Economist,* 22 October 2009. http://www.economist.com/opinion/displaystory.cfm?story_id=14699593. Accessed April, 2011.

10. A special report on China and America: Tug-of-car. *The Economist,* 22 October 2009. http://www.economist.com/node/14678523 Accessed April 2011.

11. Cookson, Clive, 2010. Building BRICS: China scientists lead world in research growth. *Financial Times,* 25 January. http://www.ft.com/cms/s/0/7ef3097e-09da-11df-8b23-00144feabdc0,dwp_uuid=9bae68fe-011c-11df-a4cb-00144feabdc0.html. Accessed April 2011.

12. The National Intelligence Council, 2008. *Global Trends 2025: A Transformed World.* Washington DC: US Government Printing Office. http://www.dni.gov/nic/PDF_2025/2025_Global_Trends_Final_Report.pdf. Accessed March 2011.

13. Developing nations' progress risks hitting the wall. *Financial Times,* 18 January 2010. http://www.ft.com/cms/s/0/841bf01e-03d1-11df-a601-00144feabdc0.html#axzz1LNttaagD. Accessed April 2011.

14. An elephant, not a tiger: A special report on India. *The Economist*, 13 December 2008. http://www.economist.com/node/12749735?story_id=12749735 Accessed June 20 2011.

15. India's surprising economic miracle. *The Economist*, 30 September 2010. http://www.economist.com/node/17147648?story_id=17147648. Accessed June 20 2011.

16. A special report on business and finance in Brazil. *The Economist*, 14 November 2009. http://www.economist.com/node/14829485?story_id=14829485 Accessed April 2011.

17. The White House, 2010. U.S.–Russia relations: "Reset" fact sheet. http://www.whitehouse.gov/the-press-office/us-russia-relations-reset-fact-sheet. Accessed April 2011.

18. Goldman Sachs, 2007. *BRICS and Beyond*. http://www2.goldmansachs.com/ideas/brics/book/BRIC-Full.pdf. Accessed April 2011.

19. United Nations, 2010. Security Council imposes additional sanctions on Iran. http://www.un.org/News/Press/docs/2010/sc9948.doc.htm. Accessed April 2011.

20. International Monetary Fund, World economic and financial surveys: World economic outlook database. http://www.imf.org/external/pubs/ft/weo/2010/01/weodata/index.aspx. Accessed April 2011.

21. Pelofsky, Jeremy, and Margolies, Dan, 2010. U.S. charges Daimler with violating bribery laws. *Reuters,* Mar 23. http://www.reuters.com/article/idUSTRE62M3TK20100323. Accessed April 2011.

22. Google in "new approach" on China, *BBC News, Business*. 30 June 2010. http://www.bbc.co.uk/news/10443648. Accessed April 2011.

23. Farchy, Jack, 2011. Libya fighting hits oil-exporting region. http://www.ft.com/cms/s/0/ce174c10-44bf-11e0-a8c6-00144feab49a.html#axzz1FRehBpN7. Accessed March 2011.

24. Oil Pressure Rising. *The Economist*, 24 February 2010. http://www.economist.com/node/18233452?story_id=18233452. Accessed March 2011.

25. Gmur, Martina, 2011. The new geopolitical reality. *World Economic Forum*, January 26. http://www.weforum.org/blog/posts/new-geopolitical-reality. Accessed March 2011.

Global Trend 3   Technological Challenges

1. Clarke, Arthur C., 1962. *Profiles of the Future: An Enquiry into the Limits of the Possible*. Henry Holt & Co.

2. de Heinzelin, Jean 1, Clark, J. Desmond, and White, Tim, 1999. Environment and behavior of 2.5-million-year-old Bouri Hominids. *Science* 284 (5414): 625–629.

3. http://www.theheartofnewengland.com/LifeInNewEngland-Ice-Harvesting.html. Accessed April 2011.

4. Christensen, C., 1997. *The Innovator's Dilemma*. Harvard Business School Press.

5. Vermeulen, F., 2011. *Business Exposed*. FT Prentice Hall.

6. World Economic Forum, 2011. *Global Risks 2011 6th Edition: An Initiative of the Risk Response Network*. http://riskreport.weforum.org/. Accessed July 2011.

7. The Health Protection Agency, 2011. Health and advice on mobile phones. The INTER-PHONE study. http://www.hpa.org.uk/Topics/Radiation/UnderstandingRadiation/UnderstandingRadiationTopics/ElectromagneticFields/MobilePhones/info_HealthAdvice/. Accessed March 2011.

8. Samkange-Zeeb, F., and Blettner, M., 2009. Emerging aspects of mobile phone use. *Emerging Health Threats Journal*. http://www.eht-journal.net/index.php/ehtj/article/view/7082 Accessed 20 June 2011.

9. Meggitt, Geoff, 2008. Taming the rays, http://tamingtherays.com/TTR3-EarlyYearsofXrayspdf.pdf. Accessed March 2011.

10. In place of safety nets: Lessons from Deepwater Horizon and Fukushima. *The Economist*, April 20 2011. http://www.economist.com/node/18586658?story_id=18586658. Accessed April 2011.

11. WebSiteOptimization, 2007. US broadband penetration breaks 80% among active internet users. http://www.websiteoptimization.com/bw/0703/. Accessed April 2011.

12. OECD, 2009. Total broadband subscribers by country (Dec. 2008). http://www.oecd.org/dataoecd/22/15/39574806.xls. Retrieved 15 July 2009.

13. Associated Press, 2006. "Digital music sales booming." *Wired News*, 19 January. http://www.wired.com/science/discoveries/news/2006/01/70045. Accessed April 2011.

14. Waters, Richard, 2011.Web firms aim to benefit from role in uprising. *The Financial Times*, 13 February 2011. http://www.ft.com/cms/s/2/4cdb4c98-37b1-11e0-b91a-00144feabdc0.html#axzz1Dwdn7jn8. Accessed April 2011.

15. OECD, 2008. Main science and technology indicators (April 2008). 2008(1).

16. Print me a Stradivarius. *The Economist*, 10 February 2011. http://www.economist.com/node/18114327?story_id=18114327. Accessed March 2011.

Global Trend 4   Climate Change

1. *An inconvenient truth: a global warning*. 2006. Written by Al Gore. Directed by Davis Guggenheim. Distributed by Paramount Classics.

2. CBS News, U.S. wilting under humid heat wave. http://www.cbsnews.com/stories/2010/07/17/national/main6687097.shtml. Accessed March 2011.

3. Eilperin, Juliet, and Fahrenthold, David A., 2010. Harsh winter a sign of disruptive climate change, report says. *The Washington Post*, 28 January. www.washingtonpost.

com/wp-dyn/content/article/2010/01/28/AR2010012800041.html. Accessed March 2011.

4. Who cares? Don't count on public opinion to support mitigation. *The Economist,* 3 December 2009. http://www.economist.com/node/14994856. Accessed March 2011.

5. Flawed scientists: the intergovernmental panel on climate change needs reform. The case for climate action does not. *The Economist,* 8 July 2010. http://www.economist.com/node/16539392?story_id=16539392 Accessed March 2011.

6. Climategate: Anthropogenic Global Warming, history's biggest scam. http://www.climategate.com/about. Accessed July 2011.

7. International Panel on Climate Change, 2011. *IPCC Fifth Assessment Report (AR5).* http://www.ipcc.ch/ Accessed April 2011.

8. International Panel on Climate Change (IPCC), 2007. *Climate Change 2007: Synthesis Report (2007) An Assessment of the Intergovernmental Panel on Climate Change.* http://www.ipcc.ch/pdf/assessment-report/ar4/syr/ar4_syr.pdf. Accessed March 2011.

9. IPCC, 2007. *Climate Change 2007: Synthesis Report. Contribution of Working Groups I, II and III to the Fourth Assessment Report of the Intergovernmental Panel on Climate Change.* http://www.ipcc.ch/publications_and_data/publications_ipcc_fourth_assessment_report_synthesis_report.htm. Accessed April 2011.

10. National Aeronautics and Space Administration (NASA), 2009. Arctic ice results are in. *Global Climate Change.* http://climate.nasa.gov/news/index.cfm?FuseAction=ShowNews%NewsID=174. Accessed June 20 2011.

11. National Aeronautics and Space Administration (NASA), 2009. The ups and downs of global warming. *Global Climate Change.* http://climate.nasa.gov/news/index.cfm?FuseAction=ShowNews%NewsID=175. Accessed June 20 2011.

12. Pidwirny, M., Lemke, K., and Faulkner, D., 2009. *Understanding Physical Geography.* http://www.physicalgeography.net/understanding/contents.html. Accessed March 2011.

13. National Aeronautics and Space Administration (NASA), 2009. The greenhouse effect. *Global Climate Change.* http://climate.nasa.gov/causes/. Accessed March 2011.

14. National Aeronautics and Space Administration (NASA). Climate change: How do we know? *Global Climate Change.* http://climate.nasa.gov/evidence/. Accessed March 2011.

15. Metz, B., Davidson, O.R., Bosch, P.R., Dave, R., and Meyer, L.A., eds., 2007. *Contribution of Working Group III to the Fourth Assessment Report of the Intergovernmental Panel on Climate Change.* http://www.ipcc.ch/publications_and_data/publications_ipcc_fourth_assessment_report_wg3_report_mitigation_of_climate_change.htm. Accessed April 2011.

16. Getting warmer. So far the effort to tackle global warming has achieved little. Copenhagen offers the chance to do better. *The Economist,* 3 December 2009. http://www.economist.com/node/14994872. Accessed March 2011.

17. United Nations Framework Convention on Climate Change (UNFCCC), Kyoto Protocol. http://unfccc.int/kyoto_protocol/items/2830.php. Accessed March 2011.

18. United Nations Framework Convention on Climate Change (UNFCCC), Status of ratification of the Kyoto Protocol. http://unfccc.int/kyoto_protocol/status_of_ratification/items/2613.php. Accessed March 2011.

19. Closing the gaps. How the world divides on a global deal. *The Economist,* 3 December 2009. http://www.economist.com/node/14994828?story_id=E1_TQJJQRNR. Accessed March 2011.

20. Stopping climate change, Rich and poor countries have to give ground to get a deal in Copenhagen; then they must focus on setting a carbon price. *The Economist,* 3 December 2009. http://www.economist.com/node/15017322?story_id=E1_TVDTSPNN. Accessed March 2011.

21. Spin, science and climate change. Action on climate is justified, not because the science is certain, but precisely because it is not. *The Economist,* 18 March 2010. http://www.economist.com/node/15720419?story_id=E1_TVSNDQTJ. Accessed March 2011.

22. Back from the brink: The UN climate conference achieved some results, albeit modest ones, *The Economist,* 16 December 2010. http://www.economist.com/research/articlesbysubject/displaystory.cfm?subjectid=348924%story_id=17730564. Accessed June 20 2011.

23. How to live with climate change. It won't be stopped, but its effects can be made less bad. *The Economist,* 25 November 2010. http://www.economist.com/node/17575027?story_id=17575027. Accessed March 2011.

24. World Economic Forum, 2011. *Global Risks 2011 6th Edition: An Initiative of the Risk Response Network.* http://riskreport.weforum.org/. Accessed July 2011.

25. IPCC, 2007. *Climate Change 2007: The Physical Science Basis. Contribution of Working Group I to the Fourth Assessment Report of the Intergovernmental Panel on Climate Change.* Solomon, S. et al. eds. Cambridge: Cambridge University Press, 996 pp. http://www.ipcc.ch/publications_and_data/publications_ipcc_fourth_assessment_report_wg1_report_the_physical_science_basis.htm. Accessed April 2011.

26. IPCC, 2007. *Climate Change 2007: Impacts, Adaptation and Vulnerability. Contribution of Working Group II to the Fourth Assessment Report of the Intergovernmental Panel on Climate Change.* Parry, M.L. et al. eds., Cambridge: Cambridge University Press, 976 pp. http://www.ipcc.ch/publications_and_data/publications_ipcc_fourth_assessment_report_wg2_report_impacts_adaptation_and_vulnerability.htm. Accessed April 2011.

27. The Ozone Hole. http://www.theozonehole.com/. Accessed March 2011.

Global Trend 5   Water and Food

1. Water as a scarce resource: An interview with Nestlé's chairman. *McKinsey Quarterly*, December 2009. https://www.mckinseyquarterly.com/Energy_ Resources_Materials/Water_as_a_scarce_resource_An_interview_with_Nestles_ chairman_2482. Accessed March 2011.

2. World Economic Forum, 2011. *Global Risks 2011 6th Edition: An Initiative of the Risk Response Network.* http://riskreport.weforum.org/. Accessed July 2011.

3. The National Intelligence Council, 2008. *Global Trends 2025: A Transformed World.* Washington DC: US Government Printing Office. http://www.dni.gov/nic/PDF_ 2025/2025_Global_Trends_Final_Report.pdf. Accessed March 2011.

4. Food and Agriculture Organization (FAO) of the United Nations, 2009. The state of food insecurity in the world. http://www.fao.org/docrep/012/i0876e/i0876e00.htm. Accessed April 2011.

5. Managing water strategically: An interview with the CEO of Rio Tinto. *McKinsey Quarterly*, December 2009. https://www.mckinseyquarterly.com/Energy_ Resources_Materials/Managing_water_strategically_An_interview_with_the_ CEO_of_Rio_Tinto_2494. Accessed March 2011.

6. Running Dry. *The Economist*, 21 August 2008. http://www.economist.com/node/ 11966993?story_id=11966993. Accessed March 2011.

7. A special report on water: For want of a drink. *The Economist*, May 2010. http:// www.economist.com/node/16136302. Accessed April 2011.

8. Water Encyclopaedia: Science and Issues, Drinking water and society. http://www. waterencyclopedia.com/Da-En/Drinking-Water-and-Society.html. Accessed April 2011.

9. United Nations Educational, Scientific and Cultural Organization (UNESCO), 2009. *World Water Development Report 3: Water in a Changing World.* http:// webworld.unesco.org/water/wwap/wwdr/wwdr3/pdf/World War DR3_Water_in_ a_Changing_World.pdf. Accessed April 2011.

10. World Health Organization, 2002. Water for health enshrined as a human right. http://www.who.int/mediacentre/news/releases/pr91/en/. Accessed April 2011.

11. Wild, Daniel, Francke, Carl-Johan, Menzli, Pierin, and Schön, Urs, 2007. *Water: a market of the future – Global trends open up new investment opportunities.* Zurich: Sustainability Asset Management (SAM) Study.

12. Food and Agriculture Organization of the United Nations (FAO). Aquastat, Water Use. http://www.fao.org/nr/water/aquastat/water_use/index.stm. Accessed April 2011.

13. United Nations Educational, Scientific and Cultural Organization (UNESCO), 2009. *World Water Development Report 3. Water in a Changing World.* http://webworld.

unesco.org/water/wwap/wwdr/wwdr3/pdf/WWDR3_Water_in_a_Changing_
World.pdf. Accessed April 2011.

14. Webber, Michael E., 2008. Energy versus water: Solving both crises together.
    Scientific American, 22 October 2008. http://www.sciam.com/article.cfm?id=the-
    future-of-fuel. Accessed April 2011.

15. International Panel on Climate Change. Climate Change 2007. Impacts, Adaptation
    and vulnerability. Chapter 3: Freshwater resources and their management. http://
    www.ipcc.ch/pdf/assessment-report/ar4/wg2/ar4-wg2-chapter3.pdf. Accessed
    April 2011.

16. Gleick, P. 2006. *The World's Water 2006-2007: A Biennial Report on Freshwater
    Resources*. Island Press, 392 pp.

17. Food and Agriculture Organization of the United Nations (FAO), How to Feed the
    World in 2050. http://www.fao.org/fileadmin/templates/wsfs/docs/expert_paper/
    How_to_Feed_the_World_in_2050.pdf. Accessed April 2011.

18. A special report on feeding the world: The 9 billion-people question. The Economist,
    24 February 2011. http://www.economist.com/node/18200618. Accessed April
    2011.

19. OECD, 1998. *Export fruit boom from the South: A threat for the North?. Organization
    for Cooperation and Economic Development*. Paris: OECD.

20. Food and Agriculture Organization of the United Nations (FAO), *Statistical Yearbook
    2009*. http://www.fao.org/fileadmin/templates/ess/ess_test_folder/Publications/
    Yearbook_2009/Statistical_Yearbook_2009.pdf. Accessed April 2011.

21. FAO, 2009. How to Feed the World in 2050. http://www.fao.org/wsfs/forum2050/
    wsfs-background-documents/hlef-issues-briefs/en/. Accessed April 2011.

22. US maize "threat" to Mexico farms. *BBC News*, 13 November 2004. http://news.
    bbc.co.uk/2/hi/science/nature/4008205.stm. Accessed April 2011.

23. Genetically modified crops. *The Economist,* 24 February 2011. http://www.
    economist.com/node/18231380. Accessed April 2011.

24. James, C., 2003. *Global Review of Commercialized Transgenic Crops: 2002
    Feature: Bt Maize*. Ithaca: International Service for the Acquisition of Agri-bio-
    tech Applications (ISAAA) http://www.isaaa.org/resources/publications/briefs/29/.
    Accessed April 2011.

25. National Research Council, 2004. *Safety of Genetically Engineered Foods:
    Approaches to Assessing Unintended Health Effects*. Washington DC: National
    Academies Press.

26. Skapinker, Michael, 2011. Patient science is GM food's best hope. *Financial Times*,
    10 January. http://www.ft.com/cms/s/0/228396e4-1cef-11e0-8c86-00144feab49a.
    html#axzz1JmTVH0Kf. Accessed April 2011.

27. UN Food and Agriculture Organization (FAO), 2009. State of the world's plant genetic resources. http://www.fao.org/agriculture/crops/core-themes/theme/seeds-pgr/sow/en/. Accessed April 2011.

28. Mulle, Emmanuel Dalle, and Ruppanner, Violette, 2010. Exploring the global food supply chain: Markets, companies, systems. *3D Thread Series*, 2. http://www.3dthree.org/pdf_3D/3D_ExploringtheGlobalFoodSupplyChain.pdf. Accessed April 2011.

29. Greaves, Felix, 2010. Combating disease: Scientists grapple with resurgent wheat fungus. *Financial Times*, 14 October. http://www.ft.com/cms/s/0/65f5c888-d65a-11df-81f0-00144feabdc0,dwp_uuid=bad439e6-d5c6-11df-94dc-00144feabdc0.html#axzz1JmTVHOKf. Accessed April 2011.

30. Special reports: business and food sustainability. *Financial Times*, 27 January 2010. http://www.ft.com/reports/food-sustainability-2010. Accessed April 2011.

31. Special Report on feeding the world. Not just calories: People also need the right nutrients. *The Economist*, 24 February 2011. http://www.economist.com/node/18200650?story_id=18200650. Accessed April 2011.

32. Special Report on Feeding the World. Waste not, want not. *The Economist*, 24 February 2011.

33. IPCC. Climate Change 2007. Impacts, Adaptation and Vulnerability Summary for Policy Makers. http://www.ipcc.ch/pdf/assessment-report/ar4/wg2/ar4-wg2-spm.pdf. Accessed April 2011.

34. Special report on water. Every drop counts: And in Singapore every drop is counted. *The Economist*, 20 May 2010. http://www.economist.com/node/16136324?story_id=E1_TGTPGPNQ. Accessed April 2011.

Global Trend 6   Education

1. Bill Gates on mosquitos, malaria and education. *TED Talks*. February 2009, Long Beach California. http://www.ted.com/talks/bill_gates_unplugged.html. Accessed March 2011.

2. Microsoft News Center: Bill Gates biography http://www.microsoft.com/presspass/exec/billg/?tab=biography .Accessed July 2011.

3. Lakeside School. http://www.lakesideschool.org/default.aspx. Accessed March 2011.

4. The EFA Global Monitoring Report Team, 2008. *Education for All. Global Monitor Report 2009*. Paris: UNESCO. http://unesdoc.unesco.org/images/0017/001776/177609e.pdf. Accessed March 2011.

5. Sir Ken Robinson lectures on changing paradigms. RSA Edge Lecture. http://www.thersa.org/events/vision/archive/sir-ken-robinson. Accessed March 2011.

6. Schultz, T. W., 1961. Investment in human capital. *American Economic Review*, 51 (1): 1-17.

7. Harbison, R., and Hanushek, E., 1992. *Education Performance of the Poor: Lessons from Northeast Brazil. New York.* Washington DC: World Bank.

8. Psacharopoulos, G., 1985. Returns to education: A further international update and implications. *Journal of Human resources*, 20 (4):583-604.

9. International Standard Classification of Education (ISCED), 1997. http://www.uis. unesco.org/TEMPLATE/pdf/isced/ISCED_A.pdf. Accessed March 2011.

10. OECD. http://www.oecd.org/pages/0,3417,en_36734052_36734103_1_1_1_1_1,00. html. Accessed March 2011.

11. The EFA Global Monitoring Report Team, 2010. *Education for All. Global Monitor Report 2010*. Oxford: Oxford University Press. http://unesdoc.unesco.org/images/ 0017/001776/177609e.pdf. http://unesdoc.unesco.org/ulis/cgi-bin/ulis.pl?catno=18 6606%gp=1%mode=e%lin=1. Accessed June 20 2011.

Global Trend 7   Demographic Changes

1. Hans Rosling, 2009. Let my dataset change your mindset. *TED Talks*, US Sate Department, Washington DC. http://www.ted.com/talks/lang/eng/hans_rosling_ at_state.html. Accessed March 2011.

2. World Economic Forum, 2011. *Global Risks 2011 6th Edition: An Initiative of the Risk Response Network*. http://riskreport.weforum.org/. Accessed July 2011.

3. Harper, CL, 1993. *Exploring social change*. Engelwood Cliffs: New Jersey.

4. Fertility and living standards: Go forth and multiply a lot less. *The Economist*, 29 October, 2009. http://www.economist.com/displaystory.cfm?story_id=14743589. Accessed March 2011.

5. Population Reference Bureau, 2009 World Population Data Sheet. http://www.prb. org/pdf09/09wpds_eng.pdf. Accessed March 2011.

6. United Nations, 2010. *World Economic and Social Survey 2010: Retooling Global Development*. New York: United Nations. http://www.un.org/en/development/ desa/policy/wess/wess_current/2010wess.pdf. Accessed March 2011.

7. United Nations, 2007. *World Economic and Social Survey 2007: Development in an Ageing World*. New York: United Nations. http://www.un.org/en/development/ desa/policy/wess/wess_archive/2007wess.pdf. Accessed March 2011.

8. United Nations, 2007. *World Population Ageing 2007*, Executive Summary. pp. xxvi. http://www.un.org/esa/population/publications/WPA2007/wpp2007.htm Accessed March 2011.

9. Cook, Chris, et al., 2009. The red ink of a greyer future. *Financial Time,* 1 April. http://www.ft.com/cms/s/0/a06a82ce-1ef0-11de-a748-00144feabdc0.html?nclick_ check=1#axzz1Hnpu35lr. Accessed March 2011.

10. OECD, 2010. International Migration Outlook 2010, www.oecd.org/els/migration/ imo. Accessed April 2011.

11. United Nations, 2009. Trend in total migrant stock: The 2008 revision. http://esa. un.org/migration. Accessed April 2011.

12. International Organization for Migration, 2008. *World Migration Report 2008,* http:// www.iom.int/jahia/webdav/site/myjahiasite/shared/shared/mainsite/published_ docs/studies_and_reports/WMR2008/Ch1_WMR08.pdf. Accessed March 2011.

13. United Nations, 2006. *International Migration Report 2006: A Global Assessment.* P. 3 http://www.un.org/esa/population/publications/2006_MigrationRep/report. htm. Accessed March 2011.

14. United Nations International Migration and Development Factsheet 2005. http:// www.un.org/esa/population/migration/hld/Text/Migration_factsheet.pdf. Accessed March 2011.

15. Remittances Data 2009, World Bank. http://siteresources.worldbank.org/ INTPROSPECTS/Resources/334934-1110315015165/RemittancesData_ Nov09(Public).xls. Accessed April 2011.

16. Migration and development: The aid workers who really help. *The Economist,* 8 October 2009. http://www.economist.com/node/14586906. Accessed March 2011.

17. International Organization for Migration, Facts and Figures. http://www.iom.int/jahia/ Jahia/about-migration/facts-and-figures/lang/en. Accessed March 2011.

Global Trend 8   War, Terrorism and Social Unrest

1. Calaprice, Alice, 2005. *The New Quotable Einstein.* Princeton University Press. p. 173.

2. World Economic Forum, 2011. *Global Risks 2011 6th Edition: An Initiative of the Risk Response Network.* http://riskreport.weforum.org/. Accessed July 2011.

3. List of wars and anthropogenic disasters by death toll. Wikipedia, The Free Encyclopedia. http://en.wikipedia.org/wiki/List_of_wars_and_anthropogenic_ disasters_by_death_toll#Wars_and_armed_conflicts. Accessed July 2011.

4. Keegan, John, 1994. *A History of Warfare.* Pimlico: Vintage, 432pp.

5. Keeley, Lawrence H., 1996. *War Before Civilization: The Myth of The Peaceful Savage,* Oxford University Press.

6. Rubinstein, W.D., 2004. *Genocide: A History.* p.12. Pearson Education Limited.

7. Clausewitz, Carl Von, 1976. *On War*. Place: Princeton University Press. p.87.

8. Casualties in the two World Wars for Combatant Nations. The BBC. http://www.bbc. co.uk/dna/h2g2/A2854730. Accessed April 2011.

9. The Cold War. History.Com http://www.history.com/topics/cold-war. Accessed April 2011.

10. The Vietnam War. The ultimate resource for the Vietnam War. Vietnamwar.Com. http://classic-web.archive.org/web/20080604140842/http://www.vietnamwar. com/ Accessed April 2011.

11. Timeline: Soviet War in Afghanistan. *BBC News,* February 2009. http://news.bbc. co.uk/2/hi/south_asia/7883532.stm. Accessed April 2011.

12. Iran-Iraq War. Encyclopaedia Britannica. eb.com. http://www.britannica.com/ EBchecked/topic/293527/Iran-Iraq-War. Accessed April 2011.

13. Peters, John E., and Deshong, Howard, 1995. *Out of Area or Out of Reach? European Military Support for Operations in Southwest Asia*. Santa Monica: RAND, 156 pp.

14. Persian Gulf War. Encyclopaedia Britannica. eb.com. http://www.britannica.com/ EBchecked/topic/452778/Persian-Gulf-War. Accessed April 2011.

15. 9/11 Health. New York City Health Department. NYC.gov. http://www.nyc.gov/html/ doh/wtc/html/background/background.shtml. Accessed April 2011.

16. A list of the 77 countries whose citizens died as a result of the attacks on September 11, 2001. US Department of State, Office of International Information Programs http://www.interpol.int/public/ICPO/speeches/20020911List77Countries.asp. Accessed April 2011.

17. Friedman, Alan, 1993. *Spider's Web: The Secret History of How the White House Illegally Armed Iraq*. Bantam Books.

18. Timmerman, Kenneth R., 1991. *The Death Lobby: How the West Armed Iraq*. New York: Houghton Mifflin Company.

19. Kepel, Gilles, 2002. *Jihad: The Trail of Political Islam*. Translated by Anthony F. Roberts (1st edition). Cambridge: Belknap Press of Harvard University Press.p.143.

20. IEDs kill more civilian Afghans in 2010. *USA Today,* 8 May 2010. http://www. usatoday.com/news/world/afghanistan/2010-08-05-1Acasualties05_ST_N.htm. Accessed April 2011.

21. US and coalition casualties. Afghanistan. CNN.com, 10 August, 2010. http://www. cnn.com/SPECIALS/2004/oef.casualties/index.html. Accessed April 2011.

22. Bumiller, Elisabeth, and Gallus, Carlotta, 2009. Admits civilians died in Afghan raids. *New York Times*, 7 May. http://www.nytimes.com/2009/05/08/world/asia/ 08afghan.html. Accessed April 2011.

23. War in Iraq. Transcript of Powell's UN Presentation. CNN.com, 6 February 2003. http://www.cnn.com/2003/US/02/05/sprj.irq.powell.transcript/index.html. Accessed April 2011.

24. In their own words: Iraq's "imminent" threat. Center for American Progress. http://www.americanprogress.org/issues/kfiles/b24970.html. Accessed April 2011.

25. MSNBC. The CIA's final report: No WMD found in Iraq. http://www.msnbc.msn.com/id/7634313/. Accessed April 2011.

26. USA and coalition casualties. Iraq. CNN.com, 16 February 2010. http://www.cnn.com/SPECIALS/2003/iraq/forces/casualties/index.html. Accessed April 2011.

27. Karon, Tony, 2010. U.S. combat in Iraq: Not over till it's over. *Time*, 6 August 2010. http://www.time.com/time/world/article/0,8599,2009027,00.html. Accessed April 2011.

28. Iraqi refugees facing desperate situation. Amnesty International.http://www.amnesty.org/en/news-and-updates/report/iraqi-refugees-facing-desperate-situation-20080615. Accessed April 2011.

29. Smalley, R. E., 2003. Top ten problems of humanity for next 50 years. *Energy & NanoTechnology Conference*, Rice University.

30. Hewitt, Joseph, Wilkenfield J., and Gurr, T., 2007. *Peace and Conflict 2008*. Paradigm Publishers.

31. Schmid, Alex, and Jongman, Albert, 1988. *Political Terrorism: A new guide to actors, authors, concepts, data bases, theories and literature.* Amsterdam; New York: North-Holland; New Brunswick: Transaction Books.

32. Ruby, Charles L., 2002. The definition of terrorism. Analysis of social issues and public policy. http://www.asap-spssi.org/pdf/asap019.pdf. Accessed April 2011.

33. Terrorism. Encyclopaedia Britannica. p.3. http://www.britannica.com/eb/article-9071797. Accessed April 2011.

34. Green, Matthew, 2010. Nato troops killed in Afghanistan crash. *Financial Times*, 21 December. http://www.ft.com/cms/s/0/cb19e084-c55f-11df-9563-00144feab49a.html. Accessed April 2011.

35. Two car bombs in Iraq capital kill 10. *Financial Times*, 19 September 2010. http://www.ft.com/cms/s/0/5081d1f0-c3c6-11df-b827-00144feab49a,dwp_uuid=17aab8bc-6e47-11da-9544-0000779e2340.html. Accessed April 2011.

36. Where will it end? The Americans, the Europeans and the Arabs must all hold their nerve. *The Economist*, 26 March 2011. http://www.economist.com/node/18441153?story_id=18441153. Accessed March 2011.

37. Delayed explosion. *The Economist*, 13 November 2009. http://www.economist.com/theworldin/displaystory.cfm?story_id=14742556. Accessed April 2011.

38. Hope, Kerin, 2010. Athens protests erupt into violence. *Financial Times*, 5 May 2010. http://www.ft.com/cms/s/0/fa96b574-5838-11df-9eaf-00144feab49a.html. Accessed April 2011.

39. Côte d'Ivoire's civil war. Coming to a crunch. Rebel troops are gaining ground. *The Economist,* 31 March 2011. http://www.economist.com/node/18491660?story_id=18491660. Accessed April 2011.

40. The scent of jasmine spreads. As protests erupt in Egypt, Arab leaders everywhere should take heed. *The Economist,* 27 January 2011. http://www.economist.com/node/18010573?story_id=18010573. Accessed April 2011.

41. Gilpin, Raymond, 2009. Counting the costs of Somali piracy. *United States Institute of Peace Working Paper.* Center for Sustainable Economies. http://www.usip.org/files/resources/1_0.pdf. Accessed April 2011.

42. Maersk Line's piracy costs to double. *Sea News,* 26 April 2011. http://www.seanews.com.tr/article/TURSHIP/CONTAINER/60328/Maersk-Piracyhtml/. Accessed April 2011.

43. No stopping them. For all the efforts to combat it, Somali piracy is posing an ever greater threat to the world's shipping. *The Economist,* 3 February 2011. http://www.economist.com/node/18061574?story_id=18061574. Accessed April 2011.

44. Dagne, Ted, 2009. Somalia: Conditions and prospects for lasting peace. *Mediterranean Quarterly,* 20 (2):95-112. http://muse.jhu.edu/login?uri=/journals/mediterranean_quarterly/v020/20.2.dagne.pdf. Accessed April 2011.

45. Drugs and crime facts. Office of national drug control policy. Whitehousedrugpolicy.gov. http://www.whitehousedrugpolicy.gov/drugfact/related_links.html. Accessed April 2011.

46. BBC Latin America & Caribbean. Mexico says 28,000 killed in drugs war since 2006. *BBC News,* 4 August 2010. http://www.bbc.co.uk/news/world-latin-america-10860614. Accessed April 2011.

47. United Nations Office on Drugs and Crime, 2009. World drug report 2009 highlights links between drugs and crime. Press release, June 24, 2009. http://www.unodc.org/documents/wdr/1/WDR09pressreleasefinal-english.pdf. Accessed April 2011.

48. United Nations Office on Drugs and Crime, 2009. *World Drug Report 2009.* http://www.unodc.org/unodc/en/data-and-analysis/WDR-2009.html. Accessed April 2011.

49. The National Intelligence Council, 2008. *Global Trends 2025: A Transformed World.* Washington DC:US Government Printing Office. http://www.dni.gov/nic/PDF_2025/2025_Global_Trends_Final_Report.pdf. Accessed March 2011.

50. Office of the Director of National Intelligence, USA, 2009. *The National Intelligence Strategy.* Foreword pp. 3–4. www.dni.gov/reports/2009_NIS.pdf. Accessed April 2011.

Global Trend 9   Energy

1. Crooks, Ed, 2009. Special report on the future of energy. Climate of opinion. *Financial Times,* 3 November 2009. http://www.ft.com/reports/futureofenergy. Accessed March 2011.

2. World Economic Forum, 2011. *Global Risks 2011 6th Edition: An Initiative of the Risk Response Network.* http://riskreport.weforum.org/. Accessed July 2011.

3. Oil Reserves. *FinancialTimes,* 11 October 2010. http://www.ft.com/cms/s/3/770b34cc-d516-11df-ad3a-00144feabdc0.html#axzz1Hnpu35lr Accessed March 2011.

4. Barley, Shanta, 2009., Why the peak oil debate is irrelevant. New Scientist, 8 October http://www.newscientist.com/article/dn17943-why-the-peak-oil-debate-is-irrelevant.html. Accessed March 2011.

5. UK Energy Research Centre, 2009. Global oil depletion: An assessment of the evidence for a near-term peak in global oil production: http://www.ukerc.ac.uk/support/tiki-index.php?page=Global+Oil+Depletion. Accessed March 2011.

6. Bernard, Steven, 2009. Understanding energy policy: Energy emitters. *The Financial Times,* 1 December 2009. http://www.ft.com/cms/s/2/db740e56-de87-11de-89c2-00144feab49a.html. Accessed March 2011.

7. International Energy Agency, 2010. World Energy Outlook 2010. http://www.worldenergyoutlook.org/. Accessed March 2011.

8. World Energy Council, 2007. *Survey of Energy Resources.* Executive Summary. http://www.worldenergy.org/documents/ser2007_executive_summary_final_18082008.pdf. Accessed March 2011.

9. International Energy Agency, 2008. Worldwide trends in energy use and efficiency. http://www.iea.org/papers/2008/Indicators_2008.pdf. Accessed March 2011.

10. BP statistical review of world energy, 2010. http://www.bp.com/liveassets/bp_internet/globalbp/globalbp_uk_english/reports_and_publications/statistical_energy_review_2008/STAGING/local_assets/2010_downloads/statistical_review_of_world_energy_full_report_2010.pdf. Accessed June 20 2010.

11. Interactive graphic: Our energy-driven world. *Financial Times,* 4 November 2009. http://www.ft.com/cms/s/0/4a33a7ae-c973-11de-a071-00144feabdc0,dwp_uuid=6cff521a-c48c-11de-912e-00144feab49a.html. Accessed March 2011.

12. Energy Security: Oil Key players and movements. *Financial Times,* 18 June 2008. http://www.ft.com/cms/s/0/74bf31bc-992a-11dc-bb45-0000779fd2ac.html#axzz1IMk0Q454. Accessed March 2011.

13. World Energy Council . 2007 *Survey of Energy Resources.* http://www.worldenergy.org/publications/survey_of_energy_resources_2007/default.asp. Accessed March 2011.

14. Culham Centre for Fusion Energy (CCFE), United Kingdom atomic energy authority. http://www.fusion.org.uk/introduction.aspx. Accessed March 2011.

15. The Joint European Torus (JET), European Fusion Development Agreement (EFDA). http://www.jet.efda.org/fusion-basics/what-is-fusion/. Accessed March 2011.

16. International Energy Agency, 2009. Launching an energy revolution in a time of economic crisis: http://www.iea.org/G8/docs/Energy_Revolution_g8july09.pdf. Accessed March 2011.

Global Trend 10   Ecosystems and Biodiversity

1. United Nations Environment Program, Convention on biological diversity introduction to the United Nations international year of biodiversity. http://www.cbd.int/2010/welcome/. Accessed March 2011.

2. International Union for Conservation of Nature (IUCN), 2010. *Red List of Threatened Species*. Version 2010.4. http://www.iucnredlist.org. Accessed April 2011.

3. World Economic Forum, 2011. *Global Risks 2011 6th Edition: An Initiative of the Risk Response Network*. http://riskreport.weforum.org/. Accessed July 2011.

4. Millennium Ecosystem Assessment, 2005. *Ecosystems and Human Well-being: Synthesis.*, Washington, DC: Island Press. http://www.maweb.org/documents/document.356.aspx.pdf. Accessed April 2011.

5. Millennium Ecosystem Assessment, 2005. *Ecosystems and Human Well-being: Biodiversity Synthesis*. Washington, DC: World Resources Institute. http://www.maweb.org/documents/document.354.aspx.pdf Accessed April 2011.

6. The Encyclopedia of Earth. http://www.eoearth.org/article/land-use_and_land-cover_change. Accessed March 2011.

7. Millennium Ecosystem Assessment, 2005. *Ecosystems and Human Well-being: Current State and Trends: Findings of the Condition and Trends Working Group*. Washington, DC: Island Press. http://www.maweb.org/documents/document.766.aspx.pdf Accessed April 2011.

8. Humans must change behaviour to save bees, vital for food production – UN report. United Nations News Centre, 10 March 2011. http://www.un.org/apps/news/story.asp?NewsID=37731%Cr=unep%Cr1. Accessed June 20 2011.

9. Black, Richard, 2010. Bee decline linked to falling biodiversity. BBC News, 20 January 2010. http://news.bbc.co.uk/2/hi/8467746.stm. Accessed April 2011.

10. A special report on forests. Seeing the wood. The Economist, 23 September 2010.http://www.economist.com/node/17062713?story_id=17062713. Accessed April 2011.

11. Food and Agriculture Organization of the United Nations, 2009. *The State Of World Fisheries and Aquaculture 2008*. Rome: United Nations. http://www.fao.org/docrep/011/i0250e/i0250e00.htm. Accessed April 2011.

12. The history of oysters in Britain. 3 April 2000. BBC Home. http://www.bbc.co.uk/dna/h2g2/A283105. Accessed April 2011.

13. Ewing, B. et al., 2010. *Ecological Footprint Atlas 2008.* Oakland: Global Footprint Network. http://www.footprintnetwork.org/en/index.php/GFN/page/ecological_footprint_atlas_2010. Accessed April 2011.

14. World Footprint: Do we fit on the planet? Global Footprint Network, 3 November 2010. http://www.footprintnetwork.org/en/index.php/GFN/page/world_footprint/ Accessed April 2011.

15. Diamond, Jared, 2005. *Collapse: How Societies Choose to Fail or Succeed.* Viking Press.

16. Harvey, Fiona, 2010. Special report on sustainable business. Saving species: Bad for biodiversity is often bad for business. *Financial Times*, 1 October 2010. http://www.ft.com/cms/s/0/ce6b8e02-cceb-11df-9bf0-00144feab49a,dwp_uuid=e55f5b88-c9f9-11df-87b8-00144feab49a.html#axzz1KuRmE5aE. Accessed April 2011.

17. World Wildlife Fund, 2010. *Living Planet Report.* http://wwf.panda.org/about_our_earth/all_publications/living_planet_report/2010_lpr/. Accessed April 2011.

18. Millennium Ecosystem Assessment, 2005. *Ecosystems and Human Well-being: Opportunities and Challenges for Business and Industry.* Washington, DC: World Resources Institute. http://www.maweb.org/documents/document.353.aspx.pdf Accessed April 2011.

19. Commission on Climate Change and Development, 2008. Ecosystem under Pressure. http://www.ccdcommission.org/Filer/pdf/pb_ecosystem_services.pdf. Accessed April 2011.

Global Trend 11   Health

1. Larry Brilliant Wants to Stop Pandemics. *TED Ideas Worth Spreading.* February 2006, Monterey, California. http://www.ted.com/talks/larry_brilliant_wants_to_stop_pandemics.html. Accessed April 2011.

2. Ernest Madu on World Class Health Care. *TED Ideas Worth Spreading.* April 2008, Arusha Tanzania. http://www.ted.com/talks/ernest_madu_on_world_class_health_care.html. Accessed April 2011.

3. World Economic Forum, 2011. *Global Risks 2011 6th Edition: An Initiative of the Risk Response Network.* http://riskreport.weforum.org/. Accessed July 2011.

4. *Constitution of the World Health Organization.* Basic Documents, 45th Edition, Supplement, October 2006. http://www.who.int/governance/eb/who_constitution_en.pdf. Accessed May 2011.

5. Article 25, *The Universal Declaration of Human Rights.* United Nations. http://www.un.org/en/documents/udhr/index.shtml. Accessed May 2011.

6. World Health Organization, 2008. *World Health Report 2008: Primary Health Care Now More Than Ever.* Geneva: WHO Press.http://www.who.int/whr/2008/whr08_en.pdf. Accessed May 2011.

7. Gapminder World Map 2010. http://www.gapminder.org/GapminderMedia/wp-uploads/pdf_charts/GWM2010.pdf. Accessed April 2011.

8. UNICEF, 2008. Releasing declining numbers for child mortality, UNICEF calls for increased efforts to save children's lives. Press release. 12 September 2008.http://www.unicef.org/media/media_45607.html. Accessed May 2011.

9. Health Maps. Public/ Private Health Spending. [online map] Worldmapper. *The World as You've Never Seen it Before.* http://www.worldmapper.org/textindex/text_health.html. Accessed April 2011.

10. U.S. Census Bureau, 2009. Income, poverty and health insurance coverage in the United States: 2008. Newsroom, 10 September 2009. http://www.census.gov/newsroom/releases/archives/income_wealth/cb09-141.html. Accessed May 2011.

11. U.S. Government Accountability Office, n.d. Health care challenges for the 21st century. 21st century challenges: Reexamining the base of the federal government. http://www.gao.gov/challenges/healthcare.pdf. Accessed May 2011.

12. The World Health Organization (WHO), 2007. The top ten causes of death. Fact sheet no. 310. http://www.who.int/mediacentre/factsheets/fs310.pdf. Accessed April 2011.

13. Taubenberger, Jeffery K., and Morens, David M., 2006. 1918 influenza: The mother of all pandemics. *Emerging Infectious Diseases*, 12(1). Centers for Disease Control and Prevention. http://www.cdc.gov/ncidod/eid/vol12no01/pdfs/05-0979.pdf. Accessed May 2011.

14. World Health Organization, 2010. Pandemic (H1N1) 2009 update 110. Weekly update. http://www.who.int/csr/don/2010_07_23a/en/index.html. Accessed May 2011.

15. Updated CDC estimates of 2009 H1N1 influenza cases, hospitalizations and deaths in the United States, April 2009 – April 10, 2010. Centers for Disease Control and Prevention (CDC). http://www.cdc.gov/h1n1flu/estimates_2009_h1n1.htm. Accessed May 2011.

16. World Health Organization, 2009. Influenza (seasonal). Fact sheet no. 211. http://www.who.int/mediacentre/factsheets/fs211/en/. Accessed May 2011.

17. Health topics: Chronic diseases. World Health Organization. http://www.who.int/topics/chronic_diseases/en/. Accessed May 2011.

18. Falfetto, Marta, and Matlin, Stephen A., 2009. Global R&D financing for communicable and noncommunicable diseases: A report to the WHO expert working group on R&D financing. http://www.who.int/entity/phi/GlobalRandDFinanceCDsNCDs.doc Accessed May 2011.

19. Global Alliance for TB Drug Development, 2011. Why new drugs now? An outdated treatment. http://www.tballiance.org/why/outdated.php. Accessed May 2011.

20. World Health Organization, 2009. Drug resistance could set back Malaria control success. News release, 25 February 2009. http://www.who.int/mediacentre/news/releases/2009/malaria_drug_resistance_20090225/en/index.html. Accessed May 2011.

21. Adams, C.P. and Brantner, Van Vu, 2010. Spending on new drug development. *Health Economics* 19: 130–141.

22. Adams, C.P., and Brantner, Van Vu, 2006. Estimating the cost of new drug development: Is it really $802 million? *Health Affairs*, 25(2): 420-428. http://content.healthaffairs.org/cgi/content/abstract/25/2/420. Accessed May 2011.

23. AVERT, Averting HIV and AIDS, n.d. AIDS, drug prices and generic drugs. International HIV & AIDS Charity. http://www.avert.org/generic.htm. Accessed May 2011.

24. Scandlyn, Jean, 2000. When AIDS became a chronic disease. *Western Journal of Medicine*, 172(2): 130-133. http://www.ncbi.nlm.nih.gov/pmc/articles/PMC1070775/. Accessed May 2011.

25. Jeffords, James M., 2004. Direct-to-consumer drug advertising: You get what you pay for. Health Affairs. http://content.healthaffairs.org/cgi/content/full/hlthaff.w4.253v1/DC1 Accessed May 2011.

26. FDA is rejecting more new drugs than in past. *Associated Press*, Aug 17, 2007. http://www.msnbc.msn.com/id/20321830/. Accessed May 2011.

27. Mellon, Margaret, Benbrook, Charles, and Benbrook, Karen Lutz, 2001. *Hogging It! Estimates of Antimicrobial Abuse in Livestock*. Cambridge: Union of Concerned Scientists (UCS). http://www.ucsusa.org/food_and_agriculture/science_and_impacts/impacts_industrial_agriculture/hogging-it-estimates-of.html. Accessed May 2011.

28. Drug-spending increase highest in four years. *Indianapolis Business Journal*, May 2010. http://www.ibj.com/drugspending-jump-highest-in-4-years/PARAMS/article/20061. Accessed May 2011.

Global Trend 12   Natural Disasters

1. International Strategy for Disaster Reduction, United Nations, n.d. *2010-2011 World Disaster Reduction Campaign*. http://www.unisdr.org/english/campaigns/campaign2010-2011/. Accessed May 2011.

2. The International Disaster Database, EM-DAT, Centre for Research on the Epidemiology of Disasters (CRED). http://www.emdat.be/disaster-list. Accessed May 2011.

3. Gramáticas, Damian, 2011. Japan tsunami: Searching for the lost in Natori. *BBC News*, 16 March 2011. http://www.bbc.co.uk/news/world-asia-pacific-12767755. Accessed April 2011.

4. Hogg, Chris, 2011. Japan quake: Disaster tests country's famed "stoicism." *BBC News*, 20 March 2011. http://www.bbc.co.uk/news/world-asia-pacific-12798799. Accessed April 2011.

5. Zernike, Kate, Wilgoren, Jodi, and Ruethling, Gretchen, 2005. In search of a place to sleep, and news of home. *New York Times,* 31 August 2005. http://www.nytimes.com/2005/08/31/national/nationalspecial/31stranded.html Accessed 20 June 2011.

6. Darryl, Barthe, 2006. After Katrina: Readers' experiences. *BBC News,* 29 August 2006.http://news.bbc.co.uk/2/hi/talking_point/5283700.stm. Accessed April 2011.

7. Nowshera, Alamzeb, 2010. Pakistan floods: Your stories. Alamzeb's diabetic mother died in Nowshera. *BBC News,* 3 August 2010. http://www.bbc.co.uk/news/world-south-asia-10829888. Accessed May 2011.

8. Alam Khan, Muhammad, 2010. Pakistan floods: Your stories. Dr Muhammad Alam Khan is unable to test for cholera in Swat. *BBC News,* 3 August 2010. http://www.bbc.co.uk/news/world-south-asia-10829888. Accessed May 2011.

9. EM-DAT: The OFDA/CRED International Disaster Database – www.emdat.be – Université Catholique de Louvain – Brussels – Belgium. http://www.emdat.be/classification. Accessed May 2011.

10. World Economic Forum, 2011. *Global Risks 2011 6th Edition: An Initiative of the Risk Response Network.* http://riskreport.weforum.org/. Accessed July 2011.

11. Natural disasters: counting the cost. *The Economist,* 21 Mar 2011. http://www.economist.com/blogs/dailychart. Accessed March 2011.

12. The World Bank, 2011. The recent earthquake and tsunami in Japan: Implication for East Asia. *East Asia and Pacific Economic Update,* 2011 (1). http://siteresources.worldbank.org/INTEAPHALFYEARLYUPDATE/Resources/550192-1300567391916/EAP_Update_March2011_japan.pdf. Accessed April 2011.

13. 2010 disasters in numbers. EM-DAT: The OFDA/CRED International Disaster Database. http://www.unisdr.org/preventionweb/files/17613_rectoversodisasters2010.pdf. Accessed May 2011.

14. Natural disaster trends. EM-DAT: The OFDA/CRED International Disaster Database. http://www.emdat.be/natural-disasters-trends. Accessed May 2011.

15. US Geological Survey: Science for a changing world, 2009. FAQs: Earthquake myths. *Earthquake Hazards Program.* http://earthquake.usgs.gov/learn/faq/?faqID=110. Accessed May 2011.

16. Guha-Sapir, Debarati, 2011. Natural disasters in 2010. *CRED Crunch* (23). http://www. cred.be/sites/default/files/CredCrunch23.pdf. Accessed May 2010.

17. US Geological Survey: Science for a changing world, 2009. 100% chance of an earthquake. *Earthquake Hazards Program*. http://earthquake.usgs.gov/learn/topics/100_ chance.php. Accessed May 2011.

18. US Geological Survey: Science for a changing world, 2011. Magnitude 8 and greater earthquakes since 1900. *Earthquake Hazards Program*. http://earthquake.usgs. gov/earthquakes/eqarchives/year/mag8/magnitude8_1900_date.php. Accessed April 2011.

19. Earthly powers. Disasters are about people and planning, not nature's pomp. *The Economist*, 24 April 2010. http://www.economist.com/node/15951696?story_ id=E1_TVJVTGJG. Accessed April 2011.

20. Quoted in CRED *Annual Disaster Statistical Review 2010.*

21. Quoted in CRED *Annual Disaster Statistical Review 2010.*

22. Hirst, Michael and McGeown, Kate, 2009. Rising sea levels: A tale of two cities. *BBC News*, 24 November, 2009. http://news.bbc.co.uk/2/hi/science/nature/8369236. stm . Accessed April 2011.

23. Sutter, John D, 2010. In search of an earthquake-proof building. *CNN*, 2 March 2010. http://articles.cnn.com/2010-03-02/tech/earthquake.resistant.building_1_building-codes-powerful-earthquake-chile/2?_s=PM:TECH. Accessed April 2011.

24. US Geological Survey: Science for a changing world, 2009. Frequently asked questions about volcano monitoring. *Earthquake Hazards Program*. http://volcanoes. usgs.gov/about/faq/faqmonitoring.php. Accessed April 2011.

25. Guha-Sapir, Debby, Vos, Femke, Below, Regina, and Ponserre, Sylvain, 2011. *Annual Disaster Statistical Review 2010: The Numbers and Trends*. Centre for Research on the Epidemiology of Disasters (CRED), Brussels. http://www.cred.be/sites/ default/files/ADSR_2010.pdf. Accessed May 2010.

26. Quoted in *CRED Review 2010.*

27. US Department of Homeland Security, 2010. What to do before an earthquake. http://www.fema.gov/hazard/earthquake/eq_before.shtm. Accessed April 2011.

28. International Strategy for Disaster Reduction,United Nations, n.d. Making cities resilient. *2010–2011 World Disaster Reduction Campaign*. http://www.unisdr.org/ english/campaigns/campaign2010-2011/documents/campaign-kit.pdf. Accessed May 2011.

29. International Strategy for Disaster Reduction, United Nations, n.d. Hyogo framework for action. http://www.unisdr.org/we/coordinate/hfa. Accessed May 2011.

30. United Nations, 2011. Global assessment report on disaster risk reduction, revealing risk, redefining development. Summary and main findings. http://

www.preventionweb.net/english/hyogo/gar/2011/en/bgdocs/GAR-2011/GAR2011_
ES_English.pdf. Accessed May 2011.

Facing Up to a Changing World

1. World Economic Forum, 2011. *Global Risks 2011 6th Edition: An Initiative of the Risk
   Response Network*. http://riskreport.weforum.org/. Accessed July 2011.

2. Diamond, Jared, 2005. *Collapse: How Societies Choose to Fail or Succeed*. Viking
   Press.

3. Schwartz, Peter, 2003. *Inevitable Surprises: Thinking Ahead in a Time of Turbulence*.
   Gotham Books.

4. The Darwin Correspondence Project. *Six things Darwin never said – and one he did*.
   http://www.darwinproject.ac.uk/six-things-darwin-never-said. Accessed May 2011.

Index

Page numbers in *italics* represent tables.
Page numbers in **bold** represent figures.